Privatization and Transition in Russia in the Early 1990s

The privatization of Russia in the early 1990s was one of the most controversial economic reforms of the twentieth century. Its objective was the formal unwinding of the Soviet administrative command economy and the founding of a market system.

Much has been written on the subject, but there is as yet no comprehensive history of the laws and events that which brought about privatization – the institutional context surrounding the debates – and the chaotic economic and administrative circumstances of their implementation. As a result, the judgments that have been passed on the reform are too often based on a superficial understanding of history they seek to interpret.

This book fills the gap, and helps to set the record straight. Written by two senior advisors who worked in Russia at the time, it disentangles the actions, the politics, the laws, the institutions and the economics that shaped, for better or worse, this momentous reform. In writing the book, the authors have had unique access not only to leading academics, but to contemporary documentation, and through interviews, to protagonists on both sides of the debate.

The book is essential reading for anyone who wishes to understand the period, or suggest lessons that can be learned from it. It will be of importance to any scholar of Russian history, and to those who study transition economics.

Carol Scott Leonard, Emeritus Fellow at St Antony's College, Oxford, UK, is Vice-Rector of the Presidential Academy of the National Economy and Professor at the National Research University – Higher School of Economics, Moscow, Russia.

David Pitt-Watson is an Executive Fellow at the London Business School. In the early 1990s he was the director responsible for Eastern Europe at Braxton Associates/Deloitte.

Routledge explorations in economic history

Edited by Lars Magnusson
Uppsala University, Sweden

1 **Economic Ideas and Government Policy**
Contributions to contemporary economic history
Sir Alec Cairncross

2 **The Organization of Labour Markets**
Modernity, culture and governance in Germany, Sweden, Britain and Japan
Bo Stråth

3 **Currency Convertibility**
The gold standard and beyond
Edited by Jorge Braga de Macedo, Barry Eichengreen and Jaime Reis

4 **Britain's Place in the World**
A historical enquiry into import controls 1945–1960
Alan S. Milward and George Brennan

5 **France and the International Economy**
From Vichy to the Treaty of Rome
Frances M.B. Lynch

6 **Monetary Standards and Exchange Rates**
M.C. Marcuzzo, L. Officer and A. Rosselli

7 **Production Efficiency in Domesday England, 1086**
John McDonald

8 **Free Trade and its Reception 1815–1960**
Freedom and trade: volume I
Edited by Andrew Marrison

9 **Conceiving Companies**
Joint-stock politics in Victorian England
Timothy L. Alborn

10 **The British Industrial Decline Reconsidered**
Edited by Jean-Pierre Dormois and Michael Dintenfass

11 **The Conservatives and Industrial Efficiency, 1951–1964**
Thirteen wasted years?
Nick Tiratsoo and Jim Tomlinson

12 **Pacific Centuries**
Pacific and Pacific Rim economic history since the 16th century
Edited by Dennis O. Flynn, Lionel Frost and A.J.H. Latham

13 **The Premodern Chinese Economy**
Structural equilibrium and capitalist sterility
Gang Deng

14 **The Role of Banks in Monitoring Firms**
The case of the Crédit Mobilier
Elisabeth Paulet

15 **Management of the National Debt in the United Kingdom, 1900–1932**
Jeremy Wormell

16 **An Economic History of Sweden**
Lars Magnusson

17 **Freedom and Growth**
The rise of states and markets in Europe, 1300–1750
S.R. Epstein

18 **The Mediterranean Response to Globalization before 1950**
Sevket Pamuk and Jeffrey G. Williamson

19 **Production and Consumption in English Households 1600–1750**
Mark Overton, Jane Whittle, Darron Dean and Andrew Hann

20 **Governance, the State, Regulation and Industrial Relations**
Ian Clark

21 **Early Modern Capitalism**
Economic and social change in Europe 1400–1800
Edited by Maarten Prak

22 **An Economic History of London, 1800–1914**
Michael Ball and David Sunderland

23 **The Origins of National Financial Systems**
Alexander Gerschenkron reconsidered
Edited by Douglas J. Forsyth and Daniel Verdier

24 **The Russian Revolutionary Economy, 1890–1940**
Ideas, debates and alternatives
Vincent Barnett

25 **Land Rights, Ethno Nationality and Sovereignty in History**
Edited by Stanley L. Engerman and Jacob Metzer

26 **An Economic History of Film**
Edited by John Sedgwick and Mike Pokorny

27 **The Foreign Exchange Market of London**
Development since 1900
John Atkin

28 **Rethinking Economic Change in India**
Labour and livelihood
Tirthankar Roy

29 **The Mechanics of Modernity in Europe and East Asia**
The institutional origins of social change and stagnation
Erik Ringmar

30 **International Economic Integration in Historical Perspective**
Dennis M.P. McCarthy

31 **Theories of International Trade**
Adam Klug
Edited by Warren Young and Michael Bordo

32 **Classical Trade Protectionism 1815–1914**
Edited by Jean Pierre Dormois and Pedro Lains

33 **Economy and Economics of Ancient Greece**
Takeshi Amemiya

34 **Social Capital, Trust and the Industrial Revolution**
1780–1880
David Sunderland

35 **Pricing Theory, Financing of International Organisations and Monetary History**
Lawrence H. Officer

36 **Political Competition and Economic Regulation**
Edited by Peter Bernholz and Roland Vaubel

37 **Industrial Development in Postwar Japan**
Hirohisa Kohama

38 **Reflections on the Cliometrics Revolution**
Conversations with economic historians
Edited by John S. Lyons, Louis P. Cain, and Samuel H. Williamson

39 **Agriculture and Economic Development in Europe since 1870**
Edited by Pedro Lains and Vicente Pinilla

40 **Quantitative Economic History**
The good of counting
Edited by Joshua Rosenbloom

41 **A History of Macroeconomic Policy in the United States**
John H. Wood

42 **An Economic History of the American Steel Industry**
Robert P. Rogers

43 **Ireland and the Industrial Revolution**
The impact of the Industrial Revolution on Irish industry and society, 1801–1922
Andy Bielenberg

44 **Intra-Asian Trade and Industrialization**
Essays in memory of Yasukichi Yasuba
Edited by A.J.H. Latham and Heita Kawakatsu

45 **Nation, State and the Industrial Revolution**
The visible hand
Lars Magnusson

46 **A Cultural History of Finance**
Irene Finel-Honigman

47 **Managing Crises and De-globalisation**
Nordic foreign trade and exchange 1919–1939
Edited by Sven-Olof Olsson

48 **The International Tin Cartel**
John Hillman

49 **The South Sea Bubble**
Helen J. Paul

50 **Ideas and Economic Crises in Britain from Attlee to Blair (1945–2005)**
Matthias Matthijs

51 **Bengal Industries and the British Industrial Revolution (1757–1857)**
Indrajit Ray

52 **The Evolving Structure of the East Asian Economic System since 1700**
Edited by A.J.H. Latham and Heita Kawakatsu

53 **German Immigration and Servitude in America, 1709–1920**
Farley Grubb

54 **The Rise of Planning in Industrial America, 1865–1914**
Richard Adelstein

55 **An Economic History of Modern Sweden**
Lennart Schön

56 **The Standard of Living and Revolutions in Russia, 1700–1917**
Boris Mironov

57 **Europe's Green Revolution and Others Since**
The rise and fall of peasant-friendly plant breeding
Jonathan Harwood

58 **Economic Analysis of Institutional Change in Ancient Greece**
Carl Hampus-Lyttkens

59 **Labour-Intensive Industrialization in Global History**
Edited by Gareth Austin and Kaoru Sugihara

60 **The History of Bankruptcy**
Economic, social and cultural implications in early modern Europe
Edited by Thomas Max Safley

61 **The Political Economy of Disaster and Underdevelopment**
Destitution, plunder and earthquake in Haiti
Mats Lundahl

62 **Nationalism and Economic Development in Modern Eurasia**
Carl Mosk

63 **Agricultural Transformation in a Global History Perspective**
Edited by Ellen Hillbom and Patrick Svensson

64 **Colonial Exploitation and Economic Development**
The Belgian Congo and the Netherlands Indies compared
Edited by Ewout Frankema and Frans Buelens

65 **The State and Business in the Major Powers**
An economic history 1815–1939
Robert Millward

66 **Privatization and Transition in Russia in the Early 1990s**
Carol Scott Leonard and David Pitt-Watson

Privatization and Transition in Russia in the Early 1990s

Carol Scott Leonard and
David Pitt-Watson

Routledge
Taylor & Francis Group
LONDON AND NEW YORK

First published 2013
by Routledge
2 Park Square, Milton Park, Abingdon, Oxon OX14 4RN

Simultaneously published in the USA and Canada
by Routledge
711 Third Avenue, New York, NY 10017

Routledge is an imprint of the Taylor & Francis Group, an informa business

British Library Cataloguing in Publication Data
A catalogue record for this book is available from the British Library

Library of Congress Cataloging in Publication Data
Leonard, Carol Scott, 1945–
Privatization and transition in Russia in the early 1990s / Carol Scott Leonard and David Pitt-Watson.
pages cm
1. Privatization–Russia (Federation) 2. Russia (Federation)–Economic conditions–1991– 3. Russia (Federation)–Economic policy–1991– 4. Post-communism–Russia (Federation) I. Pitt-Watson, David. II. Title.
HD4215.15.L46 2013
338.947'0509049–dc23 2012050412

ISBN: 978-0-415-55608-8 (hbk)
ISBN: 978-0-203-76682-8 (ebk)

Typeset in Times New Roman
by Wearset Ltd, Boldon, Tyne and Wear

Printed and bound in the United States of America by Publishers Graphics, LLC on sustainably sourced paper.

Contents

Illustrations

Figure

Tables

Acknowledgements

The authors gratefully acknowledge the important contribution to this book made by Alisa Voznaia, who, while completing her D.Phil. at the University of Oxford, graciously helped shape these chapters into a book. A special debt of gratitude is due to CEELBAS, the Consortium of UK Universities, which sponsored the conference on privatization at St Antony's College, and to our co-organizer Christopher Gerry. The authors appreciated the papers presented and discussions at that conference, with particular thanks to Ira Liberman, Vladimir Mau, Dmitry Vasiliev, Christopher Granville, Padma Desai, Anders Åslund, Marshall Goldman, Saul Estrin, Bill Tompson, Silvana Malle, Julian Cooper, Tina Jennings, Tomas Mickiewicz, John Earle, Giovanni Cornea, Phil Hanson, Judith Shapiro, Pekka Sutela, Simon Commander and Wolfram Shrettl. We thank those who worked for the EBRD/World Bank Consortium of advisers to Russia in 1992–94, in particular Joshua Bower Saul and Nicola Ramsden who have contributed appendices for this publication. The authors express appreciation for an anonymous charity research grant, which covered travel to Russia and editing of the book. The authors are grateful for support by the Presidential Academy of the National Economy and Public Administration, the National Research University – Higher School of Economics, and St Antony's College in Oxford, where the work on this book was completed.

Introduction

Background to the book

This book aims to describe, with some granularity, one of the most momentous and controversial economic reforms of the twentieth century: the privatization of Russia in the early 1990s. This involved unwinding the "great Soviet experiment – an attempt to run an entire economy ... by administrative command rather than by markets" (Gregory and Stuart 1994: 5).[1] The book should be of obvious interest to those who study Russian history, or transition economics, and it should also be of interest to anyone who wishes to reflect upon the gap between economic theory and the practical reality of economic policy and implementation. Privatization was not only an event of great importance for the people of Russia. In its rapidity and scale, it was also an experiment that created great debate among western economists about the nature and direction of economic policy.

It is now some 20 years since the passage of the 1992 Privatization Programme in Russia. This is the date when the process is typically assumed to have begun.

Initially it was seen as highly successful, as the foundation of political and economic freedom. Popular support was widespread for privatization (Nelson *et al.* 1992). But since the mid-1990s the climate of opinion among economists has changed. The process came to be seen as corrupt. The popular Russian label was *Prikhvatizatsiia* (the Grab),[2] and in English, "Piratization", as in the title of a book on reforms written by Marshall Goldman (2004). Indeed the failure of Russian economic reform in general, and privatization in particular, is often cited as evidence of the inadequacy of the liberal "Washington Consensus" as a prescription for economic reform.

As people who worked as advisers in Russia during that period, we both felt that this often heated debate failed properly to reflect our experience of what was happening on the ground. The accounts often failed to pay proper attention to the detail of either the history of events, the institutional framework for reform, or the political forces that influenced it. So, for example, they tend to overlook the degree of privatization, both de facto and de jure, which had taken place before 1992. They fail to distinguish between the many forms of privatization, some of which commanded broad support from the executive and legislature, and some of which did not. Often all Russia's economic ills are ascribed to privatization without adequate understanding of their origin in the economy to be reformed, or of the political context within which economic policy had to be developed.

Perhaps because these events were of such significance to the economic policy debate in the West, there has been a danger that, rather than drawing their conclusions from the events of the time, economists have been guilty of selecting aspects of the history of privatization to justify preconceived views.

Our aim is therefore to begin to set the record straight. To do so, we have aimed to review the privatization debate. This included hosting a conference of academics and other participants at Oxford in 2010. We have aimed to supplement this with interviews with participants from both sides of the debate. And we have had access to personal documents of the advisers to the Privatization Ministry (the GKI) during the period 1992–94. In the future, others may be able to add to this historical perspective. For now we hope that this short book will provide a record of the evolution of the policies and events, which will be of assistance to anyone who wishes to study the period, or indeed anyone who wishes to refer to these events to support a particular point of view in economic policy. Privatization in Russia is not just an important event in Russian, or indeed world, economic history. It is also one which is called as evidence to support or critique different economic policy prescriptions.

A guide to the book

For those who supported the reform, the need for private ownership derived from the assumption that with the establishment of private property rights, a key step towards efficient economic outcomes had been taken. Those who criticize the privatization policies reflect differently on the state of the Russian economy today, and see its ills emanating from the era of privatization. In Chapter 1 we review the debates over the assessment of privatization, and we find that the profound disillusionment and increasingly heated criticism show a complex and highly politicized subtext.

For example, to political journalists and non-mainstream economists the Russian government was too concerned with the liberal economic thinking behind the policy. It has not helped, in this regard, that theoretical economics most often assumes away the political context within which policy is developed. At a given moment, policy makers need to decide what to do, and that in turn is determined by what is feasible. This does not mean that privatization policy implemented in 1992 emerged out of the blue. We show in Chapter 2 that it emerged over time and was a result of both successful and failed negotiations between many interested parties and of legislation that predated the breakup of the Soviet Union. We note that the authority and room for manoeuvre of the government and, still more, of the reformers within the government, was very small. Further, privatization could not be implemented without regard for its broader consequences. Reformers had to design a policy able to dismantle the

Soviet economy without generating destabilizing unrest. We review this, and its implications for reform, in the first part of Chapter 3.

The "reformers" and those who advised them were aware of the dangers and the limitations of what was proposed. Indeed, they were aware that, on its own, privatization was unlikely to achieve the goals that the programme intended. Nevertheless, they chose to support its implementation and, to a degree, aimed to steer it away from the worst pitfalls, in particular the re-creation of a command and control structure based on the old Soviet ministries. We review this in the second half of Chapter 3.

In Chapter 4 we chronicle the progress of the implementation of the 1992 programme, why it was initially viewed as successful, and why that view proved to be short-lived.

The year 1994 marked the end of "voucher privatization" in Russia, and also the end of the period for which we have had access to privileged information. However, in Chapter 5 we move on to reflect on what happened in the period after 1994 as Russia moved to cash sales of its larger companies, and the critical similarities and differences from the earlier period.

Why is the book significant?

In Chapter 6, we summarize our objectives in writing this history. We believe they are important.

The first is to foster a more accurate history of this momentous period. In the first half of the 1990s Russia underwent the most fundamental economic and political changes. Indeed, the year 1991 witnessed the breakup of the Soviet Union and the elevation of the Russian Federation as a separate nation. Privatization was but one of the enabling reforms, and arguably not the most important. No single policy was free-standing or an end in itself; together they served as a means to a more prosperous and open economy for Russia. Understanding the successes and failures of at least one policy is of some importance in understanding the history of the country during that period.

The second is to reflect on the economic models that were used by the western and Russian promoters of reform, and their adequacy. Russian privatization is cited in the popular press as an example of the failure of aid to Russia, along with aid priorities referred to as the Washington Consensus (Freeland 2000). However, little attention is given to what alternatives to rapid privatization in Russia were actually feasible, the degree to which they were considered, and whether they would be likely to have worked. This, in turn, may help identify the adequacy or otherwise of the corpus of our economic knowledge, and where we might focus to make it more salient to policy makers operating in the real world.

Finally we argue that the issues that confronted policy makers in 1992 and bedevilled reform in Russia remain urgent in countries such as Cuba, where market-oriented structures are being introduced. Some issues related to privatization remain important even in Russia, where considerable reform has already remade the economic environment. For example, we would suggest that some of the constraints to improved corporate governance and economic growth which existed 20 years ago have now been removed, but some remain.

Privatization prior to 1992: a synopsis

In most transition countries, privatization was the third of three key reforms designed to encourage the market economy. Meant to follow in close sequence, they comprised "an incentive approach" to jump-start the economy. The first was price and trade liberalization. Only when prices reflected the real structure of costs (scarcity) would there be an incentive for a well-functioning financial system, where households could save instead of hoarding goods and investors could identify the best opportunities for the long term. Since the price shock was expected to be inflationary due to the release of repressed inflation, fiscal and monetary tightening was immediately required for stabilization; the third reform, privatization, aimed to encourage entrepreneurship and the spread of private ownership in previously command administrative economies. Privatization was the one reform of the three for which ready models existed: since the 1980s, there had been waves of "denationalization", reflecting a roll-back of post-Second World War nationalization in a liberal environment in market countries.[3] Only in a few communist countries, however, had any private sector activity been permitted, and therefore privatization was needed everywhere not in its classic case-by-case form but as a more radical and all-encompassing, decisive step. In one country in particular, Russia, radical privatization was required also because of political circumstances.

At considerable cost, Russian privatization was pushed forward in 1992 despite ongoing macroeconomic volatility and rapid inflation. Both timing and speed had to do with competition over privatization plans. In 1990 and 1991, there was evident tension between groups of government officials drawing up plans for privatization. Those who advocated essentially giving factories to the employees were particularly influential in the heart of the Soviet government; those who advocated a reform more like what was planned in Central Europe were dominant in the newly sovereign Russian Federation government.[4]

The era of market-oriented reforms had begun with Mikhail Gorbachev's reform agenda presented to the Communist Party on 10 December 1984, three months before he was elected its General Secretary (Åslund 1989: 26). In the spirit of economic revitalization, Gorbachev had introduced changes in investment policy to foster innovation, some instruments and market levers for enterprise managers, and the liberalization of foreign trade allowing even individuals to engage in profitable cross-border trade. In the name of accelerating growth and productivity, the government had embraced these liberalizing measures without fully anticipating the consequences for the management of enterprises.

They had envisioned the gradual diminution of the state sector over time and the preservation of socialism. Thus laws had enabled "individual labour activity" (19 November 1986),[5] joint ventures between state enterprises and foreign firms

(13 January 1987),[6] the transformation of enterprises from administrative to legal status (30 June 1987)[7] and a self-financing mechanism for independent "cooperatives" (26 May 1988),[8] which eliminated the barrier between cash and non-cash transactions and removed some restrictions on trade.[9] The most important law, and the beginning of what Russians call *peredel* ("the new order", or "breaking point"), associated with the economic reformer Petr Bunich, was About Rent (Leaseholding) (23 November 1989).[10] It had allowed work collectives legally to lease-to-purchase space and equipment from their enterprise and to accumulate new assets through retained earnings or bank loans (Ustiuzhanina 2001: 79). Some enabling rulings, particularly about Joint-stock and Limited Liability Companies on 19 June 1990,[11] had then allowed factory directors to shift state assets (including intellectual property rights) into the fixed capital of the new firm, thus giving shareholders possession of property of value. Managers and workers' collectives had then acquired substantial profits for reinvestment: they could borrow on their shares and, given rapid inflation, they could repay loans at a fraction of their real value. The Gorbachev regime, dominated by industrial interests, essentially had guaranteed future ownership rights to spin-offs from state firms (Nellis 1995: 8–9). Spontaneous privatization, as this was called, was certainly a way to launch a market-oriented economy in that it had led to asset seizing by the management and workers, but it had left the rest of the population without similar entitlement (Lieberman and Kopf 2007: 266; Feige 1991: 637; Abalkin and Miliukin 1990; Sutela 1991; Åslund 1997). In 1990, in some sectors, "trusts" had taken over general management of cooperatives and spin-offs under the directorship of ministry officials; these proliferated throughout 1991.[12]

Reform plans to carry out slower privatization had been proposed by one group in the Union government, headed by Leonid Abalkin. From this group the famous "500-Day Plan" by Grigory Yavlinsky and Stanislav Shatalin emerged; another group of reformers, economists working separately for the Russian Federation government under Evgeny Saburov, including such distinguished public figures as Evgeny Iasin, Aleksandr Shokhin and Vladimir Lopukhin, had also proposed a plan to Premier Ivan Silaev. Neither group had seen its proposals accepted (Mau 2010).

However, with more modest ambitions, the group in the Russian Federation, in the subcommittee for property and privatization, headed by Petr Fillipov and Petr Mostovoi, of the Supreme Soviet Committee for Economic Reform, had witnessed some success with laws passed on first reading on 24 and 25 December 1990.[13] These measures had limited the rights of workers' collectives to appropriate the profits of firms. They had clarified juridical definitions of private property and privatization, and aimed to stop spontaneous privatization by stipulating that privatization would only proceed on annual plans approved by the parliament of the Russian Federation. These laws were followed by a major law passed by both bodies, the Russian Federation Supreme Soviet and Union Supreme Soviet, in early July 1991.[14]

With this law on de-statization or privatization begins the history of the 1992 legal refinement of the process of privatization.[15] In the chaotic circumstances after the failed coup attempt of August, the July law became a mandate and resulted in the Privatization Programme for 1992, planned by members of Premier Gaidar's government, and passed by the now governing Russian Federation parliament in June 1992. This law, and the decree on the use of vouchers in the summer of 1992, so significantly transformed the process that they constituted the real first phase of legislated reform.

From 1992 to 1994, the Russian government carried out the Mass Privatization Programme (MPP), which used as its model the Czech voucher programme with some differences: for example, vouchers were made tradable. In the first phase of reform, 75,000–100,000 small-scale enterprises were created. Through the MPP, some 16,000 medium-size enterprises were privatized (Lieberman and Kopf 2007: 265).

The cash phase of privatization began in September 1994. The remaining shares left over from the MPP were sold by auction along with other enterprises. But in 1995, a different approach was taken. Some valuable properties were given to selected bidders for loans in order for the government to gain an immediate source of revenues before the elections. The final phase, which used as its instrument that classical case-by-case method, began with the auction of part of Svyazinvest, the national telecommunications company, and other large companies in a process by which the government selected suitable owners for a state-owned company.

The main focus of this book is the 1992 Privatization Programme, though the penultimate chapter discusses subsequent events. We hope to throw new light on the history and introduce more historical context so that scholars may rethink the intense economic debate that still surrounds these events.

1 Privatization and the Russian transition

Perspectives

The Russian Mass Privatization Programme (MPP) of 1992–94[1] was the largest single privatization project ever undertaken, in terms of the number of companies and employees it affected. More important, it created the foundation of a market economy in Russia.

This chapter aims, first, to provide a brief background for our history of decision making in the early 1990s. We place that decision making in the context of the economic inheritance of Russia – the political, legal and constitutional mêlée within which reform was introduced, including the attempted coup in August 1991 and parliamentary opposition in September 1993. As Appel (2004: 179) cautions in her comparison of privatization in the Czech Republic and Russia, one must not "lose sight of the context in which the region's privatizers found themselves in the early 1990s". As reform was planned, there were tectonic shifts in the configuration of actors and interests in politics, introducing an urgent practical need to bring this reform – already mandated in the summer of 1991 – to completion.

Second, we aim to show the evolution of perspectives on the reforms. Initially the response was positive; however, in later years, for many policy-oriented economists after the mid-1990s, the Russian transition seemed an example of what went wrong with the Washington Consensus. The international aid community is often held responsible for the state of the Russian economy in the mid- to late 1990s. in the Conclusion to this chapter, we see perspectives on Russian privatization as still not entirely settled.

The first step is to put some flesh on the bones of those events. We then aim to arrive at what we believe is a balanced view of this reform, warranted by the evidence, and the lessons we might learn from it.

Background to privatization in Russia

Pressure for reform, 1985–1991

Some generalizations about the economic and political context of reform apply to all the transition economies of Eastern Europe and the former Soviet Union. Decades of faltering productivity growth rates put pressure on the governments to exact radical market-oriented reform. To this pressure was added a popular desire, more apparent in some countries than others, for political reform, the creation of democratic institutions and the introduction of civil rights (Fish 1997; Pickles and Smith 1998; Fidrmuc 2003). In these countries, obtaining support for reforms by government was often a smoother process than in Russia and the Commonwealth of Independent States (CIS), where expectations could not be anchored in hopes of European Union (EU) accession.

The mounting pressure for economic and political reform in the Russian Federation was accompanied by declarations of sovereignty among the Soviet republics, which led to the fracturing of central political authority. Throughout 1991, as the Soviet economy stagnated, the soon-to-be break-away republics, including the Russian Soviet Federative Socialist Republic (RSFSR), began to execute economic reform without consulting the central authorities of the Soviet state. Both the Russian and the Soviet parliaments passed legislation that enabled private and quasi-private ownership before 1992, resulting in simultaneous policy formation at different levels of government. The process was chaotic and associated with fierce conflict over means and ends.

Mikhail Gorbachev,[2] the head of the Soviet Union, had failed to implement a clear programme of institutional or economic reform, in part because his government was focused on political reform, indeed the future of the Soviet Union (Breslauer 2002; McFaul 2004: 140).[3] Gorbachev's cautious policies and vacillation between inviting reform proposals and rejecting them showed both the power of leading communist opponents to stall and shape industrial privatization and his own reluctance on the issue of private property rights. So, in 1991, the legislation underlying ownership of Russia's industrial assets remained ambiguous. Laws emanating from both the Soviet and the Russian parliaments were incomplete and often contradictory.[4] The focus of political debate and reform was less on economic reform and more on the very existence of the country itself.

Even without a full programme, Gorbachev started the privatization process which led to "spontaneous privatization". The Communist Party of the Soviet Union (CPSU) in 1991 had agreed to remove small businesses and traders from state ownership. A Standing Socioeconomic Commission of the CPSU Central Committee report, dated 20 May 1991, advocated rapid privatization of light industries, the food industry, and trade and services; but it advocated state ownership for natural resources and leaseholding and shareholding mechanisms for the state industrial sector.[5] The speed of change was to be slow, in fear that "excessive haste, or God forbid, compulsion" might lead to serious social unrest.[6] One driver of legislation in Gorbachev's government was the formidable interests of industrial ministries, which aimed to control privatization.

After the failed August coup, Boris Yeltsin,[7] then the President of the RSFSR, showed a strong commitment to both political and economic change. He banned the former ruling Communist Party and converted the central planning economic regime to a state apparatus less engaged with the economy and more accommodating to markets (McFaul 2001: 127; Sakwa 2002: 32; Gros and Steinherr 2004:

228). He secured Gorbachev's resignation on 25 December 1991, which triggered the dissolution of the Soviet Union, and gained recognition of the United Nations for the Supreme Soviet of the Russian Federation[8] as the government of the successor state. The Russian Federation now held a permanent appointment at the Security Council.

Despite Yeltsin's political departures from the previous regime, he did not call elections for a new Congress of People's Deputies[9] and he postponed plans for a new constitution. Thus, from 1991 to 1993, parliamentary and presidential authority was derived from the constitution of the previous Russian republic, originally drafted in 1977, and subsequently amended (not least to incorporate the role of president).[10]

Without a new constitution, or a new popular mandate, Yeltsin had little choice but to work with the existing Russian parliament (Congress of People's Deputies) and with the Supreme Soviet that governed between its sessions. This strategy meant that, at least initially, he depended on key allies in the Supreme Soviet (of which he had previously been chairman), especially Ruslan Khasbulatov,[11] its current chairman, who helped Yeltsin secure temporary extraordinary powers to rule by decree in November 1991, and to push preliminary approval of the government's Privatization Programme through the Presidium of the Supreme Soviet in December 1991.[12]

Yeltsin's decision to rule by decree no doubt lessened incentives for further institutional reform and weakened the essentially democratic credentials that he held when he became president.[13] Nevertheless, he was the only figure who could claim a popular national mandate. He was the leader of the political movement Democratic Russia, had been the head of the Russian Supreme Soviet,[14] was elected the chair of the Russian Congress of People's Deputies, and, from June 1991, was the elected president of the Russian Federation.[15] Although he seized control "from the top of a tank", he did so in defence of parliamentary rights (Gustafson 1999: 29).

However, the political weight bestowed upon parliament in the early 1990s allowed it not only to award powers to Yeltsin, but also to challenge his government. In the Soviet era, there had been no separation of power between government branches, and the Supreme Soviet had made and executed the laws. Ruslan Khasbulatov on 13 January 1992 sharply criticized the reform programme as leading to a chaos that might serve a dictatorship. On 20 January, he called for the government to resign and for society "to realize the difference between the government and the Supreme Council".[16]

Against this political force, the government provided no unified front. It essentially comprised a weak coalition of conservative and reform interests. Yeltsin's non-ideological stance was reflected in the different backgrounds and opinions of the members of his own government. Yeltsin chose to stay above the fray, to the extent that it was possible. His role, as Burbulis put it, was as brakeman and regulator or arbitrator as well as locomotive.[17] Colton (2008: 247) describes Yeltsin's "migration" as president to a position where "he had done Russia a service by *shielding* it from a revolution. He preferred the emollients 'radical reforms', 'democratic reconstruction', 'reformist breakthrough', or if revolutionary verbiage could not be helped, 'quiet revolution' (*tikhaya revolyutsia*)."

From his fragmented political base, with resignations and new additions to his team, Yeltsin faced challenges in building the foundations of a market economy that were political as well as economic in nature. With the buildup of a strong lobby within the government against mass privatization of industry and favouring workers' collectives, he nevertheless had to construct a reform that would address the pressing needs of the Russian economy, while paving the way for longer-term benefits through better corporate governance and overall efficiency. Meanwhile, his foreign policy moved towards closer relations with Europe and the United States, while his domestic policy embraced reform and institutional change, replacing the command administrative system (Lane and Ross 1999; Breslauer 2002). At the time, the political challenges in Russia were considerable and pressure for legal reform was building. In Russia, as in Central Europe, mass privatization was seen as a key reform in market transformation, and its larger message, addressed to communist politicians, was that the total state ownership of enterprise was over.

Further, the economy was in a parlous state in late 1991, and the question of "when to do what" was not a political priority. As McFaul observes (2004: 141), "no one within the Russian government cautioned against going 'too fast' ". Yegor Gaidar,[18] the architect of the radical economic reforms and one of the leading politicians in Yeltsin's first government, later reflected that when Yeltsin formally assumed the reins of power at the end of 1991, the country was on the brink of catastrophe. With the collapse of the Soviet communist state and no immediate succession to a new democratic one, the country lacked key elements necessary for a functioning state and economy.[19] It was in these circumstances of institutional chaos that Yeltsin and his government set about the reform process.

The decisions

The 1992 Privatization Programme was approved by the Russian parliament within six months of price and trade liberalization. With a single, albeit incomplete, price and trade reform on 1 January 1992, the government ended the autarkic closed system that enabled the functioning of the command economy. The pace and the order of changes in Russia were forced on the government, as Anatoly Chubais explained in an interview on Russian TV with Aleksandr Radov, who asked "Why did you rush?"

> If we had had the opportunity to act as we wanted, the problem of privatization would have been resolved first. Of course, it would have been even better to restore the financial situation to health first, and only after that to free prices. We found ourselves in a situation where the economy was on its deathbed. Either we took emergency measures right away and got it out of this state, or we would quite simply be dealing with a corpse.[20]

Thus, price liberalization came first, then stabilization with fiscal tightening, then privatization. Yeltsin, who had little knowledge of economics, nevertheless knew that change was needed. And, indeed, a survey taken by the USSR State Committee for Statistics in March 1991 had found widespread appreciation of the need for "radical change".[21] Just under half (45 per cent) the population was prepared to accept the temporary hardship that would come about as a result of radical reforms. The commentator for *Izvestiia* observed: "I must repeat, however, that people are perfectly well aware that there is no alternative to a market economy and that change cannot be avoided."[22]

It was understood at the time that inflation would complicate stabilization efforts (Choksi and Papageorgiou 1986; Feige 1991). In Russia, inflationary pressure powerfully contributed to undermining the classic transition strategy. The initial rise in the price level was far higher than expected – exceeding 250 per cent – associated mostly with a larger than expected monetary overhang from the Soviet era and an underprediction of the effects of a large initial devaluation.[23] There were no doubt also structural reasons, such as the move from a dual to a unitary monetary system for the jump in the price level.[24] Difficulties also stemmed from Russia being a federative state – without the enviable fiscal control of unitary states like Poland and the Czech Republic. Autonomous regional borrowing along with discretionary budgeting imperilled fiscal stability throughout transition. For the severity of inflation, the policies of the Central Bank, headed by Viktor Gerashchenko,[25] were in part responsible. Accountable to parliament rather than to the government, Gerashchenko continued to issue credits to enterprises. Nor was it clear whether the government was united in its desire to control the budget. Yeltsin himself was "a hard sell" on the subject of controlling the money supply (Colton 2008: 243). Viktor Gerashchenko pointed out that it was "the government asking us through Parliament to provide [enterprises with] credit".[26] Where credits were not issued by the Central Bank, enterprises issued credits to one another, which resulted in huge pressure on the centre to pay the enterprises' workers. Rapid inflation persisted throughout 1992 and the decline of the economy accelerated. The rampant inflation[27] hardly provided favourable conditions for the Mass Privatization Programme, which began in the autumn of 1992.[28]

The hope had been that the effects of price shocks would only last for a limited period.[29] In a television address, Yeltsin himself told the nation, that the reform process "will be tough for us … but this period will not be long. We are talking about 6–8 months."[30] By the end of 1992, however, the turnaround in Russia's economic fortunes had failed to materialize. Gaidar had left the government. Anatoly Chubais was the leading reformer, made responsible for the execution of the Privatization Programme.

Privatization was the policy that reformers were hoping would lead to early benefits, initially in giving securities of value to the population and later in accelerating restructuring and efficiency. So, despite these inauspicious conditions, the government went through with the drafting of the Privatization Programme for 1992, passing it in June 1992.[31] It became one of the few pieces of economic reform legislation that had both parliamentary and executive approval. It included a list of categories for companies that were to be privatized. For medium to large companies, the programme laid out three alternative approaches to privatization. Controversially, one of these allowed the purchase of the majority of shares in a company by its own workforce.[32] That move, often regarded as a concession to the industrial lobby, certainly helped build a coalition in support of the programme (Boycko *et al.* 2001).

However, while the "supply side" of privatization gained parliamentary support, the demand side did not. A Presidential Decree of 18 August 1992, which authorized the issue of tradable vouchers (as opposed to illiquid privatization accounts),[33] was perceived by parliamentary opponents as contradictory to the spirit of the 1991 Privatization Law, under which the 1992 Programme was passed.

The Privatization Programme set out the terms for voucher acquisition by citizens and their redemption at auctions for shares of medium-size firms. Big companies, including companies in the extractive sector, were excluded from privatization. The voucher decree was modelled in part on the Czech experiment, but the vouchers were to be individually subscribed for, and to be tradable, thus offering Russian citizens as a whole, and not only the labour collectives, a stake in Russian industry.

The design of the voucher distribution model accorded particular privileges to insider purchasers. To some extent, voucher privatization in Russia mirrored the outcomes in the Central and Eastern European (CEE) economies, which were similarly characterized by insider trading. In Russia, however, this was also in part a decision to "trump" laws put in place under Gorbachev, which had allowed "leasing for purchase" and other forms of "spontaneous privatization", which were to be superseded by privatization. So, for example, these earlier laws had allowed managers to lease, or in other ways transfer, the value of their enterprises' assets to shell companies owned by friends or to set up joint ventures with foreign partners (Thomas 1993; Carlin *et al.* 1995; Bornstein 1999). Though vouchers aimed to involve citizens and provide a sense of fairness, and though worker ownership was in accord with the traditions of Russia, it was, as we shall show, unlikely that voucher privatization and insider ownership could, in the short term, help Russia to restructure its industry. Additionally, voucher distribution meant that the state was not going to raise any revenue from privatization. The limitations of what could be achieved through privatization were understood by policy makers at the time; nonetheless, the programme garnered support, not least because it was deemed superior to any other option available.

The Russian Privatization Programme was developed and implemented in the context of chaotic institutional transition. Its political champions navigated through the corridors of reform with lightning speed, attempting simultaneously to resolve supply and demand problems, while dismantling the Soviet command economy. Thus, while to some extent the Russian Privatization Programme paralleled similar programmes in the CEE, the political situation, the industrial structure of the country, and cultural heterogeneity complicated the reform process in Russia, making it qualitatively different to those in many other post-communist countries in the region.

Perspectives on privatization

A large body of empirical literature has addressed the outcomes of privatization in post-communist countries. It has asked if fundamentally changing the ownership structure of firms resulted in improved performance of firms, restructuring and greater efficiency.[34] It is not our objective to evaluate this literature, except in one regard. It is an important finding that after 20 years, no robust difference in performance has been established among countries as a result of different methods of privatization. Estrin *et al.* (2009: 702) write:

> Commencing with the macro studies, we find that the results suggest that privatization, especially when accompanied by complementary reforms, may have a positive effect on the level of aggregate output or economic growth. However, one of the most widely debated issues of transition (e.g., Kornai 2001), namely the effect on aggregate output and growth of rapid privatization (frequently accompanied by dispersed ownership) versus slower privatization (often with more concentrated ownership), remains unresolved.

It was widely acknowledged at the time that privatization alone was insufficient to produce positive results, which could be gained only from a larger reform strategy, by coordinating what Svejnar (2002: 5) later called "type 1" (macroeconomic stabilization, price liberalization and dismantling institutions of the communist regime) and "type 2" (legal reform and institutions for regulating a market economy, including privatization) reforms (Svejnar 1990; Lipton and Sachs 1990; Blanchard *et al.* 1991; Aghion and Blanchard 1994; Estrin *et al.* 2009). In other words, significant as it was in ending the essence of the communist state – total state ownership of the means of production–privatization was by no means enough to jump-start a well-functioning market economy.[35]

Voucher privatization has nevertheless taken much of the blame in academic literature for Russia's long recession (Wedel 1998; Black *et al.* 2000; Shlapentokh 1993; Stiglitz 2002; Woods 2006). Along with weak corporate governance in Russia, the reform is credited with the pervasive corruption observed in the country by the end of the 1990s (Varese 2005). Privatization has been credited as the main driver of recession (Black *et al.* 2000; Kolodko 2000; Goldman 2004), even though, by early 1992, Russia was already in the grip of runaway inflation and widespread seizure of firm assets. This chapter attempts to explain why this single reform – no less successful than similar reforms in other transition economies – has seemed the main factor in Russia's unfortunate and enduring economic recession, and why the authors of this reform, rather than general economic conditions and a larger policy failure, were to such an extent held to blame.

The early reputation of privatization

In the first few years of the reform, observers noted the efficacy of the decentralization process, which demonstrated the federal state's considerable capacity to transfer thousands of state-owned firms to the private sector without halting economic activity or undermining the political order in the short run (Lieberman and Rahuja 1995; Nellis 1995; Estrin and Stone 1997; Appel 2004). The reform was carried out with speed and an effective media campaign. Despite the enormous size of the country, the reform established private ownership in an economy "more heavily distorted by communist planning than most (and in an environment more intensely politicized than elsewhere)" (Lieberman and Rahuja 1995: 7, 29). An impressive all-Russian auction centre was in place after March 1993: brokerages and exchanges were established in the regions. Leeds and Harman (1995: 111) report that "despite a continuous array of roadblocks, the Russian privatization program has indeed become the catalyst for market-oriented reforms and it has established solid foundation for the development of a securities market".

To be sure, as Blasi *et al.* (1997: 2, 48) caution, short-term judgements were impressionistic: "One month Russia is all Mafia, the next months all emerging stock market, then all communism, then all entrepreneurial savvy." There was excitement in 1994 when the Russian stock market seemed to take off, but then it crashed. Russian investment privatization, or voucher funds, first drew note as they multiplied in a few years, and then disappointed the observers, who later assessed them as having been mismanaged and failed to bring about transformation (Volgin and Milner 1995: 55; Pistor and Spicer 1997).

The Washington Consensus[36] was important in the early positive reputation of Russian privatization. John Williamson's seminal Washington Consensus, a policy prescription advocating macroeconomic stabilization and the opening up of trade and investment, encapsulated the reformers' priorities, which conformed to the views of many development economists who were shaping international aid policies at the time. During this period, there was "more privatization, deregulation, and trade liberalization in Latin America and Eastern Europe than probably anywhere else at any point in economic history" (Rodrik 2006: 974).

It is important to underscore, however, that while international agencies were supportive of the Russian plans, significant international aid for Russian privatization began only in 1992.[37] Initially, the Russian government worked on the privatization programme with little help from international agencies. In March 1992, the World Bank sent a mission to Russia, providing early guidance on the use of vouchers. The mission included experts who had worked on the Czech privatization, to which the Russian programme bore some resemblance. However, the World Bank advised that "privatisation [was] not an end in itself".[38] Unlike some of the Central European countries, Russia privatized its enterprises before restructuring them, with millions of vouchers distributed to management and employees. In reviewing the Russian privatization, the US

Government Accountability Office (GAO) observed that restructuring could be complicated if the new share owners objected to it.[39] Despite reservations regarding restructuring, the GAO determined that assistance for privatization was a successful, if not cost-effective, project. More than 70 million vouchers were distributed during the course of the programme, with many of the distribution centres evolving into active market institutions.[40]

Among others who supported the highly positive international consensus, naturally, were the reformers and some of their advisers, whose works cited Russia's privatization for its demonstration of the applicability of certain "fundamental economic principles" (Boycko *et al.* 1995: vii). The achievements were indeed extraordinary. For example, Lieberman and Rahuja (1995: 7) remark that the Russian government had moved forward with impressive reform plans and implementation: "From December 1992 to February 1994, nearly 9,500 large scale enterprises, employing 11 million people, were privatized, creating 40 million new shareholders." One of the most successful of the European post-communist restorations of private ownership in law and its dominance in the economy, they wrote, the Russian programme assumed a grander scale than the more controlled reforms in Poland, the Czech Republic and Slovakia. It was more comprehensive in the sense that vouchers were more widely distributed, with over 20 million company employees gaining access to vouchers, far more than in any programme elsewhere. And the privatization took only 27 months to complete from the introduction of the bill to parliament until the closure of voucher auctions.

Russian privatization served as a model for others. Twenty-five countries used some form of mass privatization as either a primary or a secondary method (Estrin 1997). Nine countries used management-employee buyouts as their primary mechanism, with six more using them as their secondary method. Only five countries used direct sales as the primary privatization method – and these five were among the most developed and advanced transitional economies. Estrin (2002a: 109) writes:

> Mass privatization was an excellent solution to the problem that state ownership was omnipresent and domestic wealth holders were insufficient to buy the assets. The mass privatization strategy also facilitated an extremely speedy ownership change in most transition economies, as few countries had contained a private sector of any significance in 1990.

Nellis (1995: 1) wrote that Russian privatization was "the one bright spot in the generally bleak Russian economic landscape". The transformation of half the state-owned enterprises into joint stock companies with privileges for workers' collectives, he commented, although a forced compromise, designed by Anatoly Chubais, was an achievement, undermining potential opposition from workers and managers by distributing vouchers. In 1994 and 1995, the political accomplishment of Russian reform was widely viewed as one of the most significant in all respects in Central and Eastern Europe (Appel 2004: 93).

Reception of reform: mid-1990s

Views of reform grew more tentative when Russia, in common with most other countries of the former Soviet Union and in contrast to the leaders in Central and Eastern Europe, failed to recover quickly from a deep transformational recession. The costs of institutional transformation, and perhaps of early policy flaws,[41] were severe. Economists began more widely to question the appropriateness of the privatization models used and, particularly, the speed of reform. The negative appraisal worsened in subsequent years as a consequence of a growing lack of transparency in the privatization process, especially after 1994 (when the MPP had come to an end). Before the turn of the century, the condemnatory views came to dominate popular literature. Privatization is totemic in a sweeping criticism of the broader economic reform programme of the Yeltsin regime.

Internally, that is within Russia, criticism of the project emerged early among those leading the parliamentary opposition and also from within the government. Even those who might be considered reformers were critical, including Grigory Yavlinsky, an economist and the leader of the liberal Yabloko party. This domestic criticism later affected perceptions abroad, especially following the loans-for-shares (LFS) operation in 1995.[42] The review of privatization laws and policies carried out by the Audit Chamber of the Russian Federation was highly critical ("Analiz" 2004). The critics viewed the LFS, probably the seminal event undermining the positive view of privatization, as unfair, benefiting the government and the oligarchs at the expense of society as a whole. In addition to divesting the state of valuable assets at a time when their market price was low, losing substantial revenue for the state, the LFS considerably weakened the government's credibility domestically and abroad, even in the eyes of fervent supporters of the Russian Privatization Programme (Lieberman and Kopf 2007: 325–6).

The non-transparent nature of the LFS and its outcomes led some observers to call into question the actions of the elites driving the privatization and the role of international donors guiding reform policies. Freeland's *Sale of the Century* (2000), for instance, describes the pervasive corruption, which she attributes to the ambitions of the elites who supposedly exploited the chaotic conditions in the country to coordinate privatization to their advantage. She finds, further, that a small coterie around Yeltsin, led by Anatoly Chubais, the minister in charge of privatization, manufactured the LFS mainly to assist the victory of Yeltsin in the 1996 presidential elections (Freeland 2000; Goldman 2004). Freeland posits that the oligarchic elites were backed by western agencies, though to our knowledge no official international agency advised on or condoned the LFS.[43]

Like Freeland, Wedel (1998) criticizes international donors' seeming proclivity to "back people", as opposed to policies. In her book, Wedel links US aid to the Yeltsin regime and the privatization project, weaving a personal scandal into the reform narrative. According to this account, international donors made Yeltsin's government "the gatekeeper for hundreds of millions of dollars in G-7 taxpayer aid, subsidized loans, and rescheduled debt" (ibid.: 122), in essence, sponsoring a small clique around "the 'St Petersburg Clan' or the 'Chubais

Clan' ". While there is validity to the observation that western agencies come to the assistance of particular policy makers, rather than basing their assistance only on the soundness of the policies themselves, it can be argued that for transition aid to have been effective, it had to be given to reform-oriented governments and have been negotiated and managed for those governments by key individuals. This was a lesson learned from prior experience in Latin America, where economies showed little benefit from the extension of unwelcome aid (Tsikata 1998: 75).[44] So, although large areas of government were broadly and deeply affected by ongoing consultations with international advisers, in many areas, such as agriculture, international agency expert advice was limited. Furthermore, Wedel's argument that US aid to Poland and Russia comprised "too often poorly conceived and structured projects ... [which] ... led to impasse or even disaster" (ibid.: 6) shows little understanding of how aid worked and, specifically, how aid for privatization actually functioned.[45]

What went wrong?

Into the late 1990s, when the Russian economy had not yet emerged sustainably from its transformational recession – again, by contrast with the more advanced Central European states – policy analysts focused exclusively on what went wrong. Some focused on Russia's initial conditions, which predisposed it to a particular vulnerability to transition reforms. Russia had no experience with market reform, in contrast to countries in Central Europe, particularly Poland and Hungary, where there had been partial marketization in the 1980s. Russia's industrial structure and external trade patterns were initially more distorted than in Central Europe. The weakness of law enforcement institutions and the strength of the industrial lobby and other opponents of markets were attributed by some economists to legacies of the Soviet era (Gaddy and Ickes 2002; De Melo *et al.* 1997; Krueger and Ciolko 1998; Heybey and Murrell 1999; Popov 2000: 35). Others traced the failure of macroeconomic reform in Russia in large part to the state of chaos at the end of perestroika, chaos far worse than in former East Germany, Hungary, the Czech Republic and Slovakia (Dabrowski 1997: 41–2). An excessive supply of money, in combination with mainly fixed prices, led to repressed inflation and forced savings. As the planned economy disintegrated in the late 1980s, relaxed economic discipline in Russia drove the annual rate of growth of M2 up to 15 per cent and increased the velocity of money, while investment collapsed and output began to plunge.

Other economists focused on the critical policy differences between Russia and Central and Eastern Europe (Åslund *et al.* 1996; De Melo *et al.* 1996; Brenton *et al.* 1997). It was thought that the pace of privatization without prior stabilization had not been the best policy. Rogoff (2002) observed:

> Now it is clear ... creating incentives for genuine restructuring of enterprises was more important than moving property into private hands. Imposing hard budget constraints to force out the chronic loss-makers among the

> enterprises turns out to have been quite important in inducing restructuring even if the enterprises were still in state hands.

"The furious pace of the sale of assets" was also blamed for opening the door to corruption (Black *et al.* 2000; Kolodko 2000: 166). Kolodko (ibid.: 156) put it as follows:

> [W]hen assets were being dragged through the hectic process of the transfer of property rights, the distortions induced in management and corporate governance were quite serious.... Privatizations which are politically driven, hurriedly executed, and not well planned intensify rather than reduce allocative inefficiency.

To be sure, it was well known from the outset that speedy reform would not preclude self-dealing (Sachs and Pistor 1997). But alongside this disadvantage, the reformers assumed that there would be benefits: the alignment of control and property rights and the provision of incentives for less able insiders to sell the firm to better managers (Blanchard and Aghion 1996). After the fact, however, it became clear that once in control and connected to government, powerful insiders could not be constrained. For example, in Russia, the so-called "strategic" industries, including oil, gas and the extractive industries, continued to have the support of the state. In one of the most searing critiques, Black *et al.* (2000) argue with this in mind that self-dealing both discredits reform and, in the long run, prevents corrective policies.

Other major faults were found with Russian privatization. Some faulted inconsistency, for example the failure to precede price reform with currency reform (Goldman 2004: 64), the failure to decontrol energy prices (Shleifer and Treisman 2001: 2), and the failure to reform the punitive tax system (Vysokov 1995: 15; Black *et al.* 2000). As economists tabulated the negative impact of the privatization on the Russian economy, many began to reconsider the soundness of privatization as the focal point of development reform.

The consensus shift

The attack on Russia's privatization broadened to its "free market fundamentalism", as Nobel Prize-winning economist Joseph Stiglitz[46] represented the ideology of the privatizers. It would be difficult to separate this attack on Russian reform from an emerging fault line in aid policy agendas, driven by "new" Keynesianism during the late 1990s. The displacement of the Washington Consensus as the dominant paradigm followed a series of financial crises in the 1990s, affecting Mexico (1994), Asia (1997), Russia (1998) and Brazil (1999).

Stiglitz and many others attribute the poor performance of the Russian economy in the 1990s almost exclusively to the reforms, emphasizing the gap between the goals and the outcomes of privatization, particularly the failure of firms to become more profitable. The overall privatization strategy, Stiglitz (2002: 143–4) wrote,

> set the preconditions for decline. Not only was investment halted, but capital was used up – savings vaporized by inflation, the proceeds of privatization or foreign loans largely misappropriated. Privatization, accompanied by the opening of the capital markets, led not to wealth creation but to asset stripping. It was perfectly logical. An oligarch who has just been able to use political influence to garner assets worth billions, after paying only a pittance, would naturally want to get his money out of the country.

From this perspective, at least at the time, the costs of building markets by assumption outweighed the benefits.[47] However, the context of decision making is not addressed. Neither are the pre-existing spontaneous and widespread privatization, corruption and rampant inflation. Indeed, one objective of mass privatization was to stop the spontaneous privatization that began in 1990 and 1991, and clauses in the June 1992 Programme repealed previous methods of privatization. As we discuss in chapters below, asset stripping emerged in the late Soviet era due to weakness of control over firm management. It then fed on expectations of further property rights reform (Kikeri *et al.* 1992; Grigoriev 1992; Kornai 1992; Naishul 1992). The 1992 Programme, unlike subsequent waves of privatization, aimed to formalize and regularize the privatization process. It aimed to guarantee that despite "asset stripping", Russian citizens and other outsiders would gain a stake in the new market economy.

For reform policies to bear the full responsibility for poor outcomes, however, it would be necessary to show that there was a better alternative reform programme available. In essence, this would have been one that would have established the structures of a market economy before embarking on privatization. As we will show, the international institutions were aware that, if such an outcome were possible, it would indeed have been a better policy. However, to have delayed de jure privatization, however imperfect, would have risked the continuation of de facto control being taken of industrial assets, either within or beyond the law, which is precisely the process to which the critics of privatization object. Indeed, arguably, corruption within the privatization process became greater, not less, the longer the delay in its implementation.

In writings of this persuasion, curiously, examples generally given of abuse are frequently those of companies that were not part of the original Mass Privatization Programme. Rather, such examples focus on companies that were sold for cash, were privatized under special arrangements, or were sold after the mass privatization had finished.

The broad attack on Russia's policies found support among Russian opponents of the 1992 Privatization Programme and its implementation. Their critique was founded in the ideology of "economic democracy". That is, members of the academy institutes, who had long been opposed to radical reform and to unlimited private ownership, cited the western critiques in their writing (Shlapentokh 1993: 25).

For two decades from the early 1980s, privatization seemed a global orthodoxy (Megginson and Netter 2001: 5). However, it was now extensively criticized, especially in Russia. Nellis (1999: 3) describes the about-face as "a multifaceted spirit of revisionism". He summarizes the revisionist view:

> There was doubt that sufficient analytical rigor had been used in modeling privatization and in assessing empirical results; that privatization was not socially justified in all firms and contexts; and that revenues for the state and profits for shareholders had outweighed the disadvantages for the poor and the socially excluded.

Scepticism now pervades policy literature, and development theoreticians are shifting towards regionally tailored agendas. There is little question that the Washington Consensus has vanished as a descriptor of donor priorities; instead it is now associated with the negative attribution of "neoliberalism" (Rodrik 2006). The negative consequences of "neoliberal" Russian policies are now a common feature of writing about Russia. Goldman (2004: 22), for example, argues "that the faulty privatization process is responsible for many of Russia's present-day problems. The oligarchs who are a product of that privatization are responsible for much that has gone wrong".

Further reflections

From such literature, some comparative political economists have taken a more neutral stance. For example, Appel's (2004) *A New Capitalist Order: Privatization and Ideology in Russia and Eastern Europe*, discussing reform in Russia and in the Czech Republic finds much in common: a commitment to speed, reflecting to some degree a pragmatic and flexible approach, and an ideological core, which was liberal in its economic principles and committed to fairness in allowing citizens, and not only workers, to benefit from reform. Appel does not associate the pain, indeed acute suffering, following reform in post-communist societies with particular mistaken and ill-intended acts (ibid.: 178). She argues that, for complex reasons, the cost of compliance in Russia was particularly high due to the extent and organization of opposition, observing that reformers failed to employ ideological justification or use national symbols in support of the restoration of markets, by contrast with the campaigns led by reformers in the Czech Republic. As a result, their opponents reaped the advantage by seizing those instruments of national interest to undermine the reform as a "Western imposition and alien to Russians" (ibid.: 100). The two radical reform governments thus carried out similar reforms; however, for the lack of Russian identity symbolization in information campaigns, she argues, similar policies were judged very differently.

Granville and Oppenheimer (2001: 18) also offer a similar, balanced account, noting the institutional constraints to reform and the danger of misinterpreting statistics. Yet even they allow the suggestion that voucher privatization allowed a new business elite to "steal absolutely everything".

Finally, there are still economists who continue to view the Russian privatization as highly successful. Åslund (2007: 268), for example, included even the

LFS in his view that privatizations were an "unmitigated success" because leaving those enterprises in state hands would have brought about worse outcomes. More recently he has analysed the relationship between levels of privatization in different transition economies and found them to have a positive correlation with democracy and a negative one with corruption.[48]

Among those who have maintained that there was considerable merit all along are the economists at the OECD (2005: 20):

> The past thirteen years have seen a dramatic transformation of Russia's economy. An economy based on state ownership, central planning and a high degree of autarky has given way to one based primarily on private ownership, market forces and integration into the world economy. The private sector, which barely existed in 1991, now accounts for roughly 70% of GDP.

We derive the starting point for our discussion from the continuing ambiguity shrouding a clear evaluation of the Russian privatization process.

Conclusion

All this leaves open a huge question. How should we evaluate what happened in the Mass Privatization Programme in Russia? Effective? Ineffective? We believe that question is best addressed by going back to the events of the time to understand how policy was developed, what it attempted to achieve, and how it was implemented. These will be the subjects of the following chapters.

In the next chapter we are concerned with the substance of the reform. In Chapter 3 we discuss the economic rationale for the Privatization Programme, why the benefits that could be expected from it were limited in the absence of other reforms, and why it was nevertheless accepted as the best course of action. In Chapter 4 we look at the detail of policy and implementation, the dilemmas facing policy makers, and the nature of decision making. In Chapter 5 we go on to look at the later cash privatization, and in Chapter 6 we draw conclusions about how the privatization process in Russia might be evaluated and what we can learn from it.

2 The Mass Privatization Programme

The ideas, their evolution and their embodiment in law

Introduction

Summaries of the Privatization Programme in Russia often make the assumption that there was one well-defined policy; that it was clear; that it had one set of architects; that it was well prescribed in legal terms, as it might have been in an advanced market economy; and that the process of privatization was bimodal, or that one could readily distinguish the characteristics that meant a company was or was not privatized. However, closer analysis of the history of the various different attempts at privatization and quasi-privatization in Russia, of contemporary accounts of events, and of the writings of those advising on privatization reveals that the situation was considerably more ambiguous.

First, there were many versions of privatization and marketization building upon, or even reversing, one another. Few of them followed the prescriptions of any one political grouping, few were even complete, and few created definitively privatized entities. Arguably, this includes companies privatized through the Mass Privatization Programme. Second, there were many architects of different versions of privatization. In part, this was because there were many loci of power: before and after the abandonment of the Soviet Union; executive and legislative; local and national; in enterprises and in ministries. Finally, there is a tendency in the economic literature to distinguish only between private and state-owned enterprises. In fact, private enterprises can often be highly regulated and controlled by the state, whatever their apparent legal ownership. This is certainly true in the advanced market economies, where companies in certain regulated industries are deeply beholden to the state. But it was even truer in Russia, where, as we shall see, the corpus of law to protect private property was neither well defined, nor well established, nor enforceable.

The confusion about privatization law arose, in part, through disputes, both in law and in practice, arising throughout the period 1990–93 when key privatization decisions were made about who had the authority to set the legal framework (Blasi *et al.* 1997: 19–21). In the period before the collapse of the Soviet Union there were conflicts between its authority and the Russian parliament in a period called "the War of Laws".[1] The Russian Soviet Federative Socialist Republic declared in June 1990 the primacy of its laws over those of the central Soviet authority.[2] But even after the breakup of the Union and the establishment of the Russian Federation as its successor state, there were conflicts between the legislature and the executive branch of the Russian government over who had jurisdiction in issuing primary or enabling legislation or in implementing the law (Barnes 2001; Remington 2001: 84–6). Further, particularly in the early days of the new Russian state, there were substantial claims made by the regions about their own authority emerging from the 1992 Federation Treaty, which expanded the shared and residual powers enjoyed by subnational units (Lapidus 1994, 1999; Hanauer 1996; Solnick 1998: 63–6; Graney 2001: 36; Hahn 2003; Chebankova 2008). It is important that the implementation of privatization was not something that was fully controlled from the centre. As one reformer remarked, "the implementation capacity [of the Russian government] was extremely low".[3]

Therefore, many forces were involved both in the passage of the key Privatization Programme in June 1992 and in its implementation. This law was a major milestone. It was vitally important in getting a consistent privatization process going, but it was neither the beginning nor the end of that process. We underscore the comments of Frydman *et al.* (1993: 15), written at the beginning of the implementation process of the MPP:

> the legal situation in Russia is complicated by a plethora of often overlapping and conflicting laws and decrees emanating from a number of jurisdictions ... as a result the same subjects are often covered by many different and mutually contradictory normative pronouncements, and it is sometimes difficult to ascertain their ultimate validity.

This very confusion was one of the key considerations that led the World Bank and other international organizations to support the 1992 Programme, since it had the support of both the government and the parliament. Here is the view of the World Bank (1992: 69) in its 1991 report on Russia, which was published the following year:

> A fundamental difficulty for the conduct of government and the implementation of reform is the current uncertainty about the constitutional base and political future of the new state.... The powers of presidential and government decree are extraordinary. They were designed to fill the inevitable gap in time that would be created by the ordinary legislative process. Therefore decrees are often introduced simultaneously with an identical bill in the legislature and last only so long as the bill does not get passed or defeated in parliament. [This allows] state agencies as well as individuals and corporate entities to speculate about the durability and enforceability of decrees with which they do not wish to comply.

By resolving ambiguities in the primacy of laws, according to the World Bank report, a decisive action would have "a very high premium indeed" (ibid.).

In this chapter, we aim to provide an overview of the dilemmas leading up to the passage of the Privatization Programme in 1992. The chapter contains four main sections covering:

1 the history of privatization legislation and a description of who was responsible for the law and its implementation until 1992;
2 the ownership status of Russian enterprises prior to 1992;
3 the appointment and involvement of the reformers;
4 the terms of the 1992 legislation.

At the end of the chapter, we give a timeline of key events (Table 2.1), noting when various decisions were taken. Throughout the chapter and elsewhere, we refer to the June 1991 Law on Privatization of State and Municipal Enterprises in the Russian Federation as the Privatization Law. The presidential draft of the first Privatization Programme, issued in December 1991, Basic Provisions of the State Programme for Privatization of State and Municipal Enterprises in the Russian Federation, is referred to as the Basic Provisions. A version of this was enacted by parliament in June 1992; we refer to it as the Privatization Programme.

Who was responsible for privatization?

Constitutional considerations

Until 1990, there were 15 Soviet republics; Russia, by far the largest, dominated the affairs of the Union. After 1985, under Gorbachev, the decline of Communist Party control over the country encouraged nationalist mobilization in some republics, culminating in a demand for independence in the Baltics and Georgia and demands for sovereignty in Russia (Dallin and Lapidus 1991: 376; Goldman *et al.* 1992: 10). In March 1990, the Russian Republic elected a new legislature, the Congress of People's Deputies, and in May elected its president, Boris Yeltsin, who presided over its working body, the Supreme Soviet. On 12 June, confirmed by various laws in subsequent months, Russian laws were declared supreme over those of the Soviet Union. In June 1991, Yeltsin stood for and won the new post of president of the RSFSR by a landslide vote. At that time there was a proposal, which had been ratified by referendum in many of the republics, to create a more decentralized federal structure, called the Union of Sovereign States.

Its implementation, however, was interrupted by the coup attempt against Gorbachev. Instead, in December 1991 a loose association, which included Russia, Ukraine and Belarus, was formed and became known as the Commonwealth of Independent States. Other republics (excluding the Baltic states) would join later. At that point, the Soviet Union was dissolved (Suraska 1999; Walker 2003). It is remarkable that the breakup of the Soviet Union, and the resulting creation of 15 new nations, was, with the notable exception of the Caucasus, achieved with so little bloodshed.[4] In the history of nationhood, it is rare for such events to take place without long and protracted struggle, especially in the context of limited planning for such a breakup. This must surely rank as one of the great political achievements of the time.

However, state formation did not end the confusion about how things were to be done and who had the authority to control them. The Russian legal system still retained the same hierarchical structure as the former Soviet Union: first, the constitution (a document dating to 1977, which had been repeatedly amended), and second, the Fundamentals of Civil Legislation, including laws, ordinances and normative acts, the 1991 edition created by Gorbachev (Angelo 1993: 208). Among sources of confusion, for example, were how inter-regional trade was to be conducted, which government body controlled economic policy and regulated payments and banking, and whether a new currency should be created. Confusion over ownership was particularly acute. Under the former command administrative economy, ownership of the means of production in the late Soviet years was breaking down. Gorbachev's efforts at management reform resulted in a mix of management discretion and planning in the allocation of resources, and in the rise of cooperatives by the end of the 1980s, which led, for example, to the creation of thousands of new farming entities alongside the still dominant collective and state farms (Berliner 1976, 1988; Åslund 1989; Rutland 1992; Leonard 2011).

This theme of chaotic circumstances, preceding and following the Soviet breakup, is familiar in the literature (Åslund 2002; Sakwa 2002; Walker 2003). One effect was that, in the period leading up to dissolution, there was ambiguity about whether Soviet or Russian law was sovereign. So, for example, as discussed further below, Russia's 1990 Enterprise Law, passed a year before the breakup of the Soviet Union, "revoke[d] the law of the USSR on enterprises in the USSR, including its application to enterprises under Union control".[5]

Within the new Russian state there was also ambiguity about constitutional powers. On 1 November 1991, Yeltsin was granted special executive powers, which validated presidential decrees in the sphere of economic reform unless they were overturned within a week by parliament.[6] As tensions grew between the President and parliament, it became more difficult to know whether a presidential decree was likely to be valid for long. This tension is apparent in the writings of Russian reform ministers, such as Chubais and Mostovoi. So, for example, Mostovoi (1999a: 46–7) writes that the decree explaining the major issues of privatization was adopted, a temporary document meant to be in force only until the state privatization programme was accepted by the Supreme Council. On 29 January 1992, another presidential decree was passed that was drafted by his group. The programme itself later encountered difficulties in being approved by the Supreme Soviet, but the 29 January decree is associated with the launch of privatization. It "included major normative documents regulating the order of privatization … [which] … were in force during the whole period of voucher, and partly monetary, privatization until around 1996" (ibid.).

Yet, despite this apparent confidence that the rules for privatization were approved in January, in March of that year the leader of the World Bank Russia Working Group wrote to Chubais that the draft privatization law lacked "a clear description, readily appreciable by both the Russian public and the international investment community, of the processes involved" in privatization.[7]

In reality, little was done to implement a formal process of privatization until the passage of the Privatization Programme in June 1992. So, while decrees may have represented the policy position of the executive, arguably, it was not until there had been extensive negotiation and compromise to ensure the passage of the programme through parliament that a legal authority could be said to have been established. Further, even when the Privatization Programme was passed, the details of its implementation remained very unclear, potentially allowing a level of discretion that could have negated its apparent intent.[8]

Just as legal ambiguities could be used to prevent privatization, they could also be used to accelerate it, if those who had the de facto power chose to do so. Mostovoi notes that a diversity of plans for privatization were in effect at the same time, as allowed by the 1989 "resolution". This is because the 1989 resolution covered a process that was broader than just privatization, that is, de-statization, which could comprise many ways of reallocating state property:

> So, there was a law on privatisation and, simultaneously, a law on leasing was being developed.... According to *this* law, a state enterprise could also be leased. These two laws were being developed simultaneously and contradicted each other, as one law didn't take into account leases, while the other one didn't consider sales – unless it was under special circumstances. And, as such, it was assumed that whoever decided to lease an enterprise would eventually be able to purchase it.[9]

Another example is the exclusion of Moscow from the country-wide Privatization Programme, blocking the government's oversight by exempting Moscow in a special decree. Chubais objected, claiming that "shops were given to staff at residual value ... such a scheme was in crying contradiction of the law on privatization" (1999b: 153). He goes on, more forcefully, "Piyasheva and Pinsker [advocates of Moscow's privatization] prepared and pushed through 'their' decree of the President, after which an unimaginable orgy started" (ibid.: 155).

So, by the time of the passage of the 1992 Privatization Programme, although there was considerable support for the notion of privatization, there was still disagreement regarding the form that the privatization could take. Meanwhile, by using Soviet-era resolutions and laws, such as those discussed in the Introduction above, many privatizations had already taken place, for example through leasing.

The 1992 Programme was therefore not the first attempt at designing a method for privatization. Rather, its aim was to build on earlier legislation to establish a unified legal code embracing proper title to productive assets. That in turn required that it have clear political authority and support.

Institutional considerations

In addition to these legal wrangles, there were also different responsibilities assigned to different institutions involved in setting up and carrying out the privatization. The agency with overall responsibility for the implementation of privatization was the State Committee for the Management of State Property, or Goskomimushchestvo (GKI), founded in November 1990, of which Chubais became head in November 1991. It in turn depended on local GKIs to implement privatization. The GKI was responsible to the president. But the seller of the assets was the State Property Fund, and/or its local representatives, which reported to the legislature. In addition, in larger enterprises, it was a self-appointed "privatization commission" that drew up the privatization plan for an individual enterprise. Each *oblast* (region) also had its own property committee charged with small enterprise privatization.

There were good reasons for this division of powers. For example, the split between the state or local Property Funds as the owner and the GKI as responsible for the sale gave some protection against corruption. The use of privatization commissions reduced administrative burdens on the GKI and accelerated the process. However, the opportunity for confusion and argument in the process remained considerable. Frydman *et al.* (1993: 44) observe:

> in addition to the State Property Committee, its territorial agencies, the local property committees, and the privatisation commissions, a number of other state organisations are involved in the privatisation process. It is sometimes difficult to specify their involvement with precision, since Russian laws and decrees often remain without effect or contradict one another.

One effect of this was that the progress of privatization and its conduct were different in different parts of the country. So, in some areas, privatization may have progressed according to the norms and expectations of the lawmakers and GKI in Moscow. Elsewhere, the situation was very different, as illustrated in the descriptions of the process in Novosibirsk and Smolensk given in the Appendices to this book. In one extreme example, a foreign adviser to the GKI was sent to observe the process of privatization taking place in a particular city. He was turned back at the airport, and told that his life would be in danger should he decide to return.[10] One can but speculate how the process was conducted in that city.

The key point is that neither the central policy makers, nor the GKI and the reformers, should be assumed to have been in full control of what was taking place. Ellerman (2003: 15) has described the reformers as "market Bolsheviks", in the sense that they were a small ideologically driven group, intent on delivering their own prescription for Russia's problems. Rather, they might be described as a group who had limited command of the levers of power. As one of the reformers puts it:

> The government did not control anything ... I always had the sense that we were pressed, pushed, kicked, hit from all directions. And you needed to think very hard about what is crucial and essential and what you can give away.[11]

Indeed, the reformers themselves accept that their powers to implement and enforce the law were limited. Reflecting on the Moscow privatization, which was legal by exception, Chubais (1999a: 79) reflects:

> Of course, I could concentrate all my political resources (not very considerable) to achieve the rejection of the presidential decree [on the privatization of Moscow by its own method] by introducing an amendment, or start a propagandistic campaign against the Moscow programme. But I made a decision not to touch it. In pragmatic terms it was more reasonable to concentrate energy not on the wrongheaded privatization [in one region] but its absence [i.e. the right privatization] in other regions.

Thus, in considering how privatization took place, it is important not to exaggerate the degree to which the government in Moscow was united or in control of the process.

The ownership of Russian enterprises prior to the 1992 Privatization Programme

There is a tendency to think of Russia in 1991–92 as having the same economic control structures as the ones employed in the Soviet Union five years earlier, and that it was onto these structures that the Privatization Programme was superimposed. But the situation was much more confused than that suggests. As outlined in the Introduction, ambiguities arose from the fact that both the Soviet and the Russian authorities had been passing laws and decrees that both went into the code of laws, creating different forms of "private" ownership.

The enterprise acts of the late 1980s, issued both by the Soviet Union and by the Russian Republic, had allowed enterprises a degree of discretion to sell their own output. They had also allowed the establishment of new companies. For example, in 1989 and 1990, managers had been encouraged to lease the assets of the enterprise that they managed, in effect privatizing its operations without privatizing its assets. So, according to Frydman *et al.* (1993: 22), in February 1992, before the 1992 Privatization Programme was passed, 13 per cent of total production and 11 per cent of industrial employees could already be categorized as part of enterprises which were "leased". This represented approximately a twofold increase over the previous year.

A similar observation applies to the emergence of industrial "associations". The RSFSR Enterprise Law, signed by Yeltsin on 25 December 1990, set out that each enterprise should be established as "an independent economic unit", which would "independently pursue its activity and dispose of its output and profit".[12] It further required that state enterprises be set up, but while "the assets [were to] be the property of the RSFSR", the "assets [could] be transferred to the management of the labour collective of the enterprise".[13] Further, enterprises could form unions and associations. Despite the fact that Russia was then still part of the Soviet Union, as noted above, the law went on to revoke "the law of the USSR on enterprises in the USSR, including its application to enterprises under Union control".[14]

One response to this, and possibly other, legislation was the creation of "associations", which often took corporate form and frequently took the role previously assumed by the branch ministries, which would have organized the details of industrial production. Thus, the "associations" created a vast vertical of non-governmental agencies with potentially huge influence. In 1991, they accounted for 38 per cent of industrial output, including the entire oil and gas industry, the coal industry and Norilsk Nickel. In late 1991, the Russian parliament resolved to restrict the powers of the "associations", so that they were "not authorised to represent the state in the disposition and management of state owned property, and could not conclude contracts with the leaders of constituent state enterprises" (Frydman *et al.* 1993: 25). But, in December 1991, a presidential decree restored some of these powers. We will return to the issue of "associations", and the challenge they presented to the privatization process, later in the book.

The effect of these "privatizing" laws is illustrated by Johnson and Kroll's (1991) study of enterprises in Kiev, undertaken just before the breakup of the Soviet Union. They report a vibrant response by enterprises to the collapse of central authority, using the new powers conferred by recent enterprise laws. These included both centralizing and decentralizing tendencies. They observe that "managers clearly felt that if something did not technically violate the rules and they could get away with it, then they would go ahead" (ibid.: 301). Given the contradictory nature of the law, this would give ample scope to new structures. While this study was undertaken mainly in Ukraine, there is little reason to believe the situation was very different in Russia.

The World Bank's view, in a private note to Chubais in March 1992, was that "the ultimate goal [of privatization was] to create effective ownership of Russia's productive assets".[15] In 1992, this meant not only setting a framework for the development of a successful market economy, but also establishing a clear framework property rights that had become obscured by the chaos of the previous years.

The appointment and involvement of the reformers

The privatization reforms are generally attributed to the reform ministers, in particular to Yegor Gaidar,[16] who became acting prime minister in 1992, and Anatoly Chubais, the minister in charge of the GKI and, subsequently, a deputy prime minister. However, we note that Gaidar and Chubais were appointed in November 1991, after the passage of the 1991 privatization law. They only had a matter of weeks to work on the "Basic Provisions" that constituted the government's proposals for reform.[17] Though both were respected economists, neither of them had had much previous experience of high office.[18] Nor were they allowed carte blanche in designing their reform.

Gaidar was appointed as head of the reform team on the recommendation of Gennady Burbulis, Yeltsin's state secretary (July 1991–May 1992). Burbulis himself was appointed by Yeltsin to "share the total responsibility for running the country … [including] long term planning and selection … [of] personnel, leaving [Yeltsin] free to conceive the … tactics and the strategy of the immediate political struggle" (Yeltsin 1994: 151). According to Yeltsin (ibid.: 156), the reformers thought of themselves primarily as technocrats, engineers who would design an economic reform independent of the political processes necessary for reform to be effective:

> Gaidar's ministers and Gaidar himself took this position with us: your business is political leadership; ours is economics. Don't interfere with us as we do our work, and we won't butt in on your exalted councils … which we don't understand anyway.

Yeltsin presumably accepted this position. However, the consequences of the failure more effectively to link economic policy with its likely consequences were soon evident. He notes (ibid.: 158): "Soon it became apparent that the Gaidar government, which was making one decision after another, was in complete isolation. Gaidar and his people never travelled around the country to take the pulse of the nation."

In 1992, the World Bank Consortium commissioned Oxford Analytica (OA), a leading geo-political consultancy,[19] to draft a report on the political backdrop to effective privatization in Russia.[20] The OA report provides a snapshot of the politics of Russia in August 1992. This is their assessment of the position of the reformers within the government:

> The Gaidar reform team, including senior advisors with the status of first deputy ministers, consists of about 30 people. They do not constitute a dominant element in the government; they do not represent a political party; they have no significant power base in Russian society. They are in government because Yeltsin's close advisor, Gennadii Burbulis, recommended Gaidar as head of a reform team, and Gaidar brought in a group of like minded friends.[21]

Of course there were no political parties in the Soviet system other than the Communist Party. The OA report goes on to observe the chaotic conditions of political decision-making within the government:

> A lack of orderliness and of generally accepted rules of the game characterises almost all social activity in Russia today. This is as true of the running of the Russian government as it is of other activities. Western observers in Moscow agree that all officials, with a few exceptions [including Gaidar and Chubais], are very disorganised and that the situation is not improving.[22]

Gaidar, in his autobiography (1999: 97–8), confirms that many in this liberal group were newcomers to government. Talking of his appointment as deputy head of the government (6 November 1991) and minister of economy and finance (13 November 1991), he wryly notes that he had never held a government post or supervised more than his own desk (ibid.: 97). He goes on to say that "there were only two people [in the government] who combined a genuine administrative savvy with profound understanding of the essence of transformations in their relative fields": Chubais and Bulgak, the Minister of Communications (ibid.: 98).

Some political difficulties resulted from inexperience, but mainly they reflected the failure of the political process to establish consensus and clearly to delineate spheres of command. This is true even within the executive, where the Vice-President, Alexander Rutskoi, could simultaneously have oversight of agricultural reform, criticize publicly Gaidar's strategy on liberalization and stabilization, operate as leader of a political party of sorts, and bring that party into an alliance with the industrialists' party and others.

Ruslan Khasbulatov,[23] the chair of the Supreme Soviet and, ultimately, one of Yeltsin's main opponents, described the relations between the executive and the legislature in an interview for this book: "I told Gaidar and the ministers 'If you are reformers, give me the laws and I will pass them in three days'". But he claims they did not give him legislation, and he felt the executive should have taken the lead. He saw parliament's role expanding in response: "If the government can't do it, let [the legislature] come up with, coordinate and create laws. And we did make most of the laws, about 90 per cent on our own."[24]

The reformers were limited in their powers, according to the law granting Yeltsin authority to "rule by decree" in the economic sphere of policy. They were also constrained under difficult circumstances to keep Yeltsin's support. This resulted in compromises, in particular with the industrial lobby, whose interests were well represented both in the government and the parliament (Kubicek 1996: 36–7; Appel 1997: 1436; Barnes 1998: 844).

In this environment, as OA observed in 1992, Yeltsin's support for the reformers, though not unreserved, was particularly significant:

> the government rests (insecurely) on Yeltsin's personal prestige: there is public competition within the government for influence over Yeltsin.... Yeltsin's own stance is crucial. So far, he has backed the reformers, at a cost to his own personal popularity. The reformers do not take a continuation of this support for granted. From April onward they have given ground to the industrialists ... the main achievement of G7 support was to keep Yeltsin on the side of the reformers.

Yeltsin sat at the centre of the debate as it grew more intense. In his memoirs (1994: 176), he noted that by late summer of 1992 the rancour between reformers and others had "stopped the government from functioning normally ... there was a coalition government, which in our politically charged atmosphere would be explosive, and frankly, deadly".

This raises the obvious question of why Yeltsin backed the reformers, and why they were successful in pushing through the privatization reform.

Yeltsin himself identified his own reservations. Enterprise management was not improving, and there were already a confusing variety of schemes for "destatization", many of which were of doubtful legitimacy (Blasi *et al.* 1997; Buck *et al.* 1998; Puffer and McCarthy 2003). Yeltsin (1994: 156) quotes Gaidar to suggest why it went forward anyway:

> I myself could have given a perfect explanation of why, in 1992, the reforms should not have been launched ... no stable support in parliament ... no normal functioning institutions of governance ... sixteen central banks.... But ... we couldn't wait any longer. We couldn't just keep doing nothing, or keep explaining why it was impossible to do anything.

His point is simply that, particularly in situations of political chaos, the decision to do nothing has equally profound, and often less predictable, consequences than taking action. In the breakup of the Soviet Union, communism had been abandoned and a civil war averted. Yeltsin may have seen the reforms not just as a way to create an effective Russian economy, but as the only credible agenda that his government had the power to implement.

The reformers themselves went much further. Chubais underscored the urgency of preventing a return of communism (Desai 2006).[25] And, indeed, the reformers were most successful in two areas: price liberalization and privatization. Price liberalization was introduced in the face of fears of lack of supply, including food supply. It was a partial reform, and one that involved the withdrawal of state power. In other words, having passed the legislation, the government felt it had little else to do to ensure its implementation.[26] Privatization required more positive action by government, since a privatization process needed to be undertaken. Both reforms created very powerful incentives for enterprises to comply. In other areas, such as macroeconomic stabilization, bankruptcy and securities legislation, reform was to make much slower progress.

In their style of work and their descriptions of their task, reformers often seemed to see themselves as a close team, working frenetically to secure their goals and to pass and bypass other government departments and the legislature. For example, Mostovoi claimed that at the turn of 1991–92, "We worked a lot then. Usually night and day. Those capable of it worked 24 hours" (Mostovoi 1999a: 69). Chubais (1999a: 33) said of the same period, "It was our good fortune that, at the end of 1991, the government apparatus was extremely weak ... it was easier to deal with than it would be a year later".[27] It may be informative that in pushing through de jure plans, Chubais perceived the weakness of the apparatus of government as an advantage. That same weakness would later be given as the reason for the inability to implement a more comprehensive set of reforms.

There can be little doubt of the huge effort and single-mindedness that the reformers put into advancing privatization. However, as the reformers' comments suggest, they were not in full control of the process they were managing. Even if there had been broader political consensus and a capacity to implement, the economic circumstances into which privatization was introduced were challenging in the extreme. World Bank figures show that GNP fell by 12.8 per cent in 1991, and then by a further 18.5 per cent in 1992 (Blasi *et al.* 1997: 190). Inflation, which had been at 138 per cent in 1991, looked out of control in 1992 at 2,323 per cent, wiping out whatever value savings had. The IMF estimated that real wages halved during that year (ibid.). It was against this backdrop that action was taken. Gaidar successfully implemented major, though not comprehensive, price liberalization in January 1992; however, by the summer, with the appointment of a new chairman of the Central Bank (Viktor Gerashchenko), he had begun to lose control of one of the levers of macroeconomic stabilization (Granville 1993; Treisman 1998: 243; Weisskopf 1998: 177).

The one reform that did gain traction was privatization. The Privatization Programme depended on more than the commitment and hard work of the reformers. It was facilitated by the fact that the industrial lobby did not oppose, in principle, the notion that enterprises should be privatized. As OA noted in 1992, "the 'industrialists' [were] not opponents of privatisation as such. In fact they [were] carrying out their own privatisation already … they [sought] controlling interests in existing state enterprises".

So, for example, the Civic Union, a grouping of powerful "industrialist-friendly" parties, supported privatization in principle, albeit on its own terms. The same could be said of Khasbulatov.[28] Indeed, securing the support of parliament for their privatization plan was a critical element, and one of the great achievements, of the programme's designers. But while it was undoubtedly a considerable achievement for the reformers to secure the passage of the 1992 Privatization Programme, the law itself was one that reflected the views of other parties. It was not the reformers' blueprint.

In particular, there was great debate about those aspects of privatization that determined future ownership and control. The 1991 privatization law made the assumption that workers and managers would be given privileges to subscribe for 30 per cent of the share capital of the company at a discount. However, these shares would be non-voting. The programme, when it emerged, had two other "variants", the second of which allowed insiders to subscribe for 51 per cent of the company in voting shares. It was this variant which was to be chosen by most of the companies privatizing under the MPP (see below).

However, by the summer of 1992, as the privatization law was being passed, other elements of Gaidar's reform programme were being undermined. Gerashchenko, the new chairman of Russia's Central Bank, which by this time had come under the control of the parliament, had distanced himself from Gaidar's stabilization policy. In December of that year, as the first voucher auctions were taking place, Gaidar was replaced as acting prime minister by Victor Chernomyrdin, a representative of the industrial lobby, who was to be head of the Council of Ministers then prime minister until 1996. Before his appointment, Chernomyrdin had made strong statements opposing the Privatization Programme as it stood at the end of 1992. It was under his government, not that of the reformers, however, that most of the controversial aspects of privatization were implemented.

Therefore the period during which advocates of radical reform controlled the reform process lasted only a short time. It involved partial price liberalization, but little subsequent control of credit. Therefore, whether or not price shock was the right solution for Russia, it was certainly not consistently applied (Åslund and Layard 1993; Åslund 1994, 1997). The only major reform from that period that progressed beyond 1992 was privatization, which had parliamentary support. Nevertheless, whoever is deemed responsible for the contents of the Privatization Programme, it was to be the basis of policy implementation for the next two years. It was under this programme that companies employing 20 million workers were sold.

The Privatization Programme of June 1992

The Privatization Programme,[29] built on the earlier law of 1991,[30] focused on the "supply side" of privatization, establishing three things. First, it set out different categories of enterprises, detailing how and whether they should be privatized. Second, it described ownership choices available to enterprises in the MPP. Third, the programme detailed how other aspects of privatization would be affected, who would have the authority to carry them out, and how the proceeds of privatization would be distributed (see Appendix 1).

It is worth reviewing each of these.

Categories of enterprise

Three categories of enterprises were to be included in the programme.

The first category included small enterprises, employing less than 200 people. These were to be sold through auctions and tenders by the municipality in which they were based. The second included large enterprises, with the number of employees ranging between 1,000 and 10,000. These were to be converted to companies (corporatization), and their managers and workers would then submit a privatization plan to the GKI. Shares would then be sold through one of the privatization options described below, with auctions for cash or vouchers organized by the GKI.[31]

The third category comprised very large companies with over 10,000 employees and/or strategic enterprises, such as defence and drug companies, and those with monopoly positions. Their privatization required special agreement with the government or the relevant ministry. The GKI would prepare the plan for their privatization.

Critically, enterprises involved in minerals and pipelines were excluded from privatization. This is significant, as much of the criticism of the privatization programmes centred on the legitimacy and the business practices of those involved in oil and other natural resource companies. These were not privatized through a bottom-up process, as prescribed by the MPP, but through top-down approval from the relevant ministry.

Privatization options

The privatization law prescribed three options, each offering benefits to employees and managers of the enterprise.

1 Option One allowed employees a free gift of 25 per cent of the equity of the company, up to a face value of 20 times the minimum monthly wage. Initially, it was proposed that these be non-voting shares (though this was not specified in the programme; and in the summer of 1992, the GKI contemplated mandating that shares be non-voting until at least 50 per cent of the enterprise was private). Employees could also buy an additional 10 per cent of the shares at a discounted price, with three years to pay. The total amount of shares purchased in this way could not exceed six minimum wage monthly salaries. In addition, officers of the enterprise could buy a further 5 per cent of the shares. These grants to workers were proposed in the Basic Provisions.

2 Option Two prescribed an even greater distribution of shares to employees and other insiders. Fifty-one per cent of shares could be purchased, with the GKI setting the price. The GKI ultimately decided that that figure should have been 1.7 times the book value in July 1992. Thus, Option Two allowed employees and managers to take control of their enterprise, which was arguably the closest reflection of the situation in most enterprises before the passage of the law and, as we have noted, was supported by the industrialists' lobby.

3 Option Three allowed the purchase of 40 per cent of the equity of an enterprise by a smaller group of insiders willing to restructure the enterprise. This option was seldom adopted.

In addition to all the advantages prescribed by the different options, the Programme allowed enterprises to establish "personal privatization accounts", which were set up to receive 10 per cent of the proceeds of any sale of shares to outside investors. The development of these three options reflected the debate between the industrial lobby, which promoted insider control and therefore a legitimization of the status quo, and the reformers, who felt that outsiders would be required to promote the strong governance necessary to restructure Russian industry. This was well understood at the time by reformers and by observers: "As evidenced by some of their public comments, the authors of the state programme were clearly aware that the modifications introduced since the privatisation law were largely a victory for enterprise insiders and the industrial lobby" (Frydman *et al.* 1993: 57–8).

Other aspects

One critical element of the Privatization Programme was its bottom-up structure. That is, for all but the largest companies, the form of privatization was developed by the management of the enterprise and then approved by the GKI. This led to a significant transfer of power to insiders. The bottom-up approach had been strongly recommended to the GKI by the World Bank, largely on technical grounds. In a private draft note to Chubais on 25 March 1992, the World Bank Group on Mass Privatisation wrote:

> Recent experience in other countries suggests that, if such a top down structure is adopted (i) it would require the GKI to have substantial administrative organisation before the privatisation process … can begin (ii) the privatisation commissions will be susceptible to paralysis and delay and (iii) the burden of expert and affirmative obligations … is likely to be unsustainable, resulting in general institutional "meltdown".

It went on to recommend the bottom-up approach, saying:

> This approach recognises two related truths of fundamental importance: management is the one group which already has the necessary expertise to quickly move the privatisation process forward and management is also the one group that, if alienated or made defensive by outside pressures, is best positioned to cause obstruction and delay.[32]

Therefore, the Privatization Programme, passed in June 1992, was not a charter for radical reform. Indeed, it can be argued that the 1992 Programme was rather less radical in some ways than the 1991 law, which was passed before any of the key reformers were appointed to office and before any of the western advisers on privatization arrived. The 1992 Programme had been amended, both by intention and by necessity, to satisfy the demands of those in charge of the enterprises that were to be privatized. It is therefore perplexing that some writers criticize the reform and the reformers in colourful language for achieving the opposite. For example, David Ellerman (1998: 15), speech writer to Joseph Stiglitz, writes:

> To promote market driven development, reforms should find some way to formalise some socially acceptable approximation to … de facto property rights … instead the market Bolsheviks [the reformers] designed the market reforms with the exact opposite purpose to deny the de facto property rights accumulated during the communist past … the reforms were successful in denying the de facto property rights acquired during the earlier decentralising reforms.

In fact, the reverse was the case. Whatever the rhetoric of the reformers, the reality of the MPP was likely to leave control of enterprises in the same hands as before. The de facto property rights of managers and workers were upheld.

Indeed, had enterprise managers or their workers' collectives decided to subvert the law, it would not have been difficult for them to do so, albeit at the cost of losing their privileges to receive shares in the enterprise at a reduced cost.

They could have claimed to be exceptions, for example by asserting that they had dominant market positions. Alternatively, they could simply refuse to cooperate, failing to set up privatization commissions or submit plans.

The time frame for the programme was ambitious. Enterprises were to submit privatization plans by 1 October 1992, with enterprises becoming companies on 1 November. Share auctions were to take place shortly thereafter.

In its initial conception, the proceeds from those auctions were to be split between the federal and regional governments. For large companies subject to mass privatization, 35 per cent was to be credited to the federal budget, 10 per cent to municipal budgets, and 45 per cent to the regional budget. It was the intention of the federal government that its share of the proceeds of privatization would be distributed to the Russian population by way of privatization vouchers. However, the nature of the "vouchers" or "privatization accounts" had not been made explicit.

Vouchers

From the perspective of internal Russian politics, one of the most controversial aspects of the privatization was the way in which vouchers were issued. In April 1992, Presidential Decree 322 declared that vouchers would be distributed to the whole population in the last quarter of the year. The outline of how the vouchers would work was described in a further decree in August, at a time when the Duma was in recess.[33] Critically, vouchers were to be tradable instruments; that is, they could be sold.

However, according to Khasbulatov, then the Speaker of the Duma, the notion of issuing vouchers as tradable instruments had not been the intention of the original 1991 law or the 1992 Programme. Here is his description of the situation:

> We [the Duma] approved all the [privatization] programmes. [But] after the law was approved – the law that was proposed by Yeltsin's government – after it had been enacted, they made arbitrary changes to that law ... I think in England you would go to jail for that!
>
> I'm talking about these privatization vouchers. Chubais's vouchers. When we ratified the law, we designed [the vouchers] to be registered. I would be given vouchers with my name marked on them [that could not be sold]. What did [the government] do? They released these privatization vouchers.... And thousands of people – opportunists, swindlers – began to buy up these vouchers.[34]

The reformers recognized the change, if not its legal ambiguity. Gaidar (1999: 169) said that initially the legislation on privatization did not provide for any currency-like medium: "We had proposed creating a system of registered privatisation accounts ... [but the time and expense of doing so would] deprive the country of a window of opportunity."

The supply of companies to be privatized was agreed to by the executive and by parliament. However, the nature of vouchers – in particular, their tradability – was contested.

The idea of voucher privatization was to ensure that those citizens who were not workers in industrial enterprises – teachers, pensioners, doctors – received some benefit from the process. Kikeri *et al.* (1992) underscore that the overriding purpose of privatization was to transfer the property rights of owners who have incentives for defending the interests of the capital they own. Private owners would provide political support for the difficult steps in creating a market economy. At the time of the passage of the Privatization Programme, an assumption was made that shares would be sold for cash and for vouchers. These vouchers were to be distributed to Russian citizens, and could be used either as part payment in worker subscriptions or at auction, in part payment for the 35 per cent of the privatization revenues that would otherwise have gone to the federal government. The vouchers played a critical role in the justification of the process.

However, the mixture of cash and vouchers created technical complexities in ensuring that the supply of companies could be readily matched with subscriptions. For example, if vouchers were to be exchanged for shares, either at book value (as would be the case for worker subscriptions) or at an auction in place of cash, they needed to have a nominal value. If there was then a difference between the nominal value and the value of shares for which they subscribed, the proceeds of privatization represented by vouchers would be different from the 35 per cent that was due to the federal government. This problem was only resolved by extending the voucher programme to cover all sales of shares. This, in effect, meant that there was to be no money raised for any state entity through the MPP. In one stroke, one of the key objectives of privatization, that of raising money for the state, was abandoned.

Vouchers also affected the timing of the programme. Vouchers were intended as temporary instruments with an expiry date. Initially, this was to be the end of 1993. Thereafter, it might be envisaged that a second privatization programme would be launched, and a new set of vouchers issued. In fact, only one tranche of vouchers was ever issued, with their expiry date extended to 30 June 1994. Therefore, the MPP had come to an end by that date. This created huge pressure for a speedy process before vouchers expired.

The voucher programme also created considerable logistical challenges since the issuance of vouchers and the purchase of company shares needed to dovetail. Further, in the summer of 1992, the GKI had not secured the authority to control the privatization process beyond 1 November of that year, when privatization plans were to be submitted.

However, the combination of vouchers with the incentives given to workers and managers meant that there was significant pressure to move forward with privatization. From the central government's point of view, once citizens had been issued vouchers, it was necessary to ensure that there was something for them to buy. And the terms of sale for companies, as well as the use of vouchers as currency, meant that those in charge of companies were willing to put them up for sale. Most of them found ways of selling to insiders.

Discussion

The 1992 Russian Mass Privatization Programme was developed and implemented in a period of considerable turmoil. It was introduced during a time when existing laws were contradictory and legal authority was unclear. Enterprises had thus established many forms of quasi-privatization, necessary for effective functioning and encouraged by the self-interest of those in power.

The 1992 Programme built on the 1991 law, which was ratified before any of the Russian reformers were appointed to the government. This is sometimes forgotten in their writings. For example, Boycko *et al.* (1995: 1) begin their book *Privatising Russia* by saying: "In late 1991 a handful of reformers led by Anatoly Chubais embarked on a far reaching program to privatise Russian firms. At the time the idea of privatising Russia seemed to most people to be a pipe dream."

While not wishing to minimize the accomplishments of the reformers, the aim of privatization predated their appointment. The 1992 Privatization Programme, and its associated decrees, gave considerably greater influence to enterprise insiders. It introduced Option Two, which allowed the purchase of 51 per cent of the shares of an enterprise by its workers. The law and the decrees created a bottom-up privatization, in essence handing the drafting of the privatization plans to the enterprise managers. Vouchers allowed workers to finance their subscription for shares.

Some of these changes, such as bottom-up privatization, were accepted and indeed were supported by the reformers. However, at face value, the importance of the 1992 Programme was not that it provided a new blueprint for reform; if anything, it compromised to meet the demands of the industrial lobby. Rather, it provided a set of clear steps and incentives that encouraged those in control to accept a change of sorts. With extraordinary zeal, reformers pressed forward with the programme.

The Privatization Programme alone could not fulfil all, or indeed very many, of the stated aims of reform. It did not produce a hard budget constraint on companies. It did not raise cash for the government. It did not create a governance framework that was likely to make new owners enthusiastic about restructuring. It did not establish the legal framework necessary for the functioning of capital markets, for example a bankruptcy law. It did not create competition or address the problem of arbitrary taxation.

However, it did create the possibility of a framework, most of which was agreed to by the feuding parliament and President, for the transfer in law of the rights over enterprises that were already becoming controlled by enterprise managers, individually and in coalition, together with their workforce. It also offered, controversially, through a tradable voucher programme, some modest transfer of benefits to those not employed in privatized enterprises. However, like so many

Russian laws, the Privatization Programme raised many questions regarding its implementation and its likely economic effects, which were understood at the time.[35] Some of these were administrative, such as establishing timetables, while others raised questions regarding the feasibility of the programme; for example, that the lack of individual savings would mean that only the well financed (of whom there would be few in Russia) would have funds to make successful bids at cash auctions, or that the programme would allow the creation of vast holding companies. Still others point out the limitation of privatization in the absence of other regulations and institutions necessary for the effective working of capital and labour markets. The passage of the law in 1992 was therefore only the beginning of the process. Its subsequent implementation would be crucial, as would be the decisions made about those enterprises not covered by the 1992 Programme. Certainly, while the MPP gave the opportunity to establish ownership rights, which in turn was likely to be a necessary condition for an effective economy, it was certainly not, at least in the medium term, a sufficient one.

Table 2.1 Timeline, 1986–92

Date	*Law*	*Effect*	*Comments*
19 November 1986	O vvedenii v deistvie Zakona SSSR Ob individual'noi trudovoi deiatel'nosti. Postanovlenie Verkhovnogo Soveta SSSR No. 6051-XI (Decree of the Supreme Soviet of the USSR No. 6051-XI. On the Introduction of the Law On Individual Labour Activity)	Allows part-time work	
30 June 1987	O gosudarstvennom predpriiatii (ob'edinenii). Zakon SSSR No. 7287-XI (USSR Law No. 7287-XI. On State Enterprises)	Allowance for individual contracts between enterprises, initially 10 per cent, then 30 per cent; governance in theory is through the workforce, but in fact managers and bureaucrats perceived to be in charge; law unclear on ultimate powers since these are given to "the founding body together with the labour collective" (Frydman *et al.* 1993: 19)	Enterprise profits rise; however tax rates vary: "Ex-post tax rates continued to vary from zero to 90 per cent, and ministries continued to confiscate profits arbitrarily in order to cross-subsidise loss making enterprises" (IMF *et al.* 1991: 26)
26 May 1988	O kooperatsii v SSSR. Zakon SSSR No. 8998-XI (USSR Law No. 8998-XI. On State Cooperatives in the USSR)	Allows cooperative ownership in certain branches of industry, and some price freedoms; powers of co-ops restricted in December 1988	(IMF *et al.* 1991: 30)

Continued

Table 2.1 Continued

Date	*Law*	*Effect*	*Comments*
7 April 1989, 28 February 1990	Ob arende i arendnykh otnosheniiakh v SSSR.Ukaz Prezidiuma Verkhovnogo Soveta SSSR No. 10277-XI (Decree of the Presidium of the Supreme Soviet of the USSR No. 10277-XI. On Leasing and Lease Relations) Osnovy zakonadetel'stva soiuza SSR i soiuznykh respublik o zemle. Verkhovny Sovet SSSR No. 1251-I (Supreme Soviet of the USSR No. 1251-I. The Fundamentals of Legislation of the USSR and the Union Republics on Land)	Assets of enterprise could be leased; "Fundamentals" stipulated state organs should do so to the greatest of their abilities; should have been competitive, in fact leases were only made to insiders (Frydman *et al.* 1993: 20–2); leasing forbidden in 1992	By February 1992, lease enterprises comprised 11.3 per cent of industrial employment and 8 per cent of total employment
1989	Emergence of "associations".	Often formed by the enterprises themselves (acting under amendments to Soviet and Russian enterprise law); creates holding companies in the place of branch ministries, often with self-perpetuating governance structures	End of 1991, comprise 38 per cent of industrial employment; includes Rosneftigas (99 per cent of oil production), Gazprom (93 per cent oil production); attempts to restrict associations by parliament (October 1991) undermined by presidential decree December 1991

Date	*Law*	*Effect*	*Comments*
1 September 1990	Shatalin–Yavlinsky "500 Days Programme" (Programma 500 dnei) and Ryzhkov–Abalkin "On Main Directions for Development" Programme (Osnovnye napraveleniia razvitiia) compete as economic platforms for reform		
25 December 1990	O poriadke vvedeniia v deistvie zakona RSFSR O predpriiatiakh i predprinimatel'skoi deiatel'nosti'. Postanovlenie Verkhovnogo Soveta RSFSR No. 446–1 (Decree of the Supreme Soviet of the RSFSR No. 446–1. On the Introduction of the RSFSR Law On Enterprises and Enterprise Activity) O predpriiatiakh i predprinimatel'skoi deiatel'nosti'. Zakon RSFSR No. 445–1. (RSFSR Law No. 445–1. On Enterprises and Enterprise Activity)	Enterprises, including state enterprises, can be registered for any activity not otherwise prohibited; enterprises can be proprietorships, partnerships or open or closed joint stock companies; state enterprises to be established which were previously under USSR control	

Continued

Table 2.1 Continued

Date	*Law*	*Effect*	*Comments*
3 July 1991	O poriadke vvedeniia v deistvie zakona RSFSR O privatizatsii gosudarstvennykh i munitsipal'nykh predpriiatii v RSFSR Postanovleniie Verkhovnogo Soveta RF ot 3 iulia 1991 goda No. 1532–1. (Decree of the RF Supreme Soviet No. 1532–1. On the Procedure for Enacting Federal Law On the Privatization of State and Municipal Enterprises) O privatizatsii gosudarstvennykh i munitsipal'nykh predpriiatii v Rossiiskoi Federatsii. Zakon RF ot 3 iuila 1991 goda No. 1531–1. (Federal Law No. 1531–1. On the Privatization of State and Municipal Enterprises)	Establishes the GKI and property funds; mandates corporatization; suggests that "privatization accounts" (vouchers) will be part of the payment made for purchase of companies; establishes that workers can subscribe to shares at a discounted price; investment funds to be established	This core legislation is passed before appointment of Chubais and Gaidar, or the arrival of western advisers on privatization
15 November 1991	Anatoly Chubais becomes the minister in charge of the Russian State Property Committee, which is responsible for carrying out privatization in Russia.		Western advisors consulted

Date	Law	Effect	Comments
29 December 1991	Osnovnye polozheniia programmy privatizatsii gosudarstvennykh i munitsipal'nykh predpriiatii na 1992 god. Ukaz Prezidenta RF No. 341 (Decree of RF President No. 341. Basic Provisions of the State Program for Privatization of State and Municipal Enterprises in 1992)	Suggests 25 per cent of enterprise value be granted free to workers but in non-voting shares; 10 per cent to be available on terms outlined in 1991 law; 5 per cent available to management	
			1991 economic performance: GDP growth: –5 per cent[a] consumer prices: +138 per cent[b]
January 1992	Price liberalization of certain goods, though notably not of commodities such as oil O merakh po liberalizatsii tsen. Ukaz Prezidenta RF No. 297 (3 December 1991) (Decree of RF President No. 297. On Measures for the Liberalization of Prices)		Inflation is about 2,000 per cent in the following year (Blasi *et al.* 199: 190); oil price less than 10 per cent of world price throughout the year; until this point, valuations for privatization purposes were to be based on the historic values in an enterprises balance sheet; these numbers become increasingly meaningless as a fair basis for privatization
29 January 1992	Ob uskorenii realizatsii programmy privatizatsii na 1992 god Postanovlenie Pravitel'stva RF ot 29 ianvaria No. 52 (Government Decree No. 52. On the Acceleration of the Realization of the Programme for Privatization in 1992)	Specifies rules and procedures for privatization	Not implemented until passage of the 11 June law

Continued

Table 2.1 Continued

Date	*Law*	*Effect*	*Comments*
2 April 1992	O dopolnitel'nykh merakh po realizatsii Osnovnykh polozhenii programmy privatizatsii gosudarstvennykh i munitsipal'nykh predpriiatii v Rossiiskoi Federatsii na 1992 god. Ukaz Prezidenta RF No. 322 (Decree of RF President No. 322. On Additional Measures to Implement the Fundamental Provisions of the Programme of Privatization of State and Municipal Enterprises in the Russian Federation in 1992)	Vouchers to be distributed to the population	Nature and use of vouchers not yet determined; no action taken
11 June 1992	O vvedenii v deistvie Gosudarstvennoi programmy privatizatsii gosudarstvennykh i munitsipal'nykh predpriiatii v Rossiiskoi Federatsii na 1992 god. Postanovlenie Verkhovnogo Soveta RF ot 11 iunia 1992 goda No. 2980–1 (Decree of the RF Supreme Soviet No. 2980–1. On the Introduction of the State Programme of Privatization of State and Municipal Enterprises of the Russian Federation)		Establishes different classes of enterprise; defines the three options for privatization, introducing Option Two for "worker control"; defines powers over programme and how proceeds are to be distributed

Date	Law	Effect	Comments
1 July 1992	Ob organizatsionnykh merakh po preobrazovaniiu gosudartsvennykh predpriiatii, dobrovol'nykh ob'edinenii gosudartsvennykh predpriiatii v aktsionernye obshchestva. Ukaz Prezidenta Rossiiskoi Federatzii No. 721 (Decree of RF President No. 721. On Organizational Measures for the Transformation of State Enterprises and Voluntary Associations of State Enterprises into Joint-Stock Companies)	Accelerated timetable for corporatization; enterprises to be responsible for privatization plan	
17 July 1992	Viktor Gerashchenko appointed chairman of the Russian Central Bank		Makes clear that credits to enterprises and companies will continue
14 August 1992	O vvedenii v deistvie sistemy privatizatsionnykh chekov v Rossiiskoi Federatsii. Ukaz Prezidenta RF ot 14 avgusta 1992 goda No. 914 (Decree of RF President No. 914. On the Introduction of a Privatization Voucher Scheme in the Russian Federation)	Fleshes out use of vouchers for the 35 per cent of shares for which the federal government is entitled to the proceeds	

Continued

Table 2.1 Continued

Date	*Law*	*Effect*	*Comments*
14 October and 16 November 1992	O prodazhe za privatizatsionnye cheki zhilishchnogo fonda, zemel'nykh uchastkov i munitsipal'noi sobstvennosti. Ukaz Prezidenta RF No. 1228. (Decree of RF President No. 1228. On the Sale of the Housing Fund, Land Plots and Municipal Property for Privatization Checks) O razvitii sistemy privatizatsionnykh chekov v Rossiiskoi Federatsii. Ukaz Prezidenta RF No. 1229. (Decree of RF President No. 1229. On Developing the System for Privatization Checks) O prodazhe ob'ektov privatizatsii za privatzatsionnye cheki. Ukaz Prezidenta RF No. 1391. (Decree of RF President No. 1391. On Selling Objects of Privatization for Vouchers)	Vouchers can be used for all share purchases at auction; Decree 1228 (14 October) issues provisions for selling land plots, municipal property and the housing fund for vouchers; Decree 1229 (14 October) increases the scope of voucher privatization, and sets out the guidelines for sales of specific enterprises; Decree 1391 (16 November) issues instructions to the RF State Committee on State Property to confirm the list of enterprises that may be sold at voucher auctions, and set the guidelines for the forthcoming auctions	
December 1992	First privatization auctions		
14 December 1992	Gaidar's nomination for prime minister is rejected by the Congress of People's Deputies; Chernomyrdin is confirmed as the Prime Minister		

Date	*Law*	*Effect*	*Comments*
			1992 Economic performance: GDP growth: –14.5 per cent;[c] consumer prices: +2,323 per cent[d]

Notes

a See World Bank Development Indicators, GDP growth (annual percentage), http: //data.worldbank.org/indicator/NY.GDP.MKTP.KD.ZG?page=4, accessed 26 September 2012.

b See Blasi *et al.* (1997: 190).

c World Bank Development Indicators, GDP growth (annual percentage), http: //data.worldbank.org/indicator/NY.GDP.MKTP.KD.ZG?page=3, accessed 26 September 2012.

d See Blasi *et al.* (1997).

3 Reforming the communist inheritance

The goals and limits of privatization

This chapter aims to assess the likelihood that the Privatization Programme would achieve its objectives, given the economic and political context of the early 1990s in Russia. Were the goals set for the privatization reform realistic and, if so, what economic and political conditions were required for it to be successful?

The chapter begins by considering what was known about the industrial structure of Russia at the time. The reform programme, both its successes and failures, can be appreciated only in the context of understanding the economic institutions to be reformed. The chapter does not claim to do full justice to the nature of Soviet inheritance or to the state of the Russian economy in 1992. Indeed, some readers with knowledge of Soviet economics may wish to pass over the section of this chapter entitled "The command economy". However, there were unique characteristics of the Soviet industrial inheritance which were of profound significance to the likely outcome of reform, and, for that reason, we believe it is important that these are addressed.

The chapter goes on to consider the various objectives that had been set for privatization, and to assess how far these were likely to be achieved, and what conditions would be necessary for success. It concludes that, given the nature of the institutions to be reformed, the Privatization Programme alone could not have achieved the goals that were set for it.

The command economy

Privatization in Russia and Eastern Europe was qualitatively, as well as quantitatively, different from the privatizations that had taken place in market economies. This difference had profound effects on the process of reform and its expected outcomes in both the short and the longer term. As the European Bank for Reconstruction and Development (EBRD) reported to the Russia Consultative Group on 8 June 1993,

> There is no historical precedent for the process of change now underway. Prior to 1988 there was virtually no private sector in Russia or throughout the former Soviet Union. Indeed to take part in all but the most basic private

> sector activities was illegal. All productive assets, including land, industrial enterprises, homes and farms were in theory owned by "the people".[1]

In practice, however, the industrial assets of the country were controlled by a state bureaucracy. It was this body that provided many of the systems of distribution, which, in the West, would be provided by market mechanisms.

The privatization reforms were unique because of what they were reforming. The administrative economy, which developed gradually after the 1917 Russian Revolution and then more rapidly as a consequence of industrial transformation during the First Five-Year Plan (1929–34) and collectivization of farms in the 1930s, was "the great Soviet experiment of the twentieth century", an attempt "to run an entire economy of a geographically and politically significant country by administrative command rather than by markets" (Gregory and Stuart 1994: 5).

For those used to a market economy which encompasses any degree of economic pluralism, it is difficult to envisage what the Soviet experiment had produced.[2] A useful analogy is one that likens the Soviet economy to "a single, giant, multibranch multiplant corporation, whose organisational components are, however, autonomous within certain limits as far as their operations are concerned" (Spulber 1969: 1).

In effect, the entire economy was planned as one single unit. Similar to a large company, this could change over time to include greater or lesser degrees of centralization. But, in effect, the state controlled all enterprises and employed all workers.

The role of money and prices

As a result of the way the economy was planned, money had a different significance in the USSR from in the West. In particular, transactions between Soviet enterprises did not involve money as we understand it, just as a Ford factory supplying a Ford production line would not involve money. The rouble served "as only a limited medium of exchange, since it [could] be used among autonomous state-owned enterprises only for transferring specified goods at predetermined prices according to specific plans" (ibid.: 161). When goods were shipped, the receiving enterprise would have a few days to raise a complaint should the goods' quality not be up to scratch. However, if no complaint was made, the receiving enterprise had an automatic deduction made from an account at the state central bank (Gosbank) and had a credit made to the supplying enterprise. But that credit could not be cashed or used at the enterprise's discretion to buy goods or services.

There were therefore two quite separate flows of money within the Soviet economy. One was the cash paid to workers, which could be either spent or saved at the national savings bank (Sberbank).[3] The other was a bookkeeping transaction between two enterprises both of which were "owned" by the government. Within this system, prices were deeply distorted compared to those that prevailed in market economies. In general, the state's aim was to fix prices at a level that covered accounting costs and left enough aside for investment. This system could be considered similar to a cost plus transfer pricing regime at a multi-divisional company. However, such an arrangement led to considerable complications.

Administrative pricing created many anomalies. One example was the price setting for commodities, such as oil. Oil was extracted from both efficient and inefficient wells from different regions across the country. To account for the disparities among enterprises, the Soviet government introduced the concept of cost zones. The cost zones "reflected natural differences in production and transport costs in different parts of the country" (IEA 1994: 17). An average price was determined for all enterprises in a specific cost zone; however, enterprises sold their products to the state using an *individual* enterprise price. This scheme resulted in the state distribution system incurring losses when individual enterprise prices exceeded the average enterprise price and gaining profits when the individual enterprise price was below. The International Energy Agency (IEA) noted that "98 different cost zones for crude oil and natural gas with average enterprise prices varying by a factor of as much as 22" existed until 1967 (ibid.). Although the number of these extreme cases was later reduced, price distortions remained high. For example, in 1991, the international (export) price of crude oil from Russia was $133.73 per tonne. The IEA's estimate of the domestic price, on the other hand, was recorded as $1.79 per tonne (ibid.: 15). Price distortions were so great, even between the USSR and other countries in the Soviet bloc, that, as we have seen in the case of oil, divergences between Russian and international prices could be colossal. In 1991 the IMF noted that "wholesale prices have been comprehensively adjusted only infrequently … the present internal structure of prices bears little relation to world market prices across products" (IMF *et al.* 1991: II, 3).

Table 3.1, estimated by the IMF *et al.* using Soviet sources, reveals the extent of price distortion.[4]

One side-effect of the existence of two "flows" of money, together with enormous price differentials, was that they created ample opportunity – for those

Table 3.1 Relative prices of goods in the USSR and world markets, 1988

Product	*Ratio of world to Soviet prices*
Oil	1:3.15
Scrap steel	1:6.45
Ammonia	1:0.53
Wheat	1:0.42
Color television	1:0.33
Video cassette recorder	1:0.30
Personal computer	1:0.015

Source: Adapted from International Monetary Fund *et al.* (1991: 2, 14); *The Economist* (20 October 1990), based on Soviet sources.

with sufficient power – to "arbitrage" the system. An enterprise, or an individual, who could establish a mechanism by which to divert output through a company or cooperative that was not constrained in the way it used its income, or who could, for example, sell subsidized Russian output abroad, could make a huge profit. The oil industry provides an illustration, but the same sort of arbitrage would be available wherever there were price distortions. As noted above, the IEA, writing in 1991, suggests that the difference between the domestic and international price of oil amounted to more than 90 per cent of its export value. The export of one tanker, containing 250,000 tonnes of oil, purchased at Russian prices and sold at international ones could net a profit of over $30 million. In 1991, Russia exported 91 million tonnes of oil outside the former Soviet Union.[5] One can imagine the incentives to which this sort of arbitrage gave rise.

Efficiency, profitability and productivity

Another fundamental effect of price distortion was the difficulty of judging the efficiency or competitiveness of a Russian enterprise. Since both the value and, indeed, the very survival of an enterprise in a market economy depended on its competitiveness, this presented very real issues in predicting the likely outcome of privatization.

For example, in 1993, one of the authors worked on a project for Kamaz, a truck manufacturer, during a period when the company was contemplating western financing. The EBRD, which was considering financing the deal, requested a comparative calculation that would appraise the value of a Kamaz truck relative to its counterpart in the West. The analysis included a variety of comparative indicators, including the cost of the vehicle (Kamaz trucks were much cheaper), as well as its relative fuel consumption and the downtime it would suffer for maintenance, breakdowns and so on. The analysis showed that, when these factors were taken into account, a Kamaz truck, like many other Russian manufactured goods at that time, was not a competitive product. In part, this was because it had not been designed to be fuel-efficient, since fuel costs were so low.

Indeed, the lack of competitiveness of Soviet industry was revealed in the structure of its exports to non-socialist developed economies, where market forces might most strongly be in play. In the period 1980–89, around 85 per cent of the exports comprised natural resources or products from industries dependent on low-cost natural resources, such as paper or chemicals. Only 15 per cent of Russian exports during that time comprised manufactured goods or services, with half of that total dedicated to armaments (IMF *et al.* 1991: II, 70). Nor did this system of pricing create many incentives to economize on resources, particularly labour, since such resources were allocated as part of the state plan, and prices were adjusted accordingly. Generally, Soviet enterprises retained more workers than was required, with many of the enterprises employing "15 to 20 per cent more labour than was necessary to fulfil their production plans" (ibid.: 141–2). Moreover, Soviet statistics were likely to have underestimated the levels of overstaffing, "since decades of excess demand for labour may have fundamentally affected the perceptions of what are necessary labour requirements" (ibid.). Thus, the comparison of western-built plants in the USSR with matched plants in the West indicates that Soviet plants employed 50 to 150 per cent more workers (ibid.).

We will return later to these issues and to their implications for the Privatization Programme.

Credit and capital

Despite this apparent lack of competitiveness, the system was kept going by administered prices, and by the issuance of credits by Gosbank.[6] Inefficient enterprises were either granted higher prices or were financed through the issuing of credits (Kornai 1986). Gregory and Stuart (1994: 160) point out:

> Gosbank grants production credit for specific purposes: if a particular transaction is called for in the input plan, the firm is automatically granted credit for this specific purpose. Even if an enterprise builds up excessive balances at Gosbank, this liquidity still does not represent command over producer goods, unless they are specifically called for in the plan.…The demand for credit is determined as a byproduct of physical planning.

In 1992, almost all state enterprises required Gosbank financing. Put simply, there was no market for capital in Russia. Unlike western privatizations, this was not one where state enterprises were transferred to private ownership, a transactions financed by private capital markets. Privatization itself was to create those capital markets.

Commercial law

Because it was a centrally planned economy, Russia had no market-oriented commercial or financial law, which is essential in western advanced countries for allowing markets to function. In order for a market economy to function effectively, legal mechanisms protecting the rights of individuals and entities must exist and be enforceable. For instance, legal recourse must be available against those who fail to pay their bills, ultimately including a bankruptcy law. Rights of shareholders, the issuance of shares, rules concerning their subsequent trading, the responsibilities of directors, the nature of limited liability and related party dealing all must be understood, and to some degree enforceable. It needs a "calculable legal framework". But as noted in *Russian Economic Reform* (World Bank 1992: 75), "administration in accordance with formal rules [was] missing from the framework of Russian governance.… The body of civil law which regulates the economic relationships necessary in a market economy is largely missing from the corpus of Soviet law."[7]

The Russian commercial legal system in 1993 was still in its infancy.[8] Gray and Hendley (1997: 151) point out that the 1988 Law on State Enterprises was a tentative step in the Gorbachev era away from command-administrative controls on firm behaviour in favour of some autonomy, but by 1990, "both Russian and Soviet legislation recognized privately owned business organizations of various types". In the early years of the Federation, Russia's legal framework was characterized by its lack of specialized legislation. For example, there was no comprehensive securities law. The existing legislation was mostly inadequate:

> the bankruptcy law [was] an ineffective mechanism for creditors to seek redress ... the conflict between laws, and the status of different laws and decrees; for example one observer has claimed that 14,000 regulations exist at oblast (regional) level, which are in direct conflict with federal legislation ... and the considerable difficulty which exist[ed] in enforcing legislation.[9]

Just as the dual pricing system had facilitated arbitrage, so the lack of a commercial legal framework had served as an invitation to informal methods of enforcement. In the absence of an independent judiciary, enforcement may frequently have been closer to a protection racket than to legal recourse and due process.[10]

The lack of any history of private business until the late 1980s also meant that the market-based ethos and assumptions that underpin trust between actors in more advanced markets were missing in Russia.

Monopoly and transport systems

Within the Soviet system, although reform-minded governments tried to encourage it, incentives for competition were ineffective. It was largely absent since pricing and production were not subject to competitive forces. Soviet ministries coordinated production, with each industry enjoying monopolistic production.

The organization of production through ministries was monopolistic in more than one sense. Not only was there one ministry that coordinated production, often only one enterprise was responsible for the total production of a particular good. The concentration of production on a single site led to a remarkable degree of monopoly. This was the industrial structure that held up for a little over 60 years, and it had enormous institutional legacies, including failed systems of competition introduced only in its declining years as the Soviet government attempted to restore some life into productivity numbers.[11]

Concentration ratios (i.e. the share of production in the hands of top firms) for the former USSR compared with the USA show that the market share "of the top four firms in any industrial market in the USA [was] lower than the top one firm in the USSR" (ibid.). Indeed, in most sectors, industrial production was highly concentrated in one or two enterprises (IMF *et al.* 1991: II, 16). As an example, the study reported that in the machine-building sector, a single supplier delivered 87 per cent of 5,885 products to the State Supply Commission (ibid.).

Table 3.2 gives some sense of concentration in other industries. In one sense, these statistics are astonishing, particularly since the vast size of the Russian land mass would suggest that there could be many products whose transport

Table 3.2 Concentration of selected products, Soviet Union, 1991

Branch	*Number of products*	*Number of producers*				
		1 (%)	*2–3 (%)*	*4–6 (%)*	*7–10 (%)*	*>10 (%)*
Machine building	5,885	87	8	3	1	2
Metallurgy	208	28	28	21	10	13
Chemicals and wood	1,225	47	28	13	5	8
Construction	90	30	29	12	18	11
Social sphere	256	45	21	13	9	13

Sources: O. Amurzhuyev and Tsapelik (1989); Kroll (1991: 145).

would be such that many suppliers would be required: cement, for example, or biscuits.

In another sense, monopoly was the natural outcome of a centralized process, and some observers anticipated that as market forces came into play, things would change. Brown *et al.* (1994: 7) write:

> Under central planning, there was no incentive, let alone authority, for the enterprise to diversify its production. Thus, while concentration measured in terms of products will naturally appear greater than concentration measured at a more aggregated level, this disaggregation is exaggerated in the Soviet case.

Therefore Brown *et al.* propose that while the level of monopoly was very high under the planning system, it might well become competitive once enterprises were given the freedom to compete.

However, such a prediction was based on enterprise-level monopoly. In 1992, Soviet ministries were often replaced by "associations", groupings of companies. Frydman *et al.* (1993: 23, 25) observe that the associations

> usually had pre-existing links, having been under the common administration of a particular branch ministry. The formal foundation of an association among them was designed to make them largely independent of the formal administrative structure, thus also making them immune to the successive administrative decisions of the government and the ever-new restructuring attempts characteristic of the later years of the Soviet regime.... These associations accounted for 38.3% of industrial production and over 6.4 million employees. They are mostly horizontal structures and constitute extremely powerful cartels. Thus, for example, one concern (Rosneftigas) controls 99.8% of Russian oil production, while another (Gazprom) controls 93% of natural gas production ... Stankoinstrument controls 88.7% of machine tools and 81.6% of forge presses.

Russia also inherited a peculiar transport system, designed to help fulfil the plan. The railway system functioned as the key freight carrier, administered by the Ministry of Railways (MPS). The MPS was "a vast monopoly" for long-distance, intercity and inter-republican freight transport, which was incidentally also responsible for half of the world's railway freight (IMF *et al.* 1991; III, 61–3). The central grip over rail transport remained strong even when Russia began its privatization reforms, leading to conditions where freight had to be scheduled six months in advance (Brown *et al.* 1994: 34). The lack of diversified transport networks, coupled with the monopolistic tendencies inherent in the railway system, served as a further impediment to the creation of competitive markets.

Enterprise towns and the social role of enterprises

Soviet, and therefore Russian, enterprises were designed as monopoly suppliers. Often they were also significant as employers in certain towns, with almost half of Soviet cities, with around 12.2 per cent of civilian employment, featuring only one significant firm and more than three-quarters of cities having four firms or fewer (ibid.: 35). Frequently, enterprises took on social functions on behalf of their workforce that would not be undertaken by their western counterparts. These functions were often supplied to the whole community and included the provision of such benefits as housing, childcare facilities, schools, hospitals, transport infrastructure, recreational facilities, shops and sometimes farms.[13]

Labour and labour mobility

The Soviet system was designed to eliminate unemployment, with the state providing social protection by means of supplying every citizen in the country with a job (a constitutional guarantee). Open unemployment which was not associated with people changing jobs was not an acknowledged feature of the Soviet economy (Standing 1991, 1994). This is not to say that there was no unemployment. In part, it related to people changing jobs and it showed up in the informal economy.[14] Perhaps there was considerable movement between jobs, with an interagency financial study noting that "official labour turnover rates in the USSR [were] not markedly out of line with those recorded in many Western countries" (IMF *et al.* 1991: III, 143). However, there was little physical mobility. Employees may have moved job, but they did not move house. In a regular housing market, 10 to 15 per cent of units are exchanged every year. In Soviet cities, statistics suggest this rate was 1 per cent or less (ibid.: III, 327).

One reason for this was the "*propiska* system",[15] or internal passport, which had been in use in Russia since Tsarist times (Matthews 1993). *Propiska* was used extensively in the past as an instrument of "labour discipline" and of "population distribution policy and special planning" (IMF *et al.* 1991: III, 143).[16] In uncharacteristically robust language an IMF report (ibid.: III, 327) writes,

> It is a major source of inequity and economic inefficiency, often subjecting rural residents to a form of serfdom by denying them the opportunity to move to cities. The population of favoured cities like Moscow has been stabilised through this passport system, and during the recent pervasive consumer goods shortages the propiska was often used when shopping.

A *propiska* was required to acquire housing and other social benefits, enormously impeding labour market adjustments. In cities and regions where the central government chose to control population numbers, employers were limited in their ability to adjust the size of their workforce (IMF *et al.* 1991: III, 327). Population control was therefore a major impediment to labour market adjustments in the sense that in most cities whose population was controlled according to the regional and special plans, "employers were not allowed to expand their staff freely" (ibid.: III, 327).

The maintenance of the system, in combination with the widespread existence of company towns, meant that, despite relatively normal levels of labour turnover, labour markets in Russia had exceptional rigidities.

Therefore, in 1992, as reformers contemplated privatization, they were faced with an economy characterized by a high degree of monopoly containing many firms which were uncompetitive, most were overstaffed and many were the only employer in isolated towns. Transport was poor, access to capital was limited, and the labour force was relatively immobile. The country lacked a corpus of commercial law, with what legislation there was often being contradictory and/or unenforceable. These characteristics of the Russian economy posed a challenge for the privatization process not just in terms of how policy was framed and how successfully it was implemented, but whether it would ever be likely to achieve its desired outcomes.

The goals of privatization

There have been many goals suggested for privatization. We discuss them under three headings: economic, that is creating the conditions for a more efficient economy; budgetary, that is raising money for the government or for companies; and political, that is garnering support for reform, changing who was in control of Russian enterprises, and indeed ensuring that control could not be exercised centrally. However, in reality, these objectives can tend to overlap.

For example, the 1992 Privatization Programme listed six objectives for privatization:

- to help develop a market economy;
- to increase enterprise efficiency;
- to ensure a social safety net;
- to help create financial stabilization;
- to promote competition;
- to attract foreign investment.

This in itself is quite a long list of objectives. But other commentators would suggest their own views of the rationale for privatization. Åslund (2007: 144ff.), for example, divides them into important political as well as economic goals. The political ones included "the breakup of hegemonic state power" and the building of "a new middle class of educated property owning people". Economic goals included the building of a well-functioning market economy; creating "real owners" for enterprises; making companies independent; imposing hard budget constraints on companies; creating enterprise restructuring and better corporate governance; creating real capital markets; and encouraging investment.

Just combining Åslund's goals with those of the Russian parliament, therefore, creates a number of potentially conflicting objectives, and this is a far from comprehensive list. Therefore, in the following pages, we summarize what might be considered the main aims of privatization and their rationale. We then go on to consider whether, given the conditions of the Russian economy, these aims were likely to be achievable. In Chapter 4 we discuss how the design of the programme favoured one or other of these objectives.

Economic objectives

To summarize above, there are two broad economic objectives for privatization. The first aims to establish the ownership of the country's industrial assets. The second has the broader goal of seeking the efficiency and prosperity that market economies had achieved. This includes the restructuring of enterprises to make their operations more efficient.

The goal of ownership transformation at that time required significant institutional change, in regard to both formal rules and informal custom. In 1991 in Russia, clear asset ownership did not exist, although Gorbachev's 1988 Law on State Enterprises had introduced a legal framework for cooperatives and contract brigades; small farmers could own land but not pass it on to their heirs. The general understanding of ownership until then was that it was shared between citizens, workers' collectives and government agencies.[17] De facto control lay in part with managers, in part with "trusts" comprised of bureaucrats and managers from old branch ministries, and in part with local and national political figures. Therefore a key aim of the reformers was to clarify ownership and to do so as quickly as possible. Indeed the privatization legislation was framed in such a way as to create adequate incentive for those who had gained de facto control to accept the new de jure legislation.

Beyond alignment of de facto and de jure rights, the aims of privatization also implied the assumption, or reason for believing, that private ownership would lead to a more efficient and prosperous economy. Eduardo Borensztein and Manmohan Kumar (1991: 300ff.) write, "The evident failure of the central planning system has created the near consensus that the move to a market economy is necessary to achieve standards of living comparable to those of the industrial economies of the West." Efficiencies will emerge, they explain, in a competitive environment, where market prices reflect relative scarcities, and enterprises and individuals make decisions mainly in response to market signals. "Private ownership leads to the achievement of these conditions," they argue, "because the incentives for the private owners to ensure their costs of production are minimized and ... their output mix is determined in relation to market signals."

However, while privatization may be a necessary condition for effective ownership and efficient markets, it is not a sufficient one. Foreign advisers were well aware of this at the time. Borensztein and Kumar note further that,

> By this rationale privatization will, within a free competitive environment, lead to efficient allocation of resources, which will maximize the welfare of the economy as a whole. However, for this to be the case privatization ... must be accompanied by other policies to promote competition if a significant turnaround in the performance of public enterprise is to be achieved.

Similarly, at a seminar of western experts on privatization organized for the Russian reformers by the EBRD/World Bank in March 1992 (prior to the passage of the 1992 Programme), a key conclusion was that

> privatization is not an end in itself. It is one among a number of means which are crucial to the achievement of improved efficiency throughout the economy, in the service of economic growth and higher living standards for the people of Russia.[18]

The question to be asked is: If privatization was not an end in itself, what other conditions were necessary to make it work, and to what extent did they exist in Russia in 1992?

Ownership

The minimalist economic justification for privatization, then, is perhaps the establishment of basic ownership rights. The importance of ownership rights is expressed in the work of Ronald Coase, who notes that, in the absence of transaction costs, provided that asset ownership is clear, ownership rights will result in efficient outcomes (Coase 1988: 158). In 1994, "members of the team, which put [privatization] together", Maxim Boycko, Andrey Shleifer and Robert Vishny, write that reform was based on the establishment of clear property rights, which they anticipated would be achieved. Reflecting the "Coase theorem", they summarized their thinking as follows (Boycko *et al.* 1995: 19):

> When property rights over a productive asset are clearly specified and the person who decides how to employ this asset bears full costs and full benefits of such employment, he puts the asset to its most productive use. This argument provides the ultimate rationale for relying on private property as the basis for an efficient organisation of economic activity.

However, as they are aware, security of ownership rights in a market economy requires protection of property and enforcement of contracts. Yet, as we noted above, the "body of civil law which regulates the economic relationships necessary in a market economy [was] largely missing from the corpus of Soviet law". Without that corpus of law, privatization alone would be unlikely to create the conditions that those economists who focus on analysis of property rights would prescribe.

Nor is this simply a legal issue, it also has to do with the structure of ownership. Economists understand that different forms of "ownership" of companies are each likely to produce different results. For example, Adolph Bearle and Gardiner Means's classic study, *The Modern Corporation and Private* Property (1932), cited in Boycko *et al.* (1995: 20), refers to the separation of ownership and control in a public corporation as one way of rendering it inefficient, because managers make decisions and shareholders bear the costs of those decisions. Alfred Marshall (1946: 303) in a similar analysis, notes that the success of the public corporation, where ownership and management are separated, depends on a "spirit of honesty and uprightness in commercial matters".

It is therefore somewhat surprising that the initial privatization reforms envisaged separating the rights of owners as a group from those of the managers and workers of the enterprise. The aim of the government's initial privatization proposals, which were reflected in the so-called Option One of the Privatization Programme, was for managers and workers to be given shares which would not carry any voting rights in order to encourage their cooperation but not their control. It was envisaged that other shareholdings would be widely distributed, as they might be in Anglo-Saxon capital markets. It was further envisaged that all shares would be tradable, leading to the creation of up to 20,000 public enterprises (more public enterprises than would be found in the whole of the rest of the world put together).

To be sure, some of the International Financial Institutions (IFIs) recognized this issue. Writing in March 1992, before the Privatization Programme was passed, the World Bank and EBRD study team note that

> a voucher program that is not part of a wider mass privatization program risks diffusing ownership amongst thousands of inexperienced shareholders potentially dispersed over a vast geographic region.... The risk is that current management will be entrenched, free of shareholder discipline, and able to misallocate resources, or do nothing at all to enhance the prospects of the company.

They go on to advocate that no project should be approved if "it fails to provide for ownership of a control block of shares by a strategic investor group".[19]

That recommendation creates a Catch-22. Either shares were to be widely dispersed, in which case management acquired de facto power, or they were to be sold to a strategic investor. The problem, which we describe in greater detail in Chapter 4, lay in the fact that there were few candidates who could become strategic investors, save those who had had the capacity to protect the value of their savings by holding cash abroad. Such investors tended either to be foreign investors, Russian individuals and institutions who held cash abroad, possibly illegitimately, or enterprises which were to be privatized in the first place.

The problem was in part "solved" when parliament passed the Privatization Programme, including a new option, negotiated by Chubais, that allowed workers and managers to subscribe for full voting shares. This legislative change was opposed by some of the reformers. Indeed, some years later, at a lecture in Moscow, Yegor Gaidar observed that the concession to grant workers and managers control of the enterprises was a mistake.[20] The critics of privatization noted that the option of granting shares to managers and workers gave rise to factory directors gaining "control and effective ownership of most of the country's factories at minimal cost to themselves, as well as minimal benefit to the public at large" (Goldman 2004: 81).

It is paradoxical that this option, opposed by both some of the reformers and their critics, may in fact have been necessary to achieve one of the fundamental goals of privatization – a greater unification of de facto and de jure ownership rights. Put simply, the ownership of a company share, and the control rights it confers, cannot be divorced from the structure, the culture and the *modus operandi* of the economic system within which those legal rights are conferred. The reformers generally opposed allowing control rights to pass to the managers and workers of the enterprises to be privatized. Yet, in the absence of enforceable laws, it was only through this device that the reformers' key goal, that is clarifying the ownership of the enterprise, was likely to be established.

Creating a market economy

The clarification of ownership rights was a necessary goal of privatization. However, the economic objectives of the programme went much further than that.

"The foremost aim of privatisation", writes Anders Åslund (2007: 146), "was to build the foundation of a well functioning market economy.... It was this which lay behind the economic imperative for the reform programmes in Eastern Europe."

The World Bank, the group of advisers hired by the World Bank/EBRD to assist the Privatization Ministry (the Consortium) and other advisory groups were equally clear. Braxton Associates and Deloitte write: "Privatization is not an end in itself. Privatization is part of a package of measures designed to bring about economic growth and higher living standards for the people of Russia."[21]

The assertions that privatization would yield economic benefits were underpinned by over 200 years of economic thinking. By this model, it is price that is the arbiter of whether a transaction takes place. Competition ensures that those who produce goods offer them for sale at close to their cost of production. If a supplier charges too much, other producers will offer lower prices and customers will go elsewhere. There is therefore a high incentive for producers to keep pushing down costs, and push up the value delivered to customers, in order to maximize profit. This in turn creates the productivity that is the driver to economic growth. However, the model requires that prices are free to move to equate the supply and demand for goods at their "natural price".

We underscore, as economists cited above did at the time, that Russia in the early 1990s was unlikely to provide such a foundation for prices to move freely. Let us revisit some of these issues.

MONOPOLY

The classical model will only produce "efficient" solutions when certain conditions are met. First, it requires that there is competition. Monopolists will restrict output and create higher prices in order to maximize profits. Adam Smith writes on competition:

> the monopolists by keeping the market constantly under stocked … sell their commodities much above the natural price. The price of monopoly is upon every occasion the highest that can be got. The natural price, or the price of free competition … is the lowest which the sellers can commonly afford to take, and at the same time continue their business.
>
> (Smith [1776])

The degree of monopolization in Russia presented a dilemma. Monopoly existed at two levels, as noted above: the enterprise trusts, or "associations" which had replaced branch ministries; and at the level of the enterprises themselves. To some extent, the Privatization Programme could aim to weaken the trusts, or associations, as was advised: "the implementation of a privatization program must be designed carefully to ensure that existing administratively created monopolies are not merely transferred into private hands in a form that would hinder the long term efficiency of the economy."[22]

However, at the enterprise level, it could prove impossible to break up monopoly producers. "Given the large number of monopoly structures and the weak government control over the SOE's (State Owned Enterprises)," the appraisal continues, "it may not always be possible for the Government to split up the monopolies before they are privatized".

Furthermore, traditional responses to monopoly problems would only lead to ineffective policies, since they often involve price controls. Central to a successful market economy is the need for prices to be freely determined. Indeed, it is "price signals" that encourage new entrants to a market. So, by controlling prices, regulators would stifle the very market forces that privatization sought to promote.

Russia's competition policy was therefore threatened by over-intervention by the state in price regulation, with the GKAP (the Russian State Committee for Anti-Monopoly Policy and Promotion of New Economic Structures) monitoring an official register of over 2,000 enterprises, which comprise 80 per cent of industrial production and supplied over 6,000 goods and obliged enterprises to register any price increase.[23] The prevalence of overlapping laws and weak information systems in 1992 meant that even when policies were revised by the government, they did not always become effective. As an indication of the legislative difficulties that prevailed in 1992, although a *Memorandum of Economic Policy* issued by the government in early March determined that such price regulation (along with maximum rates of profitability) would be discontinued as of 1 July 1992, even the City of Moscow Anti-Monopoly Committee was not aware of this decision one month later.[24]

Given the degree of monopoly, price liberalization and privatization policies were likely to have unpredictable consequences, which might not, in the medium term, conform to the efficient markets that reformers sought. Indeed, as Adam Smith notes, privatized monopolies will raise prices and reduce output. This was the reverse of the reformers' intentions.

Just as the market for goods needs to be competitive, so does the market for capital and labour. As regards labour, in an efficient economy, workers need to be able to decide which job to take; they need to be able to move to a preferred employer should they choose to do so. Yet, as we have seen, the *propiska* system constrained labour mobility, particularly the sort of mass mobility that might occur should the sole enterprise in a factory town be forced to close.

In these circumstances, it is understandable why workers might have had particular concerns about their prospects. This was perhaps one reason why enterprises went for Option Two for privatization (which granted control to workers and managers), despite that fact that in theory workers and managers would have been better off financially if they chose a different privatization option.

RESTRUCTURING

The lack of readily available capital created a further problem. The aim of moving to a "capitalist" model of production was that capital would be given to efficient enterprises that showed a high return and were profitable, and withdrawn from those which were unprofitable. All companies should be subject to a "hard budget" constraint, that is, one where capital is only made available to projects and enterprises that will generate an adequate return for the risk taken.

However, given the level of monopoly and the distortion in prices, it was difficult to determine which enterprises were efficient and which were not. On 1 January 1992, some Russian prices were liberalized. But some were not. So, while many enterprises may have seemed profitable, this was only because the price of their sales was inflated, or other inputs deflated. Other loss-making enterprises might have been profitable had they been able to trade at world prices. Furthermore, the enterprises that were to be privatized had not been run to make a profit. Indeed, they often had explicit responsibility for running the schools, transport and housing of the town in which they were located. Until these and other issues had been dealt with, enterprises would find it difficult to determine their costs, even if Russia had had a market pricing regime.

As we have seen, in Russia in 1992, the only supply of firm credit came from the Central Bank of the Russian Federation (CB, 1990–, formerly Gosbank), or from suppliers. There were no effective alternative financing systems. Indeed, the Privatization Programme aimed to develop such a system by encouraging the creation of investment funds. However, in the meantime, a hard budget constraint would only prevail if the CB could be persuaded to enforce it. Without that constraint, all enterprises would request funds from the CB. If the CB acceded to that request, it would create "moral hazard", that is, a situation in which companies were encouraged to find ways to generate credit from the state rather than to compete in the marketplace. If the CB refused, it risked dislocating the economy. Because Russian enterprises often reflected monopolistic divisional suppliers within larger company networks, the effect on the supply chain could be significant if they were to close.

In the event, following the liberalization of prices in January 1992, no effective plan was made for how the CB was or was not to fund enterprises. As a result, enterprises essentially funded each other. Companies continued to supply one another to allow the buildup of inter-company debt. In order to overcome this problem, which itself threatened to undermine the privatization process, the CB ultimately issued credits to allow for debt to be paid. However, in doing so, it breached the purpose of privatization, which was to wean companies onto a hard budget.

DISCUSSION

It was unlikely that the privatization reforms alone could lead to the creation in the medium term of the efficient markets to which the reformers aspired. As the above discussion argues, advisers to the Russian government were well aware of this problem. As the World Bank and EBRD privatization group note in March 1992 as their first "key point", privatization needed to be seen as an instrument to generate economic growth and higher living standards and that "When options within the privatization programme are being considered, they should therefore be tested according to these criteria. The options that contribute to economic efficiency should be preferred ahead of those that impede its achievement."[25]

If privatization did create new owners, then it might nevertheless have been expected to bring about a restructuring, whatever the form of industry. If the new owners of the company sought to maximize its profits, they would have little reason to keep open unprofitable operations, to accept overstaffing, or indeed to support the various social activities that companies were involved in providing.

However, this created another difficulty for the Russian government, as we shall discuss when we look at the social and political goals of privatization. If privatization was successful, and enterprises were managed efficiently, this would cause dramatic social consequences, for which Russia was unprepared. If, however, there was to be little restructuring, then the goal of economic efficiency and improved living standards was unlikely to be realized.

In retrospect, it is difficult to make the case that in Russian conditions privatization could have led quickly to efficiency or higher living standards. This was not because of a failure of understanding by either the Russian government or its advisers of the difficulties presented by the need for institutional change prior to privatization. Rather, it was that the Mass Privatization Programme needed to be coordinated within a sequencing of reforms and of investments to restructure and liberalize Russia's economy. These included abolishing price and wage controls, creating competition, establishing rouble convertibility, creating a comprehensive and enforceable legal framework, and implementing numerous other reforms in labour, goods and financial markets. Given the structure of the Russian economy, the coordination and linkage among all these reforms would be of particular importance to the overall success of each. As we will discuss in the next chapter, such coordination did not happen in Russia in 1992.

Budgetary/investment objectives

Government budget

When the Privatization Programme was passed, it was envisaged that it would make a significant contribution to the government budget. Indeed the programme itself stated that one of the six aims was to provide the finance to create a "social safety net", where receipts from privatization could raise enough to help pay for pension, unemployment and other benefits. Indeed, receipts from privatization were envisaged as a possible sponge for the "monetary overhang" which had built up over previous years, and hence the programme was seen as a contributor in helping to "create financial stabilisation" and "an effective way to reduce the monetary overhang" (IMF *et al.* 1991: II, 394).

However, the introduction of vouchers meant that the state gave up its right to the proceeds of privatization to the voucher holders. In the June 1992 Programme, it was envisaged that this would relate only to the 35 per cent of the proceeds of large-scale privatization that were due to the federal government. However, in October, vouchers were applied to the whole programme, and all state authorities therefore received little or nothing from it as a consequence. As Goldman (2004: 93) notes critically:

> Another shortcoming in the first round of privatization was that it generated very little in the way of revenue, either to the government or the firm's balance sheet and capital. Based on my unofficial estimates the state collected a mere $160 million during the first three years of privatization.

This was, of course, a necessary consequence of choosing a voucher programme. Later, in 1995, the government moved on to monetary privatization, where objectives changed. According to one of the architects of monetary privatization, its goals were "totally different from the voucher period, [when] we had been selling off companies really for symbolic prices" (Kokh 1998: 47). During the monetary privatization, the government worked, he writes, "to sell prime companies at top prices; attract investment; maximise revenues from sales; and encourage greater participation from the West".

Voucher privatization critics like Goldman are right to point out that the programme stopped the Russian government from achieving any budgetary goal. The decision to abjure cash sales was a point upon which the government found a consensus with international advisers, however, in particular the Deloitte Consortium. They note that, unless the timing of privatization was slowed, it was difficult to see where legitimate investment monies would be found to finance the privatization. Reporting on the situation in August of the following year, the Consortium reiterated the point:

> In its original conception [the Mass Privatisation Programme] envisaged 65% of the equity of Russian companies being sold for cash. Although it is difficult to measure the value of this equity, this could well be equal to 15–30% of Russian Gross National Product, based on preliminary estimates. Raising such a sum of money from within the country could well be difficult, given the estimates of savings and other internal sources of liquid assets.[26]

The Consortium went on to welcome the extension in October 1992 of the voucher programme, which addressed this problem, and it also noted that cash sales would be likely to encourage the formation of holding companies.

> It is likely that many companies will choose their customers and suppliers as strategic investors. This will result in interlocking holding companies being formed in Russia, with significant monopolistic power. The privatization programme offers little protection against this outcome.... At this stage we have few fool proof solutions to the holding company problem. However, the following suggestions may make them more difficult to create: (a) Extend the voucher programme ... (b) lengthen the timetable of the Mass Privatization Programme (c) encourage worker control under Option Two.

Vasiliev, the Deputy Privatization Minister, made the same point:

> Price liberalization had destroyed everyone's savings, there was no money any more. That realisation led us to the conclusion that cash privatisation would lead to a cataclysm. A very narrow group would buy the whole economy. That would provoke the deep seated envy of the Russian people and could spark a social upheaval.[27]

Therefore there was a clear trade-off made in the MPP, between the raising of revenues, the practicality of trying to do so, and the future industrial structure that cash privatization would create. In 1992, the choice was made, and endorsed by western advisers to the Privatization Ministry: for both practical and policy reasons, the future structure should take precedence.[28]

In sum, therefore, during the MPP, the budgetary objective of raising cash for the government was abandoned in voucher privatization, for reasons of practicality and economics, and to protect the legitimacy and integrity of the process.

Investment by enterprises

This, of course, left open the question of where the cash would come from to re-equip companies. A potential source of capital could come from the repatriation of Russian foreign currency, held legally and illegally,[29] estimated to be worth many billions of dollars. There was, however, the danger that this would raise political issues if enterprises were sold to those whose source of funds was illegitimate; or if companies were to use their own foreign currency deposits, this would result in the holding company structures that the reforms sought to avoid.

Another possible source of new funds was foreign investors. They were in a position to provide Russia not only with much needed investment, but also with access to technology and experienced management.[30]

However, the Privatization Programme attracted little interest from foreigners. In the summer of 1992, for the State Committee on Foreign Investment, Goldman Sachs surveyed 300 companies considered likely to invest in Russia. The survey concluded that while there existed the possibility for one to three "megadeals", they were unlikely to materialize; 20 to 30 deals, ranging between $20 million and $50 million, as well as several technical exchanges, were anticipated at most.[31] As such, the likelihood of foreign investment during the first phase of privatization was small and, indeed, this proved to be so. This was not just because of limited interest by western companies, but because there was "little political support for foreign investment in tenders", since "Directors [were] concerned that direct foreign investment would mean potential loss of control", and would "prefer to JV [joint venture] in a new enterprise".

So, while in theory the Privatization Programme created structures and securities that could be used by privatizing companies to raise finance in the future, there was limited prospect in the medium term that it would achieve the goal of raising finance either for the state or for the newly privatized companies.

After 1994, as policy moved towards monetary privatization, budgetary issues came to the fore, and the issue of who was put in control of the privatized companies was set aside. We have already noted (p. 67) Vasiliev's early concern that monetary privatization would mean that a very narrow group would own the whole economy. Yet Appel, writing in 2004, cites Vasiliev as having ultimately "made explicit his preference for using sales over free transfers, arguing that property would only be valued if it were exchanged at a cost to the new owners". He went on to say of the later monetary privatization that "Our aim is to form a layer of effective owners. This is privatisation in favour of a very small circle of people" (Appel 2004: 82, 93).

It is therefore paradoxical that much of the criticism of voucher privatization is levelled at its creation of corruption and oligarchy. In fact, its aim was to stop this happening. To some extent, the MPP was implemented with a degree of bad practice, and we discuss this in the following two chapters. Nevertheless, few companies that were to have been privatized in the original 1992 Programme can be identified as major vehicles for corruption or platforms for oligarchs (Gazprom and Lukoil, initially entered in 1994, were not part of the original programme). In part, this may be because the larger companies were not part of the Mass Privatization Programme, since enterprises in the field of natural resources, aluminium and banking were excluded from it. The oligarchs' direct involvement in privatization were in the main the creation of a later era, when the ability to raise substantial financial assets became a necessary condition for participation in privatization, and the benefits skewed towards a very small circle of people (Treisman 2010).

In summary, then, the voucher privatization was never likely, in the medium term, to achieve what we have termed "budgetary goals". It is the nature of vouchers that they do not raise money.

Social and political objectives

In Russia, privatization was not just an economic policy. It also had social and political aims.

Generating popular support

First, the aim, as in voucher privatization in the Czech Republic, was in part to create political support; privatization would generate a give-away. For this to succeed, however, the benefit to be received by citizens had to outweigh the costs in terms of the pain of restructuring. The Russian government had to persuade its citizens that, despite forthcoming reductions in income and redundancies, the privatization would deliver a "dividend" to them (Kikeri *et al.* 1994: 11). In this context, the popularity of the programme rested on the financial rewards available to citizens in the short and long term, as well as on its overall fairness towards everyone in the country. It was imperative to demonstrate early successes in privatizing large strategic enterprises in order to secure popular support.[32]

In the event, large strategic enterprises were not included in the privatization. As a result, the value of the assets to be sold via MPP was not high. Additionally, in the absence of a functioning commercial law system, the rights of the new owners were also difficult to determine. So the market price of vouchers remained below their 10,000 rouble face price until the summer of 1993; in dollars their value was between $4 (in May 1993) and $20 (in November 1992) (Åslund 1994: 105). Consequently, the Privatization Programme paid little dividend to the budget. As a result, if anything, the low value of the voucher led to stories of what might have been thought of as a birthright inheritance being exchanged for a bottle of vodka.

In light of these events, public support did not last. The main objective of privatization, in other words, as Kikeri *et al.* (1992: 11) put it, "to transfer the property rights to owners who have incentives for defending the interests of the capital they own", was not achieved, or at least not in terms of creating a popular demand for restructuring where private owners supported with their votes "the painful steps for transiting fully to a market economy", including the restructuring of industry.

However, that very restructuring was likely to have social consequences which could create profound problems. These might include, if there was a radical restructuring, significant unemployment in the wake of reform.

For some reformers, a key economic benefit of privatization was to limit political control of enterprises, because politicians were arguably, *ipso facto*, inefficient owners; therefore, removal of their influence from economic life was expected to reduce inefficiency, as privatization would prevent politicians from allocating goods (Boycko *et al.* 1994: 20ff.). This, of course, tends to simplify the question of what should be the relationship between the state and the market. It also begs the question of how the social consequences would be managed if restructuring were to remake Russian companies. The consequences would include high unemployment and the companies' abandonment of the social services they previously provided to the community.

From 1989 to 1992, the Russian GDP dropped further than comparable GDP figures for the USA and Germany in the 1930s.[33] Labour figures reflected high "overemployment", as well as employment at uneconomic plants.[34] Projections suggested that the unemployment consequences of privatization could be dramatic, particularly on a local level, if the incentives for enhanced efficiency were to take effect more rapidly than could be absorbed by production and market growth.[35]

However, by summer 1992, the drop in GDP had resulted in hardly any unemployment. Furthermore, the governance structures that would come about as the result of Option Two (the option in the Privatization Programme that gave power to the management and workers) would have the effect both of stifling restructuring and of reducing unemployment, which was "a source of opposition to privatisation". This conservative attitude to restructuring was evident in the summer of 1992. A survey by the GKI asked enterprise directors about their plans for the future of their "social assets", such as housing, healthcare, education and recreational facilities. Most enterprises "did not wish to divest themselves of social assets, reflecting the fact that social, personal and political motivations, as well as classical economic motivations, will continue to play a significant part in the conduct of privatised companies".[36]

So, while the distribution of vouchers might gain some modest popularity for privatization, particularly if major enterprises such as telecoms companies were included, the value of these was likely easily to be outweighed by the initial negative economic consequences of the programme. It was another Catch-22. Either the programme brought about restructuring, its economic goal, and created a political backlash, or it avoided the political backlash but at the cost of failing to achieve its economic goal. As we shall see, the problem was resolved by the granting of ownership rights to those with the greatest interest in the preservation of the status quo: the workers and managers of the enterprises themselves.

Changing attitudes

There were two other "political" goals that cannot be ignored. The first was the aim of creating a change in attitudes. This was not an explicit goal, particularly of the economic advisers. But it was the primary positive outcome of reform that Yeltsin noted in his memoirs (Yeltsin 1994: 18). He reflects on whether the Gaidar reforms have helped cure the "sick" Russian economy, and concludes that there has been improvement. He goes on:

> I draw this conclusion not on the basis of economic indicators; they are objectively poor.... Rather I am making this analysis based on the fact that people with an entirely new psychology have emerged in our country. They have the psychology of the *muzhik*, the sturdy Russian peasant who does not expect anyone to help him and doesn't rely on anyone – not the government, the parliament or Yeltsin ... normal people – the kind of people who used to be crushed by the state – have begun to appear in our country.

It is beyond the scope of this book to assess whether Yeltsin's goal was realistic, or indeed whether it was achieved.

The end of the command-administrative economy

But there was one other important political goal of privatization on the Russian side. It sets the reform in its historical context at the end of perestroika in Russia and the emergence of independent states in Central and Eastern Europe. The powers of the command-administrative economy had been underpinned by a communist ideology, which had shown its resilience over many decades. Marshall Goldman (2004: 21) comments:

> those in charge, such as Yegor Gaidar and Anatoly Chubais, rationalise what they did by insisting that in 1992 the fate of the reform movement, even the rejection of communism, was in doubt. Therefore they felt it was essential to adopt a strategy that would reinforce the public's determination ... to reject the communist system. Whenever challenged, Chubais insists that, whatever the consequences of the ill fated reform process, preventing the communists from regaining power was justification enough.

And indeed the feeling of the end of an era was palpable.

We began this chapter by emphasizing the experimental nature of the Soviet economy and, then, its accumulation of power and institutional stability. By the end of the 1990s observers were pointing to the emergence of oligarchs who had taken over Russian companies without due process. However, in 1992, the threat was less the emergence of a group of oligarchs; rather, it was, on the one hand, a descent into anarchy, and, on the other, the re-emergence of a centralized system of control. Depending on how privatization progressed, it could influence the degree to which Russia emerged as either a pluralist or a centralized and controlled economy. However, this political goal, like the economic goals, would not be determined by privatization alone, but also by the broad interplay of political forces in post-Soviet Russia.

Summary

In this chapter we have reviewed the various goals of the Russian Privatization Programme. Few of these could be achieved by privatization alone. Rather, their achievement depended on a series of reforms: the creation of a commercial legal code; the freeing of prices; the establishment of a commercial banking system; the transition from monopoly production; the transfer of responsibility for employment and social protection. Privatization, or at least the clarification of "ownership rights", may have been a necessary condition for the achievement of these goals. But for most of them, it was not a sufficient one.

The one area of reform where privatization could be particularly important was the establishment of legal title to ownership of enterprise assets. Provided that it granted these rights to those who already had some de facto claim to the assets, it could nudge ownership in the direction of one group or another, and help marry law with practice. This had knock-on effects on the degree of power granted to enterprise workers and managers, on the one hand, or to the "associations", on the other. Granting rights to insiders also had knock-on effects for the speed with which the restructuring process would begin.

Table 3.3 summarizes the various objectives for the Privatization Programme. What is immediately apparent is that, even with a comprehensive reform programme, most of the goals would be difficult to achieve in the medium term. Even over the longer term, they would all require corollary reforms in laws and their implementation and a radical change to the economic structures of the country.

To bring about such reform required a unified and clear policy which commanded broad support in the parliament, in government, and among the people. As we shall see from the next chapter, such consensus did not exist in Russia, in regard either to reform overall or indeed to the Privatization Programme itself.

Table 3.3 Goals and outcomes: likelihood of achievement

Objective	*Key constraint*	*Likelihood of achievement through voucher privatization*	*Key issues*
Establishing ownership	De facto ownership already established?	Med/high if terms of privatization reflected de facto control structures; otherwise med/low	Insider privatization
Creating competitive/efficient markets	Monopoly, lack of capital, labour mobility	Low	Dealing with privatized monopolies
Restructuring	Unknown efficiency of enterprises; social consequences	Only high if external owners secure rights, and companies rationed for capital (q.v.); otherwise low.	Social consequences of rapid restructuring
Raising money for government	Vouchers don't raise money	Low	Removal of regional interests in enterprises to be sold
Raising money for companies	Legal framework not in place; no capital market	Low/med	Lack of legal code
Gaining political support	Social consequences; lack of value in programme	Low	Lack of immediate reward to population; lack of common policy on directions; communication of programme and its consequences
Preventing re-emergence of centralized authority	Design of programme	Med/high	Future of "associations"

4 Implementation of privatization, 1992–1994

In Chapter 3 we observed that, unless it was part of a larger coordinated programme of economic and legislative reform, the Russian Mass Privatization Programme would be very limited in what it would be able to achieve. In Chapter 2 we noted that the political consensus to achieve comprehensive reform was lacking. The executive branch was split in its approach, and was, in any case, at loggerheads with the legislature. Most of the economic reform programme was enacted by presidential decree and, as such, arguably lacked a sense of legitimacy, although parliament itself accorded the president such powers and parliament approved most decrees. The passage of the Privatization Programme through parliament on 11 June 1992 was a key instance of consensus.

As we have also noted, there was a limit to what the ratified Privatization Programme had actually established. As discussed in Chapter 2 above, the legislation defined three things: first, the categorization of "objects to be privatized"; second, the method by which the privatization should take place and the rights afforded to the workers of companies (although it did not set out the terms for workers' participation); third, who was to be in control of the process, and the length of time that their remit should run.

The Privatization Programme of 11 June 1992 did not establish the mechanics of the voucher programme, which were stipulated by presidential edicts separately, in August, October and November 1992.[1] Those later edicts made clear how and to whom vouchers should be issued, and how voucher subscriptions would work, and the logistical problem of ensuring the issuance of vouchers before companies' shares were auctioned.

In this chapter, we review the implementation of the 1992 Privatization Programme. We begin by looking at how different elements in the design of the programme influenced its outcome. We then look at the evidence of how the reforms were received on the ground, specifically addressing the context of the near-revolutionary changes which were taking place in Russia at the time. Finally, we reflect on what was achieved during voucher privatization: in terms of the "transfer of ownership", in terms of how it changed the behaviour of the companies affected, and in terms of its contribution to wider economic reform in Russia.

Implementing the 1992 programme

Privatization of small enterprises

Much discussion has been given to the effects of the privatization of Russia's large enterprises. Before addressing this question, it first may be worth reflecting on the privatization of small enterprises (those with less than 200 employees). Around three million people were employed at such enterprises.

In 1993, the GKI estimated that there were 76,884 enterprises of this size in Russia, though local estimates suggest that, once broken down to individual units, these may have numbered as many as 150,000.[2] Around 55 per cent were shops, approximately 15 per cent were restaurants, and around 30 per cent were service enterprises. They were all to be privatized by August 1993. While this was not achieved, their privatization was swift. By the end of 1992, 47,000 small enterprises had been privatized; 80,000 by the end of 1993; and 96,000 by the end of 1994 (Blasi *et al.* 1997: xvi). GKI statistics tell a similar story, with 45 per cent of small businesses privatized by February 1993 (Åslund 1995: 362, note 74).

The overwhelming majority of small enterprises appear to have been purchased by their own workers' collectives. Even in the 20 per cent of cases where sales were made by auction and without conditions, workers' collectives won 60 per cent of the bids. One would have expected a higher success rate for insiders with tenders, which made up 50 per cent of sales and had conditions about preserving the line of business and the level of employment. The 30 per cent sold on lease with the right to buy were also likely to have been purchased by insiders.

In part, this was because substantial privileges were given to collectives. First, they were given a 30 per cent discount on the price, but perhaps more significantly they were allowed deferred payment over three years, which was of particular value in a period of hyperinflation. In a paper written at the time, one of the authors of this book reckoned that this meant "the workers' collective [could] effectively purchase the enterprise for little over 25% of the cost to an outside investor".[3] Until October 1992, these purchases were for cash. After October 1992, vouchers were allowed for 45 per cent of the purchase, with local discretion to extend this amount.

Small-scale privatization was a local affair, organized through local municipal GKIs. Where local authorities wished to do so, enterprises were sold; if they did not, then, doubtless, the municipality held on to the asset. As the EBRD notes in its 1993 review, "If municipal authorities are determined not to implement privatization … under current political circumstance it may … be difficult for the Russian central authorities to enforce legislation".[4]

In general, there seems to be little criticism of small-scale privatization. There were many problems experienced by small companies, including inconsistent application of laws, particularly on tax, as well as problems of corruption and extortion. However, these have either received little comment or have been treated as exogenous to the privatization process. Similar problems experienced by larger companies have been viewed as endogenous to the privatization process.[5]

It is to the privatization of those companies that we now turn our attention.

Privatization of medium and large enterprises

In Chapter 2, we described the terms set for the privatization of large enterprises, employing some 15–20 million people. In its initial conception, the Russian Privatization Programme envisaged the selling of companies, extending particular rights to the workforce and to the citizenry through the issuance of privatization accounts or vouchers.

The use of vouchers had one critical benefit. Hyperinflation meant there were no savings, particularly legitimate savings, which could have been used to purchase Russian companies. If a substantial block of the shares in privatized companies was to be paid for in cash, then this would effectively encourage those who had avoided the effects of hyperinflation and had the ability to access cash to purchase the enterprises. Few ordinary Russian citizens were in that position.

In the initial conception of the Privatization Programme of 1992, vouchers were to account for only 35 per cent of the shares of the enterprises to be sold. The rest were expected to be sold at auction. It was therefore most likely that the 65 per cent of shares that were not to be sold for vouchers would end up in the hands of those who had cash. Following hyperinflation, few people had such money, and many of those who did had acquired it in a questionable fashion.

Further, it was initially not clear, under law, whether vouchers were to be tradable instruments. The law of 1991 had talked of "privatization accounts", and, according to Khasbulatov, it was envisaged that these would not be tradable.[6] Had that proposal for privatization accounts been pursued, it would have resulted, initially, in a largely fragmented "ownership" base for enterprises. The question of when the shares in the company would become tradable or whether those who had bought shares with their vouchers were simply meant to hold on to them in the hope of some future dividend would have arisen later. In the meantime, auctions of shares not bought with vouchers would have established larger strategic investors who were able to buy larger stakes and hence would have the capacity to exert effective control over the enterprise. The reformers, on the other hand, were keen for the equity sold through vouchers to be consolidated as soon as possible. Consequently, the voucher programme, which was established by decree, abandoned illiquid privatization accounts and made vouchers tradable.

The challenge from associations and holding companies

The Privatization Programme required that enterprises be sold as individual units, rather than bundled as holding companies. However, it did little to prevent the creation of such companies during the privatization process. In particular, the associations, which we described in earlier chapters, could use privatization as a way of recreating holding company structures. The "associations", which were born of the old Soviet system, often reflected the structure of the old Soviet branch ministries that coordinated production in various industries, and, in the chaos following the collapse of the Soviet Union they often provided valuable services to their members. In 1992, there was the very real prospect that these associations would use the privatization process to recreate the old ministry structure. A more detailed, contemporary account of the associations' activities during the summer of 1992 is included as Appendix 2 below.

It shows that associations had the power, and many had the intention, to use the privatization legislation as a way of recreating holding companies that would reflect those of the old Soviet branch ministries. As noted above, following the passage of the 1992 legislation, the reformers were anxious to prevent this from happening since it would be inimical to open and competitive markets.

A comment by Andrei Shleifer, Chubais's adviser during the privatization, in response to the proposal by Industry Minister Alexander Titkin that associations should take a central role in the privatization process suggests in its tone, as well as its content, policy differences between different government ministries:

> Minister Titkin proposes to create syndicates that will put enterprises in the same lines of business and along the same technological production chain into the same organization ... [he] believes that that such arrangements would make Russian enterprises look more like their western counterparts, stabilize the economy, encourage efficient restructuring, and promote growth and competition in world markets in the long term. On every count, minister Titkin is wrong.[7]

The complexities of decision making reinforced the "threat" that associations would undermine the purpose of the Privatization Programme. Below is a note from Bob Anderson, and others, consultants to the GKI in 1992. The note is dated 3 June, just before the passage of the Privatization Programme. It too reveals the gap in policy understanding between the reformers and officials even within their own ministry:

> I had an informative but also disturbing meeting with the machine tool trade association, holding company, or whatever they are calling themselves.... The disturbing information is that the association seems to have negotiated its own privatization program both for itself and the entire industry with [a Deputy Chairman of the GKI]. Specifically, the association has obtained permission to convert itself into a holding company, which will own all of the other enterprises in the industry. This was approved by the GKI on May 14th (decree No 160).[8] A Privatization Commission is now being created to supervise this transformation into a holding company.[9]

Anderson goes on to question whether "[the Deputy Chairman] is pursuing his own privatization strategy independent of Chubais and Vasiliev". What is also notable is that the association felt happy to be explicit about their plans with Anderson, as were the 15 other associations he visited. Clearly, they felt the approach they were taking was legitimate, which is hardly surprising given that it accorded with that of Industry Minister Titkin. Four of the 15 associations that were interviewed were hostile to the privatization process.[10] Most of the others had put together plans to create different forms of holding companies.

One of the key concerns of the reformers was to avoid the creation of such holding companies. As the Consortium notes in August 1992:

> It is likely that many companies will choose their customers and suppliers as strategic investors. This will result in interlocking holding companies with significant monopolistic power. The privatization programme offers little protection against this outcome.
>
> At this stage we have few foolproof solutions to the holding company problem. However the following suggestions may make them more difficult to create: (a) extend the voucher programme, offering more shares to small investors and funds; (b) lengthen the timing of the MPP to allow other strategic investors access to finance and company information; (c) encourage worker control under Option Two.[11]

They go on:

> Like other strategic issues … the GKI alone cannot find the solution to the problem. It will require effective anti monopoly action to be taken. This in turn is only likely to work if there is a consensus for action amongst government members.

The extension in the use of vouchers made the realization of holding companies more difficult because it distributed shares broadly among the population. Rather than simply use the cash from one organization to buy up the next, associations would have to buy vouchers and compete at auctions with individuals and voucher funds. Further, enterprises privatizing under Option Two would already have sold 51 per cent of their shares to the workforce; hence association control would be more difficult to effect.

Thus, a central issue, following the passage of the 1992 Programme, was whether the privatization process would result in the creation of holding companies, with some manager/worker participation, or whether it would result in a more pluralistic structure, albeit one where enterprise managers and workers would gain greater control. Neither of these outcomes was what the reformers wanted. However, the latter outcome was deemed preferable to the former.

In fact, the "threat" from associations was greatly diluted by the expansion of the use of vouchers. Vouchers could be used not only for that portion of the proceeds of privatization that would otherwise have passed to the federal government, but also for that which was due to *oblasts* and local authorities. Given its potential effect on regional budgets, and the degree to which it made the formation of holding companies more difficult, it is remarkable that the decree to extend the use of vouchers was not challenged. It greatly reinforced the rights of enterprise managers and workers over those of the old ministry staff linked to the associations.

In combination with the popularity of Option Two, which created worker/manager control, this, to an extent, crowded out the influence of holding companies. However, it is unlikely that cross-shareholding structures of the type envisaged by associations could have been, or were, entirely avoided, particularly given the support they enjoyed within the Yeltsin government.

In December 1992, before privatization began, the Consortium concluded that "under the options given in the MPP, Russia [would] become one of the most worker/manager owned industrial structures in the world." It also noted that, even with the extension of the vouchers, "some holding company structures [were] likely to be attempted during privatization" and that perhaps this was "not what the reformers initially intended".[12]

However, there was a limited amount the reformers could do to prevent this structure from emerging. It would depend on whether those who were developing privatization plans within the enterprises were minded to encourage the creation of such structures.

As we noted in Chapter 2, privatization in Russia was a "bottom-up" process. The Russian government did not have the capability to implement anything else; had it tried to do so, the result would most likely have been the creation of holding companies such as those planned by the associations. So the question then became a political one: Could the managers and workers of the enterprise be persuaded to privatize along different, more pluralistic lines? Could they, as some of the reformers somewhat cynically put it, be "bribed"[13] into supporting the process?

Response by enterprises

The 1992 Programme had laid out the options for privatization, as discussed in Chapter 3 above. But it had not laid out the terms on which subscriptions could be made for shares under Option Two; in other words, the price at which workers could buy the shares in their companies.

At this point, it may be worth looking in a little more depth at the terms of the privatization to address how they influenced incentives and choice of privatization options. Under Option One, 25 per cent of each company was to be granted to the workers at no cost, with a further 15 per cent to be available at 70 per cent of their *book value* on 1 January 1992. Under Option Two, workers could subscribe to 51 per cent at 1.7 times their book value on the same date.

The use of book values (i.e. historic accounting values) was necessary to strike the price at which workers could subscribe. However, given that Russia was suffering from hyperinflation, values based on historic costs could quickly become anomalously low. Nevertheless, calculations undertaken in the autumn of 1992 suggest that, from a purely economic point of view (and assuming no premium for voting shares), workers and managers would receive greater benefits by choosing Option One, which was indeed what the reformers wanted. As time went by, and inflation eroded the value of money, they may well have been more attracted to Option Two, since they could have bought a greater proportion of the shares, albeit at a higher price.

However, contemporary interviews of enterprise managers undertaken by western advisers in the summer of 1992 suggest that it was not these economic incentives that were foremost in the minds of enterprise managers. The preservation of control was the central issue in choosing which option an enterprise would adopt; their aim was to preserve the status quo. Enterprise managers tended to choose Option Two, or where this could not be afforded, versions of Option One that allowed them to preserve control. In those instances where the latter route was followed, interviewees noted that "schemes [were] being devised to have employees keep control of the majority of shares".[14]

According to these interviews with enterprise managers, the primary challenge facing management was "the general macroeconomic state" and the operational problems it had created. These "directly threaten[ed] the survival of the enterprises in the short run" and "many managers [did] not see the link between these problems and privatization".

There was "a high level of scepticism by managers about the 'real' intentions of the government's [Privatization Programme]", including the view that the government wanted to force companies to choose Option One so that it could remain in control with 60 per cent of the shares. And while enterprise management were aware of the general intent of the Privatization Programme, they were unclear on many issues, including rules on valuation and the use of vouchers. Many enterprises were seeking to implement privatization "using the newspaper reprints as their source of laws and decrees".

In these circumstances, and given the financial and other issues at stake, it is hardly surprising that different projects were hatched to take advantage of the legislation. These included creating trusts, buying workers' shares collectively, and minimizing asset values. Interviews revealed that

> some enterprises/associations ... approached the central GKI regarding the holding company idea, and were encouraged by the central GKI to pursue approaches which [lay] outside the bounds of the spirit of the current MPP approach with regard to holding companies. There appears to be conflicting central GKI policy on the issue.[15]

It should be noted that these interviews took place within six weeks of the deadline for enterprises to submit privatization plans.

Nevertheless, enterprise managers were relatively supportive of the programme. Interviews reported that less than 25 per cent of them were hostile, while over 40 per cent were supportive. The rest were described as "obedient", meaning they would comply, but without any particular enthusiasm to do so. By September, almost all enterprises had plans to corporatize, and nearly 90 per cent had formed commissions to do so.

In some ways, this is unremarkable. After all, it was the law. However, if enterprises had decided not to implement the law, many would have found it fairly easy to qualify as an "exception", claiming, for example, that they were monopoly producers. The only sanction would have been the withdrawal of the rights that the workers and managers would have enjoyed under the legislation. This proved enough to tip the balance in favour of implementation. However, that implementation was never likely to be carried out with the precision that could be expected in less turbulent circumstances. The Consortium reported in October 1992 that "Most enterprises are proposing to follow the law to some degree ... but ... lots of financial schemes [are being] hatched which may not be in the spirit of the reforms."[16] It went on to quote from interviews with two Moscow-based enterprises. One, a speciality steel company, reported that 60 per cent of its shares were to be put in trust for the workforce for later resale. The other, a textile company, reported that it "would be its own strategic investor". Neither of these proposals sound as if they were within the spirit of the Privatization Programme, though, at least in the former case, the company reported that it had discussed its plans with the GKI.

Voucher design and its effects

So far we have explored some of the issues facing enterprises. There were also problems associated with the use of vouchers by purchasers. These, in turn, affected the outcome of the privatization.

We have already noted that the use of vouchers as a mechanism for privatization addressed one very important problem. Because there was little legitimate cash with which companies could be purchased, the use of cash was likely to encourage outside purchasers, the provenance of whose funds would raise questions, or to facilitate schemes devised by associations and others to maintain control, or to lead to a combination of the two.

We have already noted that voucher tradability proved to be controversial. The 1991 law talks of "privatization accounts". Some, not least Ruslan Khasbulatov, the chairman of the Supreme Soviet, felt that the presidential decree which made the voucher tradable had frustrated the intent of the law, and that the subsequent sale of vouchers at low prices had brought the Privatization Programme into disrepute.[17] However, it is difficult to know what advantage could have been gained from privatization accounts, or indeed how they could have been used in the purchase of shares and/or of funds. If the shares that were to be bought were to be tradable, it is difficult to see why the vouchers used to purchase them should not be. And certainly, if the aim was to create strategic investors, the tradability of vouchers would help in this regard.

Only one voucher was issued to each citizen. It was given a face value of 10,000 roubles. The effect of this was that, unless they gave their voucher to an investment fund, individuals could only buy shares in one company, which could hardly be considered a sensible investment strategy. It also created some technical problems in workers' subscriptions, since it was envisaged that if the subscription was oversubscribed, excess funds would be returned to the workers. This, of course, would be impossible if the subscription had been by way of vouchers, since it would be impossible to return a fraction of a voucher to a worker.[18]

In effect, individuals had limited choice as to how to use their voucher. Either they could use it in a workers' subscription organized through their enterprise. About 30–35 million vouchers appear to have been used in this way.[19] Alternatively, they could subscribe to a voucher fund which would buy and manage shares on behalf of many individuals. This structure of shareholdings is typical in the West, and was favoured by the reformers. By 1994, about 640 voucher funds had been established and some 40–45 million vouchers had been subscribed by around 20 million individuals. The three largest funds each had more than 8 million vouchers.[20] The option of subscribing individually to one enterprise would have been quite a daunting process for a Russian with little knowledge of what those shares would cost, and what rights and value would be likely to attach to them. Many chose to sell their vouchers.

One repeated criticism of the Privatization Programme was that it was unfair in terms of the rewards it offered. And certainly, Chubais's prediction that a voucher would be worth the value of two cars proved to be very far off the mark indeed.[21] However, there were issues of fairness between those who were the workers in privatizing companies and the rest of the population. There were also issues of fairness between workers in different companies, with some workers' shares being worth many tens of times those of other workers. And a similar observation could be made about managers, albeit with much higher upside stakes involved.

The aim of vouchers had been to ensure that everyone benefited from privatization. In parliament, the main opposition to privatization was not that companies should remain nationalized, but that they should, in the Soviet tradition, be given to the workers (Appel 2004: 84ff.). Chubais countered this argument by advocating that all citizens should benefit. The argument was not just about equity; it was about who would become the owner of Russian industry in the future. Worker/manager control was seen as a conservative force, inimical to the restructuring that would be necessary to make the Russian economy efficient. However, as discussed in the paragraphs above, the key goal of managers was to ensure stability and to retain control. The preferential terms on which workers could subscribe to shares gave ample scope for managers to ensure that enterprise insiders stayed in control. On average, about 20–25 per cent of vouchers seem to have been subscribed by workers and managers.[22] By using these, and by raising cash, it is estimated that by 1994 they held 65 per cent of the shares in privatized enterprises; managers were likely to have held some 25 per cent and workers 40 per cent of these shares. The 116 million vouchers that were tendered at auction received around 20 per cent of the equity.[23] So the programme was very advantageous for the workforce when compared to the rest of the citizenry. However, it is unlikely that many workers appreciated that benefit, as there was little change in the behaviour of the company of which they were now the owners.

The value of privatization benefits varied greatly between workers in different companies, depending on the number of workers and the competitiveness of the enterprise. Given the lack of competitiveness of Russian companies, shareholdings were unlikely to be of immediate financial benefit. But many workers would not have seen them that way. The point of owning shares in one's own company was to stay in control, not to reap a capital gain. Nevertheless, the difference between the benefit accorded to a worker at Gazprom or Lukoil, which became part of the voucher programme in 1994, and that of a worker in an average Russian company was very considerable.

There were also anomalies. One story, whose reliability cannot be checked, is of the janitor of a research institute in St Petersburg, where others had objected to privatization and boycotted the auction. At the subsequent sale, the janitor's was the only voucher tendered, and hence he became the owner of the enterprise. The technical issues associated with vouchers were considerable. During the period of privatization, Russia went through a major constitutional crisis, and relations between the centre and the regions were deeply strained. In this context, vouchers were expected to be distributed fairly; they needed to be available in time for the auction of companies; those company auctions had to be known about so that investors could buy the shares on offer, and vouchers had to be successfully cancelled after use. Broadly speaking this appeared to happen. However, the ease with which things could have gone wrong is perhaps best illustrated by an anecdote told by Dmitry Vasiliev.[24] During the confrontation with parliament in October 1993, offices around the parliament building were occupied, and in many cases their contents ransacked or stolen. One office contained millions of vouchers belonging to voucher funds, placed there as collateral for their bids at voucher auctions. Apparently they were not in a safe. Had they been discovered and distributed, this could, according to Vasiliev, have undermined the entire privatization programme.

Implementation on the ground

There were substantial issues related to the implementation of privatization in the different regions of Russia, reflecting in part the uncertain constitutional settlement between the centre and the periphery. During 1992–94, the Consortium sent representatives to selected regions to assess their progress. Two recollections from senior western consultants give a sense of the different approaches to be found and the role of the local administrations in determining what actually happened on the ground. Like many events in Russia at the time, they reflect the pervading chaos which led to situations that were highly unusual. They are included in full in Appendix 4 below.

The first was from an investment banker employed to help with the auctions in Smolensk, a region that was generally deemed to be progressive. Even here, the local officials kept things close to their chest:

> We ... were bemused to find ourselves kept generally at arm's length from the auctions themselves.... We received detailed reports of the outcomes

> after the event. The official in charge of these ... was a master of stone-walling impassiveness.... We asked a Russian member of the team to investigate what was really going on and he soon confirmed that the process in Smolensk was similar to that being reported elsewhere. The general directors of many of the firms being auctioned had bought or bartered vouchers from their employees so that by the time the auctions took place, they (and/or their family and friends) could bid for a controlling stake.

A similar picture emerges from other regions. Novosibirsk is one example. The consultant sent to that region again noted that local officials were very much in charge of the process. The resulting ownership structures were therefore not only determined by the law, but also by who was in control.[25]

The temptation for local officials to take over the privatization process was aided by the lack of legal clarity about who was in charge and for how long. In Chapter 2, we discussed the ambiguities about who was in control of privatization. These continued throughout the period. The GKI was led by reformers and reported to the president, with its local agencies being granted the right in law to "effect privatization". On the other hand, the Property Fund reported to the legislature and was the sole vendor of enterprises. Even as late as the autumn of 1992, there was no timetable for privatization beyond November, and it was unclear whether the GKI would remain in charge of the process beyond that date.

Given the political debates raging at the time, there was little certainty about how long privatization would last. Even if it continued, it was not immediately clear what assets would be privatized. As we discuss below, Russia was experiencing constitutional turmoil in which the powers of president and parliament were disputed. Throughout the period 1992–94, parliamentary opponents threatened to derail privatization. When Gaidar resigned in December 1992, there were concerns that the process would be reversed by Chernomyrdin, who had previously been particularly critical of the programme. The powers that were accorded to the GKI were time-limited and extended on an ad hoc basis. They were, in any case, dependent on a bottom-up process initiated and framed by enterprise directors.

Despite this, as Table 4.1 illustrates, privatization took place with continuous momentum. Table 4.1 shows that voucher auctions proceeded uninterrupted between the spring of 1993 and June 1994. Indeed, there was a jump in auctions in that final month, which we discuss below. These auctions took place in a period of extraordinary political turbulence, as illustrated in Table 4.2 at the end of this chapter. By the time Yeltsin won the referendum on economic reform in April 1993, 70 out of Russia's 86 regions were already participating in voucher auctions. These continued unabated during September and October, and were not halted by the return of a conservative parliament in December of that year.

What was being sold and how?

Not only were there questions regarding who was in control of the privatization process, there were also questions related to the time frame of the Privatization

Table 4.1 Outcome of voucher auctions

	Enterprises sold	*Regions involved*	*Thousands of employees*	*Thousands of vouchers accepted*
December 1992	18	8	43	158
January 1993	108	26	188	159
February	197	41	200	611
March	450	58	556	2,284
April	611	70	837	4,147
May	576	73	598	4,306
June	909	80	821	4,362
July	916	82	782	6,691
August	895	82	830	4,489
September	811	83	826	5,069
October	959	83	910	4,598
November	1,005	83	906	3,133
December	1,054	83	1,026	3,546
January 1994	738	84	664	3,130
February	779	86	1,285	4,549
March	975	86	1,072	8,982
April	1,084	86	1,283	13,502
May	1,212	86	1,170	8,828
June	3,165	86	7,822	33,851
Total	**16,462**	**86**	**21,819**	**116,395**

Source: Blasi *et al.* (1997: 192).

Note
Some of the figures may contain dual counting, if an enterprise had more than one auction.

Programme, as well uncertainty regarding what companies were to be included in the privatization. More broadly, there were issues about what value a share in a company could have when the legal and political situation was so uncertain.

In early 1992 reformers had in mind that there would be waves of privatizations. The 1992 Programme was to be the first of these. As it became clear just how challenging the timing of the programme was going to be, and how difficult it would be to agree a second wave of privatization, the period of validity of vouchers was extended. More controversially, at the end of the programme, companies that might be thought to be excluded from privatization were included within the scope of voucher auctions. So, for example, in March 1994, it was announced that Gazprom and Lukoil were to be included despite the fact that natural resource enterprises were expressly excluded from the Privatization Programme.

In any well-organized capital market, such changes to a programme of company sales would be unthinkable, not just because of its questionable legality but also because it would make the pricing of securities nearly impossible. So, for example, the value of a voucher depended on the value of the companies being sold, since the total value of vouchers and the total value of the shares purchased with them would need to equate. Further, those willing to use insider information could make considerable gains. For example, someone with knowledge of the fact that there would be "late entries" to the Privatization Programme could take advantage of the likely price spike that this would cause at the end of the programme. Doubtless, many did just that, since there was, of course, no effective law to prevent them from using insider information.

But in the extraordinary chaos of 1993–94, such criticisms might have been considered niceties. Privatizers would have pointed out that, throughout 1993, the entire programme was in danger of being derailed. In parliament they were debating an Option Four which would have given still more rights to workers and managers; in October the same parliamentarians attempted a coup against the President. Opponents of the privatization, on the other hand, would have said that the actions to introduce new companies to the privatization were simply illegal, as they were in breach of the programme parliament had passed. Both had a point. In the context of Russia in the early 1990s considerations of insider trading[26] and similar abuses, which would today create outrage in developed western capital markets, were considered of comparatively minor significance.

That level of disorder meant that the benefit of being a shareholder in a newly privatized company was not immediately clear. This is perhaps best illustrated by voucher prices. Each voucher had a face value of 10,000 roubles and, in closed worker/manager subscriptions, could be exchanged for equity of that book value. When used in open tenders, the value of the voucher was equal to the value of the shares it could purchase. Therefore, the aggregate value of the vouchers was equal to the aggregate value of the shares that were to be included in the Privatization Programme. Figure 4.1 tracks the value of the individual voucher.[27] It can be compared with Table 4.2. So, for example, when the reformers lost political momentum, one would expect voucher values to fall, and, contrariwise, during periods when privatization appeared to be on course to continue with new assets being added to the programme, values would be expected to rise. Surprisingly, Figure 4.1 is insensitive to political events. For example, there was little change as a result of Yeltsin's referendum victory in April.

But, starkly, at no time does the total aggregate value of the voucher programme equate with the true value that would be represented by full equity ownership of the companies whose securities were for sale. Vouchers varied in value from a low of about \$5 to a high of around \$20. So the entire voucher programme was worth between \$750 million and \$3 billion. In 1992, this would be equivalent to the value of a single company in the West. Admittedly, only 20 per cent of the equity of privatized companies was sold at auction, with 116 million vouchers thus tendered. Even so, that would suggest the total value of Russian enterprise equity to be worth between about \$3 billion and \$11 billion, a trivial sum for companies employing 22 million people.

In part, this low value may be attributed to the lack of available savings to buy vouchers and, thus, companies. In part, it can be attributed to the fact that many Russian enterprises were simply uncompetitive and, hence, valueless. However, the main reason for these low values must surely be attributed to the fact that ownership of equity in a Russian company conferred only modest

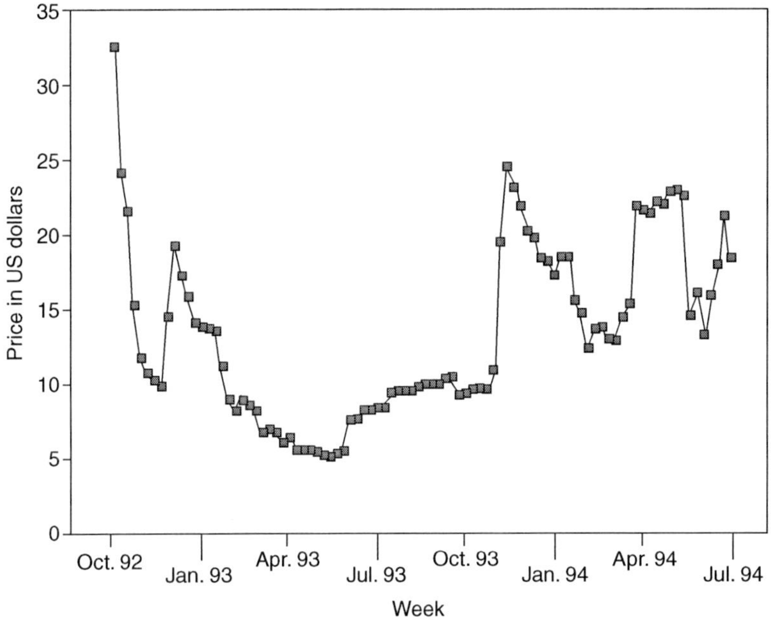

Figure 4.1 Voucher prices (source: Boycko *et al.* 1995: 102).

property rights. To be a minority shareholder in a manager/worker-controlled enterprise was of limited value, particularly where there are few laws conferring rights or courts in which they can be enforced. So while privatization, and the issuance of shares, may have been a necessary condition for the exercise of ownership rights, it was very far from a sufficient one. In 1992–94, few would have believed that, even if they had a controlling interest in a Russian company, this would have allowed them to close it down, or to liquidate its assets, as would be possible in the West. Therefore, the Privatization Programme did not sanction a "new" set of owners, in the sense of selling the legal right of control. At the beginning of the programme, in October 1992, Chubais had said, "property in this country belongs to whoever is nearest to it" (Steele 1994: 310). Perhaps privatization did not change that very much. But it did establish de jure what was happening de facto, and favoured the interests of enterprise insiders over those from the old ministries who controlled the associations. It provided a first stepping stone for Russia to establish ownership on the basis of the rule of law.

What was achieved?

Indeed, given the confusion of events, laws and institutions in Russia at the time, comparisons that talk of "privatized" or "not privatized", and that ascribe "ownership rights" without understanding the social and legal context within which these rights were granted, are unlikely to give an accurate picture of what was attempted and what was achieved, or of the difficulties that needed to be overcome.

By 1994, 16,000 companies had been created in Russia. In theory, all of them were supposed to have tradable shares. That would have meant that Russia, a country in which a few years earlier all private sector activity was illegal, would have created more than twice as many publicly traded companies as the USA, Japan and the UK combined. Further, this was going to take place in a period of hyperinflation. There was no precedent for the creation of capital markets in a hyperinflationary environment.

Indeed, the whole system of trade and exchange was under deep stress. Companies were trading on barter. The banking and payments system had collapsed – in part because enterprises were no longer profitable, in part because the bank clearing system had collapsed, and in part because the market created a proliferation of enterprises and banks – but there was no system of payments that responded to these new demands. However, the Russian government proved incapable of organizing an effective response to this crisis.[28]

In the meantime, new financial institutions were being established. However, the necessary underlying legal structures were not in place. Those operating in western financial markets are well aware of the complexity of the regulation necessary to ensure that financial institutions behave properly. New banks were established in Russia during the period of privatization. Investment funds were created. Both allowed their managers to access cash without the need to generate a profit. A cursory analysis of how the "oligarchs" made their early start suggests that these sorts of activities proved to be a more fruitful breeding ground than the take-over, even at a discount, of the industrial companies, which were the core of the Mass Privatization Programme.[29]

In summary, though by July 1994, 16,000 enterprises employing 22 million people had been transformed into corporate entities with shares, the number of their shares sold to outsiders was no more than 20 per cent of the equity. The majority of the shares were in the hands of managers and workers, whose main objective was to preserve the status quo. Thus, privatization was going to have a limited effect on reforming the economy. Certainly it managed to help establish ownership, although it did not put an end to the many devices by which managers could use or abuse their position. It did little to encourage restructuring; the new owners were likely to be very conservative in this regard. It did not raise money for the government or for the companies. It did not succeed in creating competitive markets; indeed, against the prescriptions of what would be taught in an introductory economics course, it allowed the creation of a vast number of private monopolies. And, while they may have been privatized companies, they were not capitalist ones in the sense that the government remained the main source of capital.

Noting these limitations, the extraordinary plaudits received in the first half of the 1990s by the programme, described in Chapter 1, should be taken in a mainly political context. The rights of "ownership" conferred under the Privatization Programme had actually gone to those who were least likely to support the restructuring of industry. For the long-run development of the economy, the reformers had achieved an extraordinary victory. But for the short and medium term, the victory was Pyrrhic in that the new owners were likely to be opposed to the rapid restructuring of industry.

Indeed, the behaviour of Russian companies in the post-privatization period reflected the motivation of their new owners. They did not restructure in a way that would have been expected of a private company in a market economy. All companies faced an acute liquidity squeeze; the GNP had dropped precipitously. A private company would have cut costs, including labour. Indeed, that problem was considered so acute that some advisers recommended that the programme be slowed. In 1992, Sir Alan Peacock and Michael Hay led a UN Mission to Russia to advise on "how a suitable social policy might be devised to accompany the changes associated with the move to a market economy" (Hay and Peacock 1992: 60). They concluded: "There is one thing upon which Western experts and senior Russian ministers are in complete agreement. That is, that unemployment will become perhaps *the* major economic, social and political problem in the decade ahead" (ibid.). They went on to quote Jacques Attali, then President of the EBRD, who referred to "the potentially explosive problem of unemployment".

Although economic conditions in Russia in the early 1990s were grim, there was no resulting mass unemployment in the short run. In large measure, this was because Russia was not a market economy. And those who owned its newly privatized companies were not private profit-maximizing owners, but workers and managers whose motivation was to stay in control in a deeply hostile environment. The 1992 legislation allowed them to do so. Perhaps as a result, unemployment did not immediately become "*the* major political, economic and social problem". Had it done so, the consequences could indeed have been traumatic.

Writing before privatization took place, the Consortium observed that

> if there has been a 25 per cent historic fall in production, 20 per cent over-employment and 20 per cent company bankruptcies, this would suggest that over 50 per cent of the industrial workforce could be laid off if privatised enterprises were to restructure in a way which reflected the motives of profit maximising market companies.

They went on: "unemployment should already be happening as a response to the fall in output, but it isn't because the motives of Russian enterprises are different to those of their western counterparts. They retain labour."

The 1992 Privatization Programme made little immediate change to that position. Had it done so, it would indeed have undermined political stability in Russia, and one can only speculate about the consequences The 1992 Privatization Programme was therefore a deeply conservative reform in the sense that it did not trigger radical change.

However, that does not mean that it was uniform, or indeed negative, in its effects. Commentators sometimes talk as if the managers of the companies hoodwinked the workforce, managing the companies for their own private benefit. In fact, the lack of layoffs suggests that they gave considerable weight to the interests of the workforce. Such would have been the tradition of Soviet management.

Indeed, there were instances where members of the workforce used their shares to change the management. One example would be the tractor works in Vladimir where Josef Bakalenik stood and was elected as general manager of the factory, in a contested election against the incumbent. Bakalenik had previously served as the enterprise's finance director, and was one of the first Russians to have graduated from Harvard Business School. His election was supported by an investment fund, but the deciding votes were with the workforce.

It could be argued that in Vladimir one insider replaced another with the support of the workers and external investors. Evidence suggests that there was considerable resistance to uninvited intervention by outsiders. For instance, in 1996, USAID commissioned a programme of support from western consultants to assist eight Russian companies in restructuring. All companies were concerned about outside investors attempting to buy shares and, where this was felt to be a particular threat, they had set up systems to buy back their own shares, despite the fact that many were suffering from severe liquidity constraints. It is yet another irony that the issuance of shares, which should have served as a device that would allow companies to raise more capital, had in fact resulted in some of them feeling they had to spend their money to buy back their shares in order to stay in control.

The 1992 voucher programme came to an end in June 1994. On paper, the transformation was huge. In reality, the framing of the law, and the choices made in its implementation, meant it was a conservative reform. Factory managers and employees, who had been gaining increasing de facto power over the previous few years, gained de jure ownership. Yet they were still beholden to the state for access to capital and to nationalized enterprises for energy and power. A competitive market infrastructure and an enforceable code of law were yet to be put into place.

And, despite the October 1993 showdown between President and parliament, a consensus on the direction of economic reform had not been achieved between those two bodies. No clear path existed for the direction of a broader economic reform. There was no agreed programme for future privatization, and indeed parliament opposed any further privatization taking place. Nor could the terms of the 1992 Programme readily be repeated for the enterprises that might yet be privatized, such as the utilities and the natural resource companies. It would have been inappropriate to offer such valuable assets for sale with similarly generous terms to the management and workforce.

Further, political storm clouds were gathering. Yeltsin would be up for election in 1996. The economic collapse of the country and his own failing health were hardly helping his electoral popularity.

Like a walker who has decided to cross a river on stepping stones, the reformers found they had taken one or two steps but remained precariously balanced, and it was far from clear how the reform process would unfold.

Table 4.2 Timeline, 1993–early 1994

Date	*General events*	*Privatization events*
1993		
5 January	New government reintroduces price controls	
21 January		GKI announces further list of enterprises to be privatized
1 February	Chernomyrdin declares that the fight against inflation is key economic objective; aim is a "social market economy"	96% of vouchers distributed by end January
11 February	Yeltsin opens negotiations with parliament over his proposed April referendum on a constitutional settlement	
9 March	Gerashchenko blames government for allowing borrowing by enterprises from the Central Bank	
12 March	Motion passed in parliament opposing Yeltsin referendum, and overwhelming vote accusing Yeltsin of "adventurism"	
20 March	Yelsin declares presidential rule; pushes ahead with referendum	
28 March	Yeltsin survives impeachment vote	
25 April	Yeltsin wins personal backing, and backing for economic reform programme, but not for early elections	
5 June	Yeltsin summons special assembly to draw up new constitution	
12 August	Draft of new constitution approved	
24 August	Yeltsin threatens to dissolve parliament unless it agrees to elections	
17 September	Gaidar returns to government	
21 September	Yeltsin dissolves parliament and calls for December elections; parliament occupied and surrounded by militia; constitutional court declares Yeltsin's action illegal	
22 September	Yeltsin approves parliament's hyperinflationary budget	
October	Parliamentary supporters break out of cordon and begin violent attacks which are quashed by army	
12 December	New constitution and parliamentary elections: on party lists nationalist Zhirinovskii wins 24%; Communists and Agrarians 26%, Russia Choice 15%; Russia Choice does much better in constituency section and is largest party, but other blocks critical of reform; Yeltsin does not back RC as "presidential party"	
1994		
17 January	Gaidar resigns	
20 January	Chernomyrdin announces new government; Fedorov resigns	
23 February	Parliament releases the coup plotters	
March		Announcement that 62% of Lukoil to be sold in investment tenders; 28% of Gazprom
April		Collective farms able to sell land
1 July		Vouchers formally expire

5 Implementation of privatization after 1994

Introduction

In this chapter we look at the progress of privatization in 1994 and beyond, after the voucher programme ended. In doing so, we have not had access to inside information from western advisers on policy, as we had for the material in previous chapters, in part because neither the Russian government nor any of the international agencies asked for policy advice from such advisers (though they were used on occasion for case-by-case implementation). This chapter is nevertheless important for illustrating how mass privatization and loans-for-shares came to be seen together as a failure and a corrupted process, despite being separate policies with different agendas.

The progress of privatization during this period faced many of the challenges and dilemmas of earlier years. For example, there was an overwhelming difficulty in reaching the sort of political consensus necessary for the fair allocation of undisputed property rights, and this forced a tradeoff between different privatization objectives, in particular between the need to raise funds and the limited sources of legitimate funds available in Russia following hyperinflation. Throughout this period there was a growing sense that privatization and other aspects of commercial life were conducted in a way that benefited the privileged few. Nevertheless, throughout the period, the irreversible nature of the market economy became more established, both by law and in terms of the political debate.

As noted in Chapter 2, the voucher programme had involved the sale of numerous companies, but few of any value. Thus, although it granted shares to insiders, this involved a limited transfer of wealth. It was always assumed that the more valuable companies – in natural resources and utilities – would be privatized for cash. And in the mid-1990s that cash was greatly needed by the government of Russia, which was running a substantial deficit.

So one of the key goals of the cash phase of privatization was to fill budgetary gaps. When voucher privatization ended on 30 June 1994, the government proposed to the Duma a new law whereby companies were to be sold through cash auction as the normal procedure. It was rejected by the Duma in July, in part because of failure to agree on how the proceeds were to be split between the centre, the regions and the municipalities.[1] A few days later, Yeltsin nevertheless signed a decree allowing privatization for cash, justified by the urgency of making funds available for restructuring and, particularly, for the government budget (Blasi *et al.* 1997: 72–3).[2] As Sergei Pavlenko, director of the Center for Economic Reform, underscored to journalists: "We are not talking reforms. We are talking revenue generation" (Kennet 1995).

Unlike voucher privatization, which promised to raise no money, the cash phase aimed to do precisely that. Also, it opened the possibility of avoiding a diffuse insider-dominated ownership structure. Furthermore, it aimed to create new owners who would pay firms' debts, particularly their tax liabilities, and who would promote productivity improvement, particularly in export sectors. Lastly, as earlier in the 1990s, this phase had political objectives to further dismantle the state sector in advance of parliamentary and presidential elections.

We see this period as a turning point. From June 1994 until the presidential elections of 1996, the government struggled to continue to implement a reform agenda. In order to do so in the face of parliamentary and other opposition, reformers paid a price. That was the transfer of even more production to even larger insider-controlled industrial giants, whose regional power was consolidated by new Financial Industrial Groups (FIGs). However, this was not a defeat for the government as a whole, rather a victory for those within the government who saw the creation of such enterprises as beneficial for industrial policy.

Despite, indeed in part because of, parliamentary opposition to privatization and rising concern for national security in strategic sectors including oil, the government resorted to the device of loans-for-shares, successfully transferring shares in a number of companies to consortia of banks by offering the shares as collateral for loans which were unlikely to be repaid. "Loans for shares", Treisman (2010: 216) writes, "was a way to circumvent the Duma's ban on privatizing oil companies and get private entrepreneurs into management positions." Kokh (1998: 105), who was involved in the implementation of the LFS, writes that the government would not repay the loans: "after all, the point was to inject huge sums of money into the budget, not to pay them out".

The LFS programme, which was developed during 1995, was initially opposed by reformers including Dmitry Vasiliev and Anatoly Chubais.[3] But it was to open up the sale of firms of significant value even in strategic sectors.[4] It brought revenue to the state and great profit to the banks that held the shares. Further, by backing the banks in their plans to address management problems at the enterprises that had been sold, the government did help restore the momentum for privatization, which had been slowing since 1994.

However, the LFS device had a cost. In its execution it became a poster child for insider dealing and corruption. The subsequent appointment of Vladimir Potanin as a deputy premier to the 1996 Yeltsin government only reinforced the view, fair or otherwise, that Russia was yielding some considerable political control to the bankers who had benefited from cash privatization.

To be sure, the corruption of some aspects of the privatization process was especially visible during the LFS scheme. This in turn raised further questions about the legitimacy of the buyers, which was, as discussed in Chapter 3 above, the problem of cash privatization: if cash was to be used in privatization, this could benefit only those who had cash. But hyperinflation had wiped out any cash that ordinary Russians might have had. Thus, only those who had been able to protect their money, by legitimate or corrupt methods, could bid for privatized firms. However, privatization did not cause corruption in Russia; nor did it create a special elite of oligarchs, especially given that the red directors were the main beneficiaries of privatization (Treisman 2010), as discussed below.

We have seen that, even during voucher privatization, proposals were being put together by "associations" of companies, often modelled on the old Soviet ministries. These plans were supported by members of the government, but were to some extent hindered by the design of the voucher privatization programme.

In August 1994, a similar proposal for the creation of Financial Industrial Groups (FIGs emerged from the State Committee on Industrial Policy) envisioned the creation of two or three such groups in each sector. Cash privatization facilitated this process since companies could use their own cash to buy one another. Particularly in the regions, cash privatization assisted the consolidation of powerful and politically connected formal and informal FIGs, which were given considerable policy support in view of their potential infusion of investment resources into firms. Barnes (2006: 119–40) shows that FIGs established strong links in this period with regional authorities through cash privatization, thus advancing the business-political nexus in the regions, as well as fostering nepotism.[5] Lieberman and Kopf (2007: 326) tie the LFS auctions to a clearly emerging industrial policy in the Chernomyrdin government:

> The LFS transactions deepened the government's commitment to an industrial policy focused on large regional and national FIGs. This policy implied an increase in the concentration of corporate ownership, less competition, and more government intervention in the economy. The Russian economic model, therefore, was not modeled after competitive Western markets but Japanese *keiretsus* and Korean *chaebols*.

The creation of large industrial holding companies was not an objective of cash privatization. There were other government policies (which during 1992–94 the reformers had resisted) that encouraged the establishment of FIGs. However, any cash privatization that aimed to fill budgetary gaps, but that de facto excluded foreign buyers, would discover that the only likely sources of income were the enterprises themselves. The LFS, therefore, was only one part of a far from coherent industrial policy.

Finally, the course of privatization cannot be divorced from larger political events. The Yeltsin government was losing popularity. Its decision to go to war in Chechnya in December 1994 made things worse. The war was opposed by reformers in parliament, and this would have done little to ingratiate them with the government. The subsequent poor showing of the reformers in the December 1995 parliamentary elections further weakened their influence. Throughout the period, Russia was plagued by economic problems, and, by early 1996, those around Yeltsin were more focused on winning the summer presidential election, a campaign that was headed by Anatoly Chubais, than on promoting a coherent reform programme.

We begin our review of privatization after 1994 with the controversies raised in the literature about the LFS. We then summarize the arrangements in 1995 – the LFS scheme that emerged in response to a proposal by a consortium of bankers in March 1994. We then emphasize the historical context of Russian decision making in 1995, which influenced outcomes of privatization programmes of the mid-1990s.

Interpretations

Most works on transition Russia see 1995 as a turning point in the specific sense that corruption, seemingly, became suddenly widespread. Treisman (2010: 208) summarizes the general view as follows:

> Widely condemned, it became a symbol of all the errors and sins – real or alleged – of Yeltsin's reformers. The program was a "Faustian bargain", wrote one journalist, a "fiendishly complicated scheme", in which the liberal ministers had sold their souls to a cabal of unscrupulous tycoons, who – switching metaphors – quickly metamorphosed into a "Frankenstein's monster". It "deformed the economy", "impoverished" the population, and laid "a corrupt, inegalitarian foundation for everything that came after it" (Freeland 2000: 22–3, 169–89). Under loans for shares, contended one Nobel-prize-winning economist, the country's best firms were stripped of their assets. The enterprises were left on the verge of bankruptcy, while the oligarchs' bank accounts were enriched (Stiglitz 2002: 160).

Three entire books (Freeland 2000; Klebnikov 2000; Hoffman 2002), drawn from interviews with journalists, oligarchs and other observers, contend – in a widely accepted understanding – that LFS created the oligarchs (Barnes 2006: 110). They argue that the oligarchs thereafter dominated the economy and entered politics in the late 1990s, and thus LFS caused the widespread corruption in the late 1990s.

In our view, and in accord with Treisman (2011) and others (Guriev and Rachinsky 2005; Barnes 2006), this postulate regarding how the oligarchs emerged is overly simplistic.[6] Former Soviet-era directors were the main beneficiaries of the LFS, not the "new" oligarchs (Guriev and Rachinsky 2005; Treisman 2011). Moreover, in terms of their impact on output, pledge auctions resulted over time in performance improvement by those firms managed by the new outsiders. The same cannot be said about firms managed by so-called red, former Soviet-era, directors (Treisman 2010: 218).

Treisman observes that the scale of the programme was more modest than has been suggested. Initially, 29 enterprises, including Gazprom and UES, were to be part of the LFS process. By the end of the programme, only 12 auctions had taken place, with some projects being removed because of managers' resistance and others because no bids at all were offered (Treisman 2010: 209). Perhaps more importantly, privatization was not the only, or even the primary, means by which insiders siphoned value from companies.

Another contentious point is that the LFS enterprises were thought to have been abandoned in a near bankrupt state to oligarchs, who proceeded to strip their assets. To the contrary, the story of Norilsk Nickel suggests that those who were in control before the pledge auctions were siphoning off funds. Before Oneximbank acquired its shares, a huge proportion of the company's output was sold through related companies. Glencore, a major western purchaser, claimed that it had been unable to buy Norilsk Nickel output for five years except through intermediaries. The suggestion must be that the intermediaries were acting on behalf of company insiders, but not in the interest of the company itself.[7]

Economists would rightly point out that such practices were exactly what one would expect when control rights are divorced from cash flow rights. Those in control simply channel valuable assets through companies that they own. No investment is encouraged. With ownership of the enterprise in the same hands as those entitled to control, it makes sense to invest. Thus, some oligarch-controlled companies were subsequently transformed. As Treisman (2010: 220) notes:

> Between 1998 and 2003, annual – upstream – investment in the two oligarch-controlled oil companies Yukos and Sibneft increased by about 140 per cent.... In the first 10 months of 2003 (before the Kremlin's assault), Yukos' upstream investments came to $1.1 billion, substantially more than those of any other Russian oil company. By 2005, Noril'sk Nickel was investing more than $700 million a year. There is no evidence here that the oligarchs' companies were increasing their capital spending more slowly than their counterparts.

This said, and as discussed below, the LFS procedures were very shady. Bidders were excluded, often on what seemed like invented technicalities. Foreigners in particular were not allowed to bid in many of the auctions, while the bankers who organized the auctions also bid for (and won) the assets at the stage of loan granting, and then subsequently when the shares were sold. This side of the LFS has been closely tracked by Ira Lieberman (Lieberman and Kopf 2007). Since Lieberman also focuses on the LFS agreement as part of a critically important development beginning around this time – regional support for the emerging powerful FIGs – it is worth touching on how the LFS programme worked.

Summary of the LFS arrangement

In March 1995, a consortium of nine banks proposed to supply a loan of nine trillion roubles ($1.84 billion) to the government, holding as collateral the shares in valuable enterprises. These were to be held in trust until the loan was repaid (initially by 1 January 1996, though this deadline was later extended to 1

September 1996, after the presidential election, thus marrying the fortunes of the banks to the electoral fortunes of the then unpopular President). In the event that the government defaulted, the shares would be sold, and the banks repaid from the proceeds. In addition, the banks would receive 30 per cent of any profit made on the sale.

The proposal emerged as the government was struggling politically and attempting to find a solution to the lag in privatization receipts. In April of that year, privatization had raised only 100 billion roubles out of an annual target of 9,000 billion. By August that figure had only grown to 200 billion.[8] The proposal was also attractive because it circumvented the Duma. It was not clear that the government had the power to privatize these companies. However, it did have the right to offer their shares as collateral and to default on the loan. As Kokh (1998: 105) noted, "at the expiration of the term of the loan in a future year ... the ban on the sale of oil shares that our friends in the Duma had hung around our necks would have expired".

Given the strength of opposition in the parliament, foreign investors were excluded from many of the auctions. Those likely to benefit were the leading bankers who were, as we have noted, among the few investors in Russia with sufficient cash to offer credit. Many of them were already part of FIGs, and had the expertise to demand change and, of course, to serve later on as financial intermediaries in the sale of these assets (Radygin 2000).

The banks proposed to undertake enterprise restructuring, to pay delinquent arrears of taxes and wages, and to forgo interest. Their returns promised to be substantial in profits from later privatization (Brown *et al.* 1999). The leader of the consortium of banks that proposed the loan, Vladimir Potanin,[9] president of Oneximbank, assured the government that even as "temporary" owners, the banks would make investments in Yukos, Sidanko and Sibneft, Lukoil and Surgutneftegaz, where improved productivity would show the benefits of privatization to the electorate. Some government officials agreed. The Minister of Finance Vladimir Panskov commented that, moreover, the LFS would set appropriate incentives for the banks and, if successful, strengthen the banking sector,[10] since, if the government did not repay the loans, the financial sector would gain by an infusion of 30 per cent of the capital gains, with the rest going to the government. At the time, the banking sector in Russia was very unstable[11] and had begun to expand into insurance and real estate, rather than providing resources to the real economy.

The consortium of banks also seemed likely to be useful for political and policy objectives. Support by powerful bankers could help overcome arguments for renationalization. By pitting the weight of the banking sector, whose owners had interests in the media, against the opposition, the government may have hoped further to secure their political backing for the presidential election, although bankers would scarcely have promoted Communist candidates (Treisman 2010).

Reformers diverged in their views about whether to accept the proposal. Some were not convinced.[12] Privileges in the economy being offered to a small group of bankers, writes Dmitry Vasiliev, then deputy chairman of the Federal Commission on Securities and Capital Markets, are not "helpful for Russian economic transformation.... Monopolization is what we've been fighting for a long time" (Kaban 1995). Chubais took a similar position. From the affected sectors and regions, also came a vigorous and effective defence of preserving the state sector as it was: industrial ministers strongly opposed the proposal, laying a foundation for their refusal to participate, firm by firm.[13]

In the end, from a list of 29 firms to be pledge auctioned, the bankers in the consortium obtained mostly minority tranches of shares in 12 large, state-owned corporations in return for loans to the federal budget of about $800 million. By 1 January 1996, 12 pledge auctions were completed. Besides Surgutneftegaz, the companies included oil corporations Lukoil, Yukos, Sidanko and Sibneft, as well as nickel producer Norilsk Nickel, and Mechel and Novolipetsk Steel Works. Notably, UES and Gazprom were taken off the list of companies in the LFS programme.

In its final form, the government decree of 31 August 1995, together with further amendments, showed, at least on paper, that the government had listened to some of the criticism in the months after it was proposed. The banks would not be allowed to sell their shares until after 1 September 1996, and the auctions were opened up in principle to include other bidders – both foreign and domestic – with the assurance of a transparent, open and competitive process (Lieberman and Kopf 2007: 303). However, there was a huge gap between any notion of a fair process and what actually took place.

The historical context

1994

In October 1993, Yeltsin won the showdown with parliament. But in the subsequent elections for the Duma in December, the Communists, the Agrarians, and Zhirinovsky's anti-reform party received 50 per cent of the list vote.

In theory, the agenda of the reformers was straightforward. As Vladimir Brovkin, a historian of the Mensheviks, described the task in principle:

> What the democrats must do is to reshape economic policies in accordance with the wishes of the electorate. This means, in practical terms, to put an end to corruption, stop mafia control of retail trade, create a functioning banking and credit system and regulate privatization in the interest of common people rather than mafia bosses.
>
> (Brovkin 1994)

Realpolitik was much more difficult. There was little consensus on what to do; even the views of Prime Minister Victor Chernomyrdin, who had once compared voucher privatization to Stalin's forced collectivization of agriculture in the 1930s, were shifting. At that time, in December 1992, as Chernomyrdin was chosen to take over the government, there was the real possibility that the programme would be halted. In fact, the reformers were strong enough to maintain the voucher programme, which Chernomyrdin endorsed, choosing to work with the reformers. However, in January 1994, Yegor Gaidar and Boris Fedorov, two of the key reformers, both resigned. Gaidar's replacement as first deputy prime minister was metallurgist Oleg Soskovets, who "lobbied unabashedly for state credits, bailouts, and tariff barriers" during the next two years that he worked under Yeltsin (Colton 2008: 336). Chubais was the only reformer in a senior government position, as deputy prime minister in charge of privatization.

In March 1994, Chubais announced that some of the country's largest companies from the energy sector and once top-secret military factories would be made available to investors. Hoping to encourage the use of vouchers before they expired at the end of June before the start of cash privatization, he declared: "In an unprecedented move, we will present the super-effective, super-profitable firms for the final stage of privatization" (Tolkacheva 1994). But later, the cash privatization plan met with resistance from parliament, which rejected it on first reading in July 1994. The programme thus went into effect by decree, but, effectively, privatization became voluntary (Liesman 1994).

Moreover, the pool of small investors threatened to shrink throughout 1994 amidst numerous scandals and schemes.[14] The most spectacular of these scandals, and one which perhaps serves as a metaphor for the state of the capital markets in Russia at the time, was the collapse of MMM, which turned out to be a Ponzi scheme. A Ponzi scheme is an investment operation in which depositors' money should be protected but is instead used to pay dividends to earlier investors. Of course, it all ends in tears when new investors cannot be found and depositors realize their money is lost. It is estimated that MMM resulted in losses for at least five million Russians. It had advertised on state television channels, its advertisements featuring one Lyonya Galubkov, who claimed that, with MMM's investment returns, a "common man" had bought a Paris apartment. MMM sponsored the Russian football team, provided free travel on the Moscow underground, and encouraged its share certificate to be used like cash. The price of MMM shares had risen from 1,600 roubles in March to 115,000 roubles in July. But the authorities either had little legal recourse or chose not to use it. As numismatist Peter Symes points out: "Although the Russian authorities had investigated [MMM] on several occasions, they had done nothing to alert people to [its] activities. Simply put, a pyramid scheme was not illegal in Russia."[15]

MMM's fantasist director, Sergei Mavrodi, was eventually brought to book on tax evasion charges in August 1994. However, he successfully shifted the blame, at least in the eyes of the populace, claiming that the government had "provoked the panic among MMM investors to eliminate what had become a powerful political force".[16] The government, for other reasons, had indeed failed investors in its ineffective watchdog, the Commission on Securities and Stock Funds (Gustafson 1999: 152). The collapse of the scheme thus boosted Mavrodi, now a household name, and he gained a seat in special parliamentary elections in October.[17]

Meanwhile, the Russian economy was weak. To be fair, inflation was declining, but from 839 per cent in 1993 to just over 410 per cent in 1994. But export revenues were weak. The government cancelled tax exemptions for oil exporters in May, and discussed through the summer the critical step of scrapping oil export quotas and licences to improve the budgetary situation. The summer ended, however, with continued support for the agricultural lobby in large credits going to agriculture. Output and investment continued to fall.

Nevertheless, even during this period there were some promising developments. In the summer, the State Committee for Statistics declared that one million new businesses had been created in Russia since 1992. Gazprom announced its intention to sell 9 per cent of its shares to foreign buyers to pay for pipeline upgrades (OADB, 11 August 1994). But more critically, the Duma passed a new Civil Code, which, in theory, as McFaul (2001: 253) remarks, "established the legal and economic institutions to guarantee both private property rights and the enforcement of contracts". He goes on to suggest that "progress on this monumental code suggested that the agenda of parliament had changed fundamentally … the question was no longer whether but rather what kind of market economy would develop".

That said, by the end of 1994, prospects for privatization looked bleak (Treisman 1998: 245). In October, the rouble collapsed in the panic of Black Tuesday, raising risk for strategic investors. In the same month, the state had reached only one-quarter of its privatization target (Barnes 2006: 115). The number of mid-sized and large privatized enterprises actually declined in 1994 (Blasi *et al.* 1997: 189). Some 40 per cent of Russia's enterprises had not yet been privatized, with the state still holding large stakes in those that had (Barnes 2006: 114–15).

October also brought strengthened calls in the parliament for renationalization, leading in November to the removal of Anatoly Chubais as head of privatization. He was promoted to deputy prime minister for economic affairs, but was saddled with Vladimir Polevanov, an unknown, as head of the GKI. Polevanov had formerly served as the acting head of the Amur region and was a geologist with no previous experience in Moscow and no economics education.[18] His first public remarks alluded to privatization as a threat to national security (Kokh 1998:74).[19] He proposed a Federal Nationalization Law, for example, to enhance the role of the state in strategic sectors and attacked voucher privatization as having "weakened national security". He proposed to reverse privatization in oil and aluminium.[20]

Then, in December, Yeltsin approved the invasion of the breakaway republic of Chechnya: "A military disaster", one observer called it (Durden Smith [1995]). Russian forces moved against Grozny from December 1994 to March 1995, destroying the city. The Russian forces became demoralized when the Chechen populace threw their support behind their own leader, Dzhokhar Dudayev (Lapidus 1998). In the Duma, Russia's Choice, Gaidar's reformist party, generally opposed the invasion, thus distancing itself from Yeltsin.

1995

Nevertheless, in early 1995, reformers succeeded in getting Polevanov dismissed, and a privatization programme of sorts continued. In April, the IMF approved one of the largest loans it had ever given, a $6.8 billion stand-by credit. Approval came with Russia's commitment, as Michael Camdessus pointed out, to "a strong program, which, if fully implemented, will achieve macroeconomic stabilization and accelerate structural reform".[21] However, the terms of disbursement were stiff. The IMF imposed a monthly, instead of a quarterly, review for disbursement of tranches of the loan, and among conditionalities were the reduction of the deficit from over 10 per cent to 8 per cent of GDP and a fall of the monthly inflation rate to 5 per cent.[22]

The uncertainties about outcomes of the 1995 privatization programme grew, as the investment environment worsened. The attraction of Russia as an investment target was fading with continued inflation, uncertainties over the disbursement of the loan, news of the war in Chechnya, the collapse of the Mexican peso and parliamentary enthusiasm for renationalization. At the beginning of 1995, forecasting a seriously weakened economy, Jeffrey Sachs and one of Yeltsin's own analysts, Mikhail Deryagin, felt it was possible that Russia was no longer on a steady course towards stabilization (Treisman 1998: 245).

Privatization slowly continued. Little cash was being raised, and according to Blasi *et al.* (1997: 74), " 'auctions' were wide open to domination by insiders and back room deals". In May, due to pressure on the federal government, Yeltsin issued a decree that diminished the proportional amount that the regional governments could take from sales. This only decreased incentives for regional governments to participate. The sale of some 136 large companies had to be postponed (ibid.: 73–4). Numerous problems arose in this new phase of privatization: the setting of excessive minimum prices for large stakes, which discouraged buyers, and the reverse – the selling of smaller stakes at excessively low prices – which promised to lead to no capital investment. The one instance when the government chose to display a careful and transparent approach, the attempted privatization of 25 per cent of Svyazinvest, a holding company that held over one-third of the stock in 85 regional telecommunications firms, carried out by Maxim Boycko, then head of the Russian Privatization Center, with the assistance of N. M. Rothschild & Sons, failed when Stet of Italy, the winner of the tender, wanted to put its $640 million in an escrow account and the Russian government broke off negotiations.[23] The government proceeded with the sale only in 1997.

By autumn 1995, privatization targets looked less and less achievable. By year's end, block sales had produced only 1.5 trillion roubles, instead of the expected four or five trillion, from the sale of valuable enterprises. In 1995, only 6,000 enterprises in all were privatized (5 per cent of the total number privatized) and most of these were small (fewer than 200 employees). Only 20 per cent of them were in industry (Radygin 1996: 5). Only in August 1995 did the private sector surpass the state sector in regard to total number of enterprises, and the share of the state in manufacturing still exceeded that of the private sector.[24] The bond market was active, but Russia's deteriorating assets were not attracting strategic investors. Foreign direct investment in 1994 totalled $1.2 billion, one-sixth of the IMF loan, and by August 1995, in view of the continuing deterioration of the country's "legal and tax mess", the situation looked far worse, with only $500 million invested from abroad.[25]

The bankers' LFS proposal, first made in March 1995 and effected by decree at the end of August, was therefore timely, and it was accepted in a period when the government believed privatization to be failing. The reformers, some of whom initially opposed LFS, as noted above, had little alternative. At the end of 1995, the pro-reform party was defeated in the December parliamentary elections, with opposition parties winning a greater share of the vote. In other words, the new parliament was even more conservative than the 1993 parliament. Gaidar's party won less than 4 per cent of the vote, down from 15.5 per cent in 1993. Chernomyrdin's party, Our Home is Russia, was the main beneficiary.

In this context, again, the presumed political rationale of LFS – that is, the threat that privatization might be reversed if Yeltsin lost – emerges. In February 1996, Zyuganov had declared his intention to undo the "criminal" sales, should he become president, thus doubtless putting further offside the influential group of bankers.

Indeed, by 1996 the presidential election campaign was the political priority. But Yeltsin signed a land decree, confirming private property rights to arable land. This was a major step towards rural markets, and it was possibly designed to appeal to rural voters. But at the same time, he criticized the Chernomyrdin government for "focusing on financial stabilization and forgetting about people living on wages and pensions".[26] He indulged in giveaway economics with promises ranging from the payment of pension arrears to the fixing of church roofs. Indeed, so perilous was the financial situation that the government had to pass an emergency law in June 1996 to "raid" the resources of the Central Bank.

In political terms Yeltsin's campaign, which was run by Chubais, was a huge success. He won the first ballot narrowly, but then proceeded to bring the nationalist, General Lebed, into his coalition and won the second round handsomely. He now had a coalition, which was generally supportive of market reform. Indeed, Potanin, the architect of the LFS, was brought in on 14 August as one of the three first deputy prime ministers under Chernomyrdin. In the meantime, Chubais was appointed as the head of the presidential office. So a banker who had organized the LFS was now inside the government as loans were defaulting and the shares were being put up for auction.

Whether or not Potanin used his power during late 1996 and early 1997, shares pledged under the LFS were sold to the banks that had extended the loans, despite the clear presence of a conflict of interest. Moreover, the purchase prices, at market prices at that time, were certainly regarded as low.[27]

Following Yeltsin's victory, further privatizations by auction took place under the leadership of Alfred Kokh, the new head of the GKI appointed in September

1996. On his appointment, he reflected that he "saw a space wide open for maneuver" and he "used it to the fullest extent possible" (Kokh 1998: 161).

However, the continuing privatizations brought new friction with the Duma; a Duma Commission even recommended the abolition of the GKI in April 1997. Nevertheless, in July of that year, the government and the Duma seemingly agreed on a new privatization law. It stipulated that there would be an agreed privatization plan each year. By that time, the principle of privatization seemed no longer to be in dispute. However, as regards the law itself, no agreed plans emerged and while privatization continued, the law itself was not fully enforced. The sales of shares also generated conflict between the banks themselves, particularly when Oneximbank won the Svyazinvest auction in the summer of 1997. Indeed, disputes within the government might have been increasingly interpreted as squabbles between contending oligarchs (Sakwa 2008: 188; Rutland 2009: 164).

For example, when Kokh resigned, he was replaced by Maxim Boycko, who had a reputation as an honest broker. Boycko, together with his mentor Chubais, was soon under attack over purportedly illegitimate advances for a book. The newspapers publicizing the story were associated with Boris Berezovsky, implying a feud between Berezovsky and Oneximbank's Potanin, Chubais's colleague.[28]

The apparent warring between different business elites within the government was cited as one of the reasons why Yeltsin removed Chernomyrdin from his post as prime minister in March 1998, replacing him with Kiriyenko, a young reform-minded technocrat. Whatever the motivation, privatization continued, but there was little sense of a proper separation between financial interests and those of the government, which was supposed to regulate them.

The year 1998 ended with Russia defaulting on its debt, as tax revenues dried up. The rouble was devalued, and Kiriyenko was removed as prime minister. The pace of privatization slowed. But the relationship between private business and government remained unhealthily intertwined.

The period in perspective

McFaul (2001: 246) describes the period 1994–96 as "the end of market romanticism and the beginning of oligarchic capitalism". In the first four chapters we described why the reformers might have been described as "romantic". The objectives set for the Privatization Programme were well beyond what it could ever achieve within the reality of Russian political and economic institutions. As the programme moved to cash privatization, the stakes were raised, and the lack of that institutional infrastructure became ever more apparent. The demand for more cash to finance the government budget became a shuttlecock between the Duma, which wanted to spend but objected to privatization, and the government, which wanted privatization.[29]

Yet it would be wrong to see privatization as uniquely responsible for the way in which industrial and political power developed during that period. The level of insider dealing was noted throughout Russian industry. However, like most activities of this nature, such dealings were often kept obscure. Insider dealing is encouraged when those who have control of an enterprise do not themselves own it and therefore have little incentive to manage it well, and instead direct it in a way that enhances their private advantage. This was what was happening in Russia. Indeed, one aim of privatization was to help reduce such mismanagement. We have already noted these practices being apparent at Norilsk Nickel, prior to Oneximbank's intervention. Another example would be Gazprom, a company that Marshall Goldman focuses on in his book *The Piratization of Russia* (2004). Most of the scandals he describes at Gazprom are the result not of its privatization, but rather of the "lack of government ownership and lack of outside directors [which] allowed the management to treat the company as a cash cow for their personal projects" (Goldman 2004: 95).

During the period, opposition to the principle of privatization lessened. The key objections raised by parliament and others concerned the wrong-doing in its implementation. For example, in February 1996, parliament announced a full-scale investigation into privatization practices from 1992 to 1996.[30] Favarel-Garrigues (2011: 241–4) cites cases of corruption in the cash privatization era, including information about auctions conveyed only to a single interested party, assets negotiated before the auction process, fraudulent bankruptcy not covered by criminal legislation at the time, managers ostensibly acting as outsiders buying shares and benefiting from conditions normally reserved for workers' collectives (ibid.: 243). Such instances were common throughout the privatization process.

However, the response to the inquiry was not to stop privatization, but rather to pass a new law requiring binding conditions for those who won the bidding and transparent procedures.[31] Indeed, since parliament did not approve the privatization programme for that year, in fact the new law did not go into effect, and opposition to corrupt practices continued. So, at a time when markets were becoming accepted in Russia, privatization became symbolic of increasing abuse of power. Note that abuse in the privatization process may have actually required no more contravention of law than would be natural in other spheres of life. Khodorkovsky, for example, talking to *Frontline* about how he made his money, observes: "I made a choice for myself: I said that I will not break the law … I did not break Russian law, but everything else wasn't my concern. If I saw a loophole I'd take advantage of it."[32] Without a proper legal or even cultural framework, the enterprises of Russia, state or private, offered a cornucopia of loopholes, which could be exploited by those who had the power to do so.

What went wrong with privatization in Russia was the absence of appropriate laws, routines and embedded culture required for well-functioning auctions in market economies. Blasi *et al.* (1997: 172) write:

> The leading industrialized nations focused on privatization with the intensity of a laser beam and ignored the wide-ranging institutional development Russia sorely needed.… Much more should have been done more quickly

> to accelerate the development of stock markets, private bank lending to enterprises, mutual funds for citizens, investment banks, and clear and coherent reforms in Russian law, taxation, domestic and foreign investment, and trade unions.[33]

In many senses, Blasi *et al.* are right; privatization was not "an end in itself". To make sense in policy terms, changing the ownership of an entity will only create beneficial results if other conditions about governance, law, labour, goods and capital markets are met. But, in another sense, they are wrong. Western aid may have focused particularly on privatization, but advisers from the West were at pains to point out the need for corollary reform, and Russians in government committees were exhaustively working on building draft laws for many other reforms. And no western policy adviser suggested adopting the LFS programme or designed or oversaw its execution; and Russian reformers initially rejected the idea. There is scant evidence that private companies and privatization were unique in nurturing the improper practices that blighted this period. Rather, such practices, often more openly displayed in the privatization process, were apparent throughout commercial life in Russia. The laws, the institutions, the culture and the morality needed to sustain a market system were simply not in place.

What did cash and pledge privatization accomplish? In a limited way, in regard to selected pledge auctions, they brought much needed finance to the government and, subsequently, to a key export sector that had previously experienced a serious lag in productivity, deteriorating financial conditions, and infrastructure starved of investment. Coordinated with major reforms, opening the export sector to competition was a key positive outcome of the 1995 deals. In regard to the rest of the firms struggling with bankruptcy and the need for capital, policies of this period gave increasing support to the FIGs, which extended their influence over regional authorities and transformed regional politics in varying ways.

It cannot be said that Russia's fragile market institutional development was ignored by lawmakers: Russian budget practice rapidly improved (Sinel'nikov 1995); a remarkably western Company Law was passed in 1995 (Black and Kraakman 1996). However, in Russia, as in other countries of the CIS, institutional transformation was slow. This was largely because the scale and complexity of the newly required institutions and structures were enormous. Finding legal "transplants", and getting them to be accepted, in law, in enforcement and in practice, was an enormous task. Even if, as Blasi *et al.* (1997) suggest, foreign aid had focused first and most effectively on Russia's market institutions, it is not at all clear that Russians would have been willing, for example, to adopt an equivalent of the EU framework that assisted transformation in accession countries of Central Europe. The Russian legal expertise that Russian reformers relied on had a strong base in imperial Russian and Soviet legal codified tradition. Informal arrangements based on legal understandings from the past, in extremely difficult conditions for Russian enterprises, contributed to the spread of shady practices, just as formal privatization procedures provided much of the opportunity for using such practices to advance.

Perhaps what is most important is that despite these problems, despite Russia's history, and despite the strength of the opposition parties during this period, the fact that there was to be some sort of market economy in Russia became less and less an issue of political contention. McFaul (2001: 267) sees this taking place immediately after 1993. One might argue that the consensus was already building before that, and that those "defeated" in October 1993 were not advocating a return to the planned economy. Indeed, consensus might have been reached earlier had relations between the government and the Duma been better, had there been a clearer view of how policy would develop, and had there been a leadership more focused on what good enterprise management involved. But such was not the case, and it is not our purpose here to discuss counterfactual history. Rather, we would note that even with cash privatization, whatever its faults, money was raised, ownership was changed, and the political consensus did swing further away from any thought of a return to the planned economy of the past.

Table 5.1 Timeline, 1994–99

Date	*General events*	*Privatization events*
1994		
17 June	Dudayev, the president of the breakaway Chechen republic, regains control of Grozny from rebel forces	
13 July		The Duma rejects government plan for second wave of privatization, which was to be by cash auction; much of opposition relates to municipalities' ownership of land and other assets
22 July	Tax police close down MMM Ponzi scheme; an estimated 5–10 million investors are believed to have been deceived by this scam, which was advertised on state TV networks	
1 August		UK investment bank Robert Fleming announces fund to invest in Russian shares;[a] Notes that Lukoil capitalization per barrel of reserves is at 5 cents, Shell's is $5.36[b] State Committee for Statistics reports that there are two million businesses in Russia, one million newly created since 1992 (OADB Russia, Financial Stabilisation, 6 September 1994)
1 September	Central Bank announces its ability to intervene in failing banks; over 2000 banks, mainly very small, now established	
11 October		State Committee for Industrial Policy publishes concept note envisioning the creation of giant FIGs, with two or three groups in each sector[c]
15 November		Vladimir Polevanov replaces Anatoly Chubais at the GKI; suggests that oil and metals firms be renationalized; sacked on 24 January 1995[d]
11 December	Russian invasion of Chechnya over the following 20 months, around 5500 Russian troops are estimated to have been killed, and many tens of thousands of Chechens; war unpopular; Chernomyrdin distances himself from it	

continued

Table 5.1 Continued

Date	*General events*	*Privatization events*
1995		
1 January	New requirements on accounting standards, including annual external audit come into force (OADB Russia Accounting Standards, 10 January 1995)	
16 January	Government confirms its intention to help create FIGs, including transferring government shares and loan write-offs	
30 March		Nine banks suggest the LFS arrangement with the government in exchange for stakes in companies as collateral for loans; Chubais opposes the plan on 3 May, Aleksandr Livshits, Yeltsin's economics adviser, backs it
April		Proceeds from privatization behind budget, with only 100 billion roubles raised out of an annual target of 9 trillion roubles
14 June	Budenovsk hostage seizure	
18 July		Takeover bid for Red October Chocolate Company raised to $9.50; defended (inter alia) by management and workforce opposition
24 August	Interbank trading collapses in Moscow; later restored with Central Bank action, it reveals the fragility of the Russian banking system	
31 August		Yeltsin signs decree authorizing the LFS;[e] auctions scheduled for October
28 September		Lukoil sells 320,000 convertible bonds, raising $320 million; US oil company Arco purchases $250 million worth of shares[f]
October		Commencement of the LFS bids; 29 companies originally scheduled for sale; many resist and are taken off list; giants Gazprom and UES excluded; rumours abound of likely insider dealing. Of budget of 9 trillion roubles for privatization receipts, 200 billion raised by August. Duma commissions audit of the process and passes law outlawing the action, but does not receive presidential assent

Date	*General events*	*Privatization events*
1 November		Decree passed that sale of shares in the LFS auctions cannot be disposed of until September 1996, after the presidential election (OADB Russia, Auction Controversies, 6 December 1995)
30 November		New law signed encouraging the creation of Financial Industrial Groups[g]
17 December		Duma elections. Gaidar's party fares badly. Opposition parties stronger than they had been in 1993
1996		
1 January		New companies law comes into force, defining role of the board (law originally adopted on 24 November 1995 by the Duma)[h]
16 January	Chubais resigns from the government[i]	
January/February		Development of stock markets remains weak: Gazprom, capitalization of $2.1 billion, has daily turnover of $10–20,000; bid/ask spreads very large; ZIL, for example, is over 100 per cent; shares are seen as for control, not for finance (OADB, Russia, Share Market, 8 February 1996)
23 February	Yeltsin increasingly reverts to populist economics in the run-up to the presidential election in June; cticizes the Chernomyrdin government for "focusing on financial stabilization" and "forgetting about people living on wages and pensions",[j] Chubais returns to help Yeltsin's re-election having resigned from government	
15 March	Zyuganov, the Communist challenger for the presidency, supports Duma vote to repeal the breakup of the Soviet Union	
7 March		Yeltsin land decree outflanks the Agrarian Party by confirming direct ownership rights to members of the collective, rather than ownership through the collective;[k] 75 per cent of farmland is managed through collectives

continued

Table 5.1 Continued

Date	*General events*	*Privatization events*
10 April	Yeltsin makes an overture to Dudayev, the Chechen leader, seeking peace in Chechnya	
13 April		Dispute between Oneximbank (OB) and Norilsk Nickel (NN) (supported by the regional governor); Chernomyrdin removes board of NN; OB uncovers inappropriate practices at NN, including that Glencore had been unable to buy NN output for five years, except through intermediaries
21 April	Dudayev killed in a Russian air raid; peace process destabilized	
May		Zyuganov economic policy announced; it is unclear on privatization, stating that large-scale privatization will be halted and "illegal" privatizations subject to renationalization
Presidential campaign	Populist agenda: Yeltsin offers ad hoc payments from tax relief for defence plants in Archangel, to church repairs; also payment of wage and pension arrears; compensating savers for inflation; exemption of enterprise tax arrears; child allowances; low airfares to the Far East Tax arrears rise as federal tax take drops below 8 per cent On 5 June, emergency law passed to "raid" reserves of the Central Bank	
16 June	Yeltsin wins first round of presidential election; appoints General Lebed, who came third, as head of Security Council	
July	Continuing concern by authorities at the bad debt of certain banks	Strengthening of securities oversight with establishment of stronger Federal Securities Commission on 1 July
15 July		Chubais appointed as chief of presidential administration
14 August		Vladimir Potanin (former head of Oneximbank), who was closely associated with LFS, becomes deputy prime minister with responsibility for economic policy
31 August	Chechen Peace Accord signed	
29 October		Boris Berezovsky is appointed as deputy chief of the security council
19 November		Opening of first registered and regulated mutual funds

Date	*General events*	*Privatization events*
23 November	Yeltsin orders the remaining Russian troops out of Chechnya	
23 December		Sale of 8.5 per cent of electric utility UES to consortium of Russian banks, including the banks of Gazprom and Lukoil
December 1996–February 1997		Oil company shares transferred under LFS are sold to the banks that made the loans, against the intent of the LFS programme
1997		
April		Duma Commission highly critical of 1992–96 privatizations; recommends abolition of GKI; does not impact government action (OADB Russia, Privatization Plans, 2 May 1997)
21 July		New privatization law passed[l] Establishes case-by-case privatization, including use of government's "golden share", with specific rights; the LFS and lease buyout no longer sanctioned; annual privatization plan to be agreed by Duma; sanction for breach is restitution (statute of limitation is 10 years)
25 July		After much controversy, 25 per cent of Svyazinvest, the state telecoms holding company, is sold to Oneximbank
5 August		Further 38 per cent of Norilsk Nickel sold to Oneximbank; like many such auctions, it sparks controversy; sale organizers controlled by purchaser, in possible contravention of decrees
13 August		Kokh, chairman of the GKI, resigns amid controversy regarding the sale of state assets; he is replaced by Maxim Boycko, a former Chubais aide
15 November		Boycko removed from office. A few days later, the auction for VNK raises over $2 billion, well in excess of expectations, although the agreement later falls apart

continued

Table 5.1 Continued

Date	*General events*	*Privatization events*
20 November	Chubais accused by media controlled by Berezovsky of an illegitimate book deal; steps down as finance minister but stays as deputy prime minister	
1998		
January	Price of oil falls in the wake of the Asian financial crisis; Central Bank uses reserves to hold fixed rouble exchange rate	
23 March	Yeltsin dismisses Chernomyrdin; replaced by Sergei Kiriyenko	
May	Miners' strikes across the country; financial crisis mounts over the summer, despite IMF support	
August	Devaluation; default on domestic debt; 90-day moratorium given to the banks; several banks close; Kiriyenko replaced by Evgenii Primakov	
1999		
January–	Economy improves as global oil prices rise	
19 December		Privatization slow; includes sale of 2.5 per cent of Gazprom shares

Notes

a Neil Bennett, "Fleming Launches Russian Fund", *The Times*, 1 August 1994, accessed 1 October 2012 from Factiva Database.

b Peter Marber, "Banking the Bear: Financial Marketization in Russia", *Columbia Journal of World Business*, 29 April 1994, accessed 1 October 2012 from Factiva Database.

c "Russia to Create 10 New Financial-Industrial Groups", 14 October 1994, *BBC Monitoring Service: Former USSR*, accessed 1 October 2012 from Factiva Database.

d Mikhail Dubik, "Yeltsin Fires Property Chief. Polevanov", *Moscow Times*, 25 January 1995, www.themoscowtimes.com/news/article/yeltsin-fires-property-chief-polevanov/343693.html, accessed 1 October 2012.

e O poryadke peredachi v 1995 godu v zalog aktsii, nakhodyashchikhsya v Federal'noi sobstvennosti, Ukaz Prezidenta Rossiiskoi Federatsii No. 889.

f "Russia's Lukoil Says It Sold 320,000 Bonds for $320 Million", *Reuters News*, 28 September 1995, accessed 4 October 2012 from Factiva Database.

g O finansovo-promyshlenykh gruppakh, Federal'nyi Zakon Rossiiskoi Federatsii No. 190-FZ.

h Ob aktsionernykh obshchestvakh, Federal'nyi Zakon No. 208-FZ.

i Julia Rubin, "Leading Russian Reformer Chubais Resigns", *The Associated Press*, 16 January 1996, accessed 4 October 2012 from Factiva Database.

j "In State of Nation Address, Yeltsin Threatens to Sack Government", *Jamestown Foundation Eurasia Daily Monitor*, 2(40), 26 February 1996, www.jamestown.org/single/?no_cache=1&tx_ttnews%5Btt_news%5D=8439&tx_ttnews%5BbackPid%5D=210, accessed 4 October 2012.

k O realizatsii konstitutsionnykh prav grazhdan na zemlu, Ukaz Prezidenta RF No. 337.

l O privatizatsii gosudarstvennogo imushchestva i ob osnovakh v privatizatsii munitsipal'nogo imushchestva v Rossiiskoi Federatsii, Federal'nyi Zakon Rossiiskoi Federatsii No. 123-FZ.

Conclusion

Introduction

In previous chapters we describe in some detail the background, objectives and implementation of the 1992 Russian Privatization Programme, as well as the subsequent waves of privatization.

We emphasize, in an effort to provide a precise narrative, that the 1992 Programme was designed for implementation of a prior law passed almost a year earlier by the Russian Supreme Soviet. This background is better known in Russian than in western literature on the subject. The programme itself was a compromise, not a unified construct. The sponsors of the Privatization Programme of 1992 had only a limited ability to ensure that it was implemented in spirit and letter, in part because Yeltsin's "rule by decree" gave reformers power only in regard to "economic reform", in part because of their lack of long and clearly established authority, in part because of conflicts with the parliament, and in part because privatization was a decentralized reform, and much lay at the discretion of local authorities and enterprise managers.

We also observe that privatization was unlikely to achieve its goal of creating efficient markets or do much to help Russian industry to become effective and efficient, since the structure of the Russian economy meant that these goals were not possible through privatization alone. No market economist would suggest that efficiency is likely to result from the privatization of monopoly companies where there is immobile labour, inadequate transport systems and ineffective capital markets and even payment systems. What was true for voucher privatization was equally true for the subsequent cash privatization. We trace the implementation of the 1992 and subsequent programmes, including the apparently successful voucher privatization and the subsequently flawed loans-for-shares and later cash privatizations.

We use findings from existing literature on the topic and contemporary sources. We establish a clear timeline of events, separating different phases of the privatization programme. Some chapters rely on the archives of western advisers to the international lending institutions and to the Russian government at that time, which have not previously been consulted in assessments of privatization. Our writing is informed by a conference held in Oxford[1] on 12–13

November 2010, which brought together a number of experts and participants in the privatization process. We have supplemented standard sources with interviews with people including Petr Mostovoi[2] and Maxim Boycko,[3] who were closely involved in the drafting and implementation, and also individuals often portrayed as hostile to aspects of radical reform: Ruslan Khasbulatov, the chairman of the Supreme Soviet, and Viktor Gerashchenko, head of the Central Bank.

We believe that our analysis suggests the following.

1 There needs to be a close historical reappraisal, at least of the Russian mass privatization, if not of the subsequent cash sales. In particular, there is considerable distortion in the way its short-term effects and medium-term outcomes are often portrayed. Privatization was not the only, or even possibly the major, change to the Russian economy at the time. It did not meet the expectations that were raised by information campaigns and policy pronouncements. But, equally, those who condemn the programme need to offer a credible policy option that would have better served the chaotic conditions of Russia in 1992.
2 The debate about privatization in the 1990s keeps in clear view still important questions about how realistic the economic understandings behind the policy were for Russia. This is a theme frequently raised in writing critical of privatization.[4] We speak from a somewhat different perspective from that criticism, however. We do not argue, as some of the literature insists, that mass privatization was the wrong policy for the time.

Economic policy in Russia was influenced by models of privatization elsewhere in the transition region, albeit on a much smaller scale, and we underscore that such models are inevitably used as the basis for policy development and advocacy. However, effective policy will also be shaped by institutional specificity, requiring compromise with stakeholders. In Russia, the political calculus, perhaps the single most important part of preparation for reform, had to be carried out on the spot, with time constraints. Expectations exaggerated the transformative power of property rights as a political instrument – without accompanying and facilitating market-based reforms – given Russian circumstances. Thus, experiments in Latin America and the Czech model may have provided insight for policy makers at the time of transition, but they offered no guarantee of success.

Across the transition region, the degree of success of privatization depended upon the range of legal and social support for competition, contestability, open markets and ownership. In Russia, institutional complexity was magnified by the scale of the country and by different and outmoded legal, institutional, political and social arrangements by sector and by jurisdiction. The Civil Code from the previous regime (1964) somehow remained in force in 1991–92, for example.[5] If there was ever a need for economic policy based, in the words of Ronald Coase, on "the world that exists",[6] it was at that time in Russia.

In the Yeltsin regime, economic reformers were isolated in large part because their role in legislation was confined by law to the economic sphere, and, thus, their policy formation was divorced from the politics and culture of the society it affected – conducted as if it were exogenous to the rest of the political system. It is ironic that even the most fundamental objective of privatization, which was to secure undisputed legal title, was done in a fashion so isolated from political reforms that its own legitimacy can be, and still is, called into question.

3 The economic debate calls into question some of the language used. For example, to talk of two paradigms, those of public and private "ownership", requires clarification of what is implied by those descriptions. Private ownership encompasses many types of legal forms, each of which may be expected to create a different outcome. In our conclusion, we address the ongoing philosophical debate in the literature about the degree to which simple paradigms, or expectations for the short run based on those paradigms, were useful in building an effective political economy in Russia.

These three considerations, politics, economics and philosophy, are of course at the core of public policy making. In concluding, we treat each in turn. We suggest that even a short history such as this can illustrate how, in the disordered circumstances of policy making in the early 1990s in Russia, the three interacted with one another to influence the ultimate outcome.

Let us take each of these observations in turn.

Politics

The 1992 Privatization Programme in Russia emerged during a period of economic and political chaos in the country. Within only a few months, reformers found it necessary to develop a "programme" based on the general mandate passed in the 3 July 1991 Russian Federation law.[7] They found it necessary to forge an agreement on the programme so that it could be approved by both the executive and the sharply divided parliament. Finally, they were constrained by confused responsibilities assigned to the former Union and Republican agencies and, perhaps most of all, by the lack of implementation capacity. Few today would argue it was a perfect reform. However, the context of its implementation is of fundamental importance to what was and was not achieved.

Criticism of the reform coming from those who generally supported it finds fault with its failure as a comprehensive package of economic reforms to do more than it did.[8] One critic, for example Marek Dąbrowski,[9] an economist sympathetic to the reformers, writes that they could have and ought to have seen the importance of certain supplementary reforms: the Russian government rejected, he argues, the full programme offered by Central European experience and foreign advisers there (Dąbrowski 1997: 47). Criticism of the exact path taken in economic reform is standard in the literature about Russia's early years of transition.[10]

To some extent, this literature is insufficiently appreciative of the political context of Russian privatization.[11] Reflecting on conditions and constraints, the director of the Russian Privatization Center (1993–96), Maxim Boycko, who wrote about the design of privatization in his co-authored "Privatizing Russia" (1993), said in an interview:

> There may be many criticisms of privatization. But some that I reject are those made from the assumption that there was a government of the quality, of the stability, of the sophistication of the British or the US governments. Had that been the case these would have been very questionable things to do.... Given that the government did not control anything, given that these enterprises were quite bad, given that nothing was going on except a lot of stealing ... getting enterprises privatized as quickly as possible was the priority.
>
> In terms of implementation capacity, the government could do nothing, had no control. It was political. There was no political base at all, it's mindboggling.[12]

The point Boycko is making is one that Chubais has also made in interviews: the key choices made in the Mass Privatization Programme were political, not economic.[13] Presented with the opportunity to establish comprehensive market-based "rules of the game", it is likely that the reformers would have chosen a different path. But they were constrained. They both lacked consensus on what a more comprehensive package of reform would look like and they lacked implementation capacity.

What we note here is the constraints forcing that political choice. Illustrating this point, we again cite Boycko, who spoke of the difficulties of achieving a consensus on most other issues. Indeed, the privatization reform was unique in the sense that it was the one policy on which the government not only had a specific objective but was also able to reach consensus, and could get it enforced. Whatever else might not be done, privatization was a way in which private property rights could be established as the basis for whatever economy was to emerge in the future. It symbolized as well as brought about Russia's move towards a market economy.

The problem plaguing privatization originated from the fact that many corollary policies, and institutional changes necessary for the establishment of a productive, competitive and pluralistic Russian economy, were not put in place because of this lack of consensus on the broader reform programme. To summarize, the failure was not really one of economics; many analysts and policy makers understood the need for a more comprehensive reform. It was one of politics; such a reform programme was being drafted through diverse legislative projects with limited coordination, only some of which made their way successfully through the parliament in the 1990s.

Why did it prove so difficult to create political consensus? For those who opposed the reformers, the issue sometimes seemed to be the lack of experience, as evoked in Vice-President Rutskoi's disparagement of them as "little boys in pink pants".[14] Gaidar, Chubais and some of the others were indeed much younger than those who ruled Russia in the communist era, and they were appointed for their economic understanding,[15] rather than their political experience. However, by the end of 1992, the Russian prime minister was Chernomyrdin, a man of considerable experience as head of Gazprom. His appointment did not result in a transformation in the capacity of the government. As Mau[16] drily observed in 2012:

> In November 1991, there was no one who wanted to be premier of the government. In November 1992, there was a line of those who wanted to be. And this is such an important indicator that there had appeared a country in which one could govern.[17]

So Yeltsin himself was effectively the prime minister in November 1991, with Gennady Burbulis appointed "state secretary" and his effective deputy (Yeltsin 1994: 152). It was Burbulis who introduced Yeltsin to Gaidar. There were few others so confident in economic reform and Yeltsin's leadership.[18] Gaidar and the other reformers shared an optimistic, even kamikaze, attitude that was required in the era following the ambitious, though somewhat vague, "500 days" programme.[19]

Khasbulatov, who was not selected as premier, expressed frustration that the government failed to introduce as many reforms as he wanted to parliament. "When Gaidar was in charge, I asked him 'which laws would you like us to adopt? What are your projected laws?' But they were unable to develop them … they wouldn't give me any legislation."[20] In that the parliament was developing and passing its own legislation, he went as far as to suggest that parliament was "doing the government's and the President's job".[21] One might take this view with a pinch of salt, not least because, as mentioned above, by the end of 1992, the highly experienced industrialist and politician Chernomyrdin had become prime minister, and that did not demonstrably result in comprehensive and integrated reform being introduced.

Some critics of the reform, aware of its limitations and lack of supportive political reform, have suggested that the privatization ought to have been delayed (Kolodko 2000: 156; Roland 2000; Cornia and Popov 2001; Åslund 2007: 43–4). Indeed, some advisers considered and even promoted this option.[22] But if that option had been pursued, when should privatization have happened? Should a more modest 1992 Programme have been put before parliament? If so, a rare moment of consensus would have slipped by. Should the programme have been passed but its timing delayed? If so, the government risked losing momentum and control of the process.

In any such counterfactual analysis, it is difficult to be confident that any better path was available. Given that spontaneous privatization was already taking place, it is hard to envisage that such delay would have resulted in a better outcome. Contemporary documents demonstrate that the limitations of the programme were understood by reformers and their advisers, but their judgement was that delay would have worse consequences than a decision to proceed.

Given this background, it is surprising that privatization has been blamed for so many of the subsequent ills of the Russian economy. Those who make this argument must surely place themselves in the position of those at the time, and propose, even with hindsight, what alternative path was available to Russia which would have had better consequences.

To summarize, the political objective of the reformers was to prevent a return in future years to the old communist structures, even if privatization could not, on its own, create an effective market economy. Privatization could bring Russia to a point of no return. Such an argument may or may not hold water; a failed reform effort might equally have been likely to generate a desire to return to the old system. Reformers in Russia may well have believed that they had a short time to make reform irreversible and to revive the Russian economy, which was viewed as a "corpse". Given their political as well as economic objectives, one might ask why Yeltsin and his coalition of ministers did not proceed simultaneously with as uncompromising a political agenda as well. To be sure, they did not have powers to "rule by edict" in political affairs. Still, it is evident that there is no one document that outlines in broad terms the reformers' political, economic and social roadmaps. Had there existed a consensus to implement such a programme, it would surely have been hugely valuable for the government to have had an indicative plan of what reform was needed and when. The absence of such a document speaks volumes about the lack of agreement and coordination within the government.

This in turn raises the question of why Yeltsin did not try to establish a broader political legitimacy for economic reform, once his powers to rule by decree ended. For example, in early 1992, he could have tried to pass a new constitution or could have called for a parliamentary election. For such a strategy to have succeeded, Yeltsin would have needed to be sure that the subsequent elections would return a more unified body of legislators. He could have had little confidence of this, since, even in December 1993, when, after the coup attempt, parliamentary elections did not result in the same kind of mandate Yeltsin had secured earlier (Russia's Choice, the party closest to Yeltsin, gained only 15 per cent (McFaul 2004: 38–9)). In short, neither the elections nor the constitutional change in 1993 created the kind of consensus that would have strengthened the reform base. Reform parties were fractionalized, and the social base, around which support for Yeltsin could coalesce, was not yet present (Moser and Thames 2003; Troxel 2003; Treisman 2009).

And finally, had there been consensus, there would still be a question of Yeltsin's willingness/mandate to proceed by edict with political, as well as economic, reforms. To repeat, there was only a certain range of reforms over which his executive decree powers extended. Equally important, although in the early, active years of his presidency, it was clear that he strongly supported change towards a more liberal society and democratic structure, Yeltsin was not an institutional economist, or any kind of economist for that matter. Even later, he failed to develop a "grand plan" or manifesto of social and political change to which he and his supporters could subscribe.

Mass privatization was one policy that, with great fanfare, appeared to have positioned Russia to take a bold step in the right direction. The scale and complexity of the operation would have been impressive in any country. In the disorderly conditions of early 1990s Russia, it was doubly so. It was a very pragmatic reform, however, and by most accounts, it did not result in the ownership structure the reformers had, in concept, wanted.[23] Yet initially it seemed to have been a success, appearing to create a remarkable bridgehead to a market economy. But it was only, and could only have been, a bridgehead.

There is little doubt that from a political point of view, the privatization reforms were a critical element in Russia's crossing the Rubicon towards a market economy. But, throughout the 1990s, the nature and success of that market economy were still very much in doubt.

Economics

The economic reforms needed to transform Russia into a market economy were profound, with privatization being only one of them. Privatization, per se, was not the ultimate goal, but rather a means towards the creation of a more prosperous economy. The reformers in the Privatization Ministry may well have understood the dilemma, however; the world they faced was not one where they were in control of creating broader reform. The questions they needed to address were immediate ones: how to get a programme implemented against what seemed like impossible time scales.[24] Like soldiers in a battle, they had been given their objective. If the battle was to be won, they had to focus on that goal, not on the strategy for winning the war.

Contemporary and subsequent evaluations by economists, as discussed in previous chapters, tend to agree that the ultimate goal of privatization was the creation of markets, where competition for capital, labour and resources would encourage efficiency and help underpin political pluralism. Indeed, the political imperative for accepting economic transformation ultimately rested on the ability of a market economy to deliver these benefits. However, the structure of the Russian economy meant that this goal was not possible through privatization alone. As we have argued, no market economist would suggest that efficiency was likely to result from the privatization of monopoly companies in that environment.

For the reformers at the Privatization Ministry, as Boycko *et al.* (1995: 19) write, the main objective in this battle was to clarify property rights: "When property rights over a productive asset are clearly specified, and the person who decides how to employ this asset bears full costs and enjoys full benefits of such employment, he puts the asset to most productive use." The aim, in theory, was to unify "control rights and cash flow rights" (ibid.: 22).

Yet even here there was a gap between theory and action. The reformers backed a privatization Option One that would have distributed shares to outsiders. It was as a concession to the industrial lobby that they agreed on Option Two, which gave ownership to workers and managers. Much discussion has taken place about the decision to allow Option Two. Yet it is this option that best unifies cash flow and control rights. In Option One, which was supported by the reformers, insiders, including both workers and directors, acquired a minority stake with the rest of the shares distributed to outsiders in part through the voucher programme and in part through state targeting of preferred outsider owners. This model aimed to produce a separation of management from ownership, which is one classic objective of the firm, although the reformers' economic theory might actually prescribe avoiding it.

More broadly, in the absence of other profound reforms, privatization did not, and could not, play its part in the creation of efficient market structures. It is therefore unremarkable that the review of the findings for all transition countries thus far by Estrin *et al.* (2009) finds little relationship between ownership structure and efficiency, except in regard to new and foreign-owned firms. But, at least, privatization did go some way to define the ownership of companies; it may have helped put a stop to "spontaneous privatization" and, in its voucher phase, skewed that ownership towards the more pluralistic worker and manager control, rather than the re-creation of Soviet ministries through the "associations". These are significant achievements. However, they were never likely to create an efficient market economy alone. Nor can they be blamed for all the features of the Russian economy that emerged in the late 1990s.

This brings us once again to the political significance of the reform. Privatization was a symbolic policy. Communism in the Soviet Union was based on state ownership of productive assets. Privatization was the clearest possible demonstration that this economic regime was at an end. The private ownership of assets therefore had to be at the heart of the new market economy.

But the complex institutions required to run a successful market economy, and the variety of ownership models available, were, perhaps out of necessity, often overlooked. In part this was because there was little political room for them to be discussed. But in part also, it was because Russia had little practical experience of how capitalist financial institutions worked. Insofar as policy makers or even enterprise managers had any training in the workings of a market economy, it would by necessity have been from academic study rather than from direct experience.

Was there an alternative reform agenda that emerged at that time? One might examine the writings of Yavlinsky, an early reformer who had helped draw up the 500-Day Plan during the Gorbachev era. He had been a reform politician and therefore his position, which we discuss below, might be taken to represent an alternative reform programme to that of the Gaidar government.

Braguinsky and Yavlinsky (2000: 191) recognize the need to build institutions found in developed market economies, call for a "new social contract", and attack the architects of Russian reform, "as well as many Western advisors", for "simplistic prescriptions which derive their strength from an a priori ideal scheme". They consider the Russian privatization programme one of the most spectacular failures in the history of economic reform (ibid.: 10, 123).

Yet their alternative proposal for reform is not a blueprint for a comprehensive set of market institutions. Rather, it is a plan that involves the extension of markets into law enforcement. The state, they write, should offer its services to the highest bidder and "commercialise the most important economic function played by the government, that of protecting property rights" (ibid.: 224). Reformers should, in their view, create a Federal Property Protection Service (FPPS) "as a kind of 'supermafia'" (ibid.: 232), such that privatization of services provides economic incentives to ensure the rule of law.

We underscore, in response to Braguinsky and Yavlinsky, that Russian reformers understood the need for institutions that protect property rights. However, they reasoned that the enforcement of property rights naturally followed from their establishment. It was assumed that privatization would foster the new owners' defence of those rights; that is, demand for law enforcement would naturally emerge. Goldman (2004: 74) criticizes them for this assumption:

> [Reformers] took for granted that the existence of property rights automatically guaranteed that the state would enforce those rights. This assumed that there was something like the "rule of law" and that the state would not be in a condition of near anarchy.

But Goldman does not have it quite right. The reformers anticipated that the defence of property rights would follow from the entitlement. Thus, both the reformers' views and those of Braguinsky and Yavlinsky on this issue seem to have rested on the belief that economic forces would create the law and institutions needed to enforce property rights and efficient markets. The former anticipated that privatization would naturally result in enforcement; the latter assumed that the enforcement of property rights could be sold to the highest bidder. Neither explicitly considered the institutions, incentives and cultures needed for the effective functioning of a market economy, or how variations in these elements would change the nature of the economy and society that were created.

These assumptions, at least as expressed in their published works, take economic incentives as their starting point, and assume that political, social and legal change will follow. In complex political and policy situations, such as those that confronted Russia, understanding the interplay of politics and institutions which are rooted in history and culture is also critical for effective policy.

Philosophy

The Russian privatization process, as virtually every critical commentary on privatization has observed, raises questions about the way economists sometimes apply conceptually useful models to more complex public policy. In particular, classifications for conceptually simple models can be inappropriate for the more disorderly reality. Much of the theoretical economic literature tends to distinguish between private and state-owned enterprises, for example. Among supporters of Russian privatization, the former were to be promoted, since private enterprises were expected to encourage efficiency, restructuring and pluralism in both economic and political terms.

In Chapter 3 we argued that the likelihood of privatization achieving the government's goals was low, given the circumstances of Russia in the early 1990s. Privatization can only create economic benefits when other market mechanisms are in place. In circumstances where a country lacks capital, competition and the rule of law, privatization is likely to fail in delivering those benefits. Indeed, it may have the reverse effects. In Russia, there was a great need for broader reform.

However, there is also a deeper conceptual question that needs to be addressed. In economic taxonomy, private companies are assumed to have a certain structure, which will deliver positive behaviour: they respond to market forces; they are constrained by capital; those who own shares have ownership and control rights that are exercised. But although Russian companies approximated the legal structures of private companies, empirical studies show that they did not, either individually or collectively, create the desired behaviours (Estrin *et al.* 2009).

The notion that there is one paradigm legal structure which will foster similar outcomes in all markets is a considerable simplification of the actual world, as is well known in the literature on accountability and ownership and on corporate governance in different forms of ownership (Berle 1931–32; Alchian and Demsetz 1972; Jensen and Meckling 1976; Williamson 1979, 1985; Milgrom and Roberts 1992; Hansmann 2000).[25] This is particularly the case in countries where market mechanisms are not in place. Even in the West, if we look at the universe of non-state organizations, we may find some of the features of the paradigm private company, but only to a limited extent. In many private companies capital may not, except in extremis, be a constraining factor on management action. In large public companies, shareholders often exercise little influence. Private enterprises are of many different legal types: companies, partnerships, charities, non-governmental organizations. Even within each of these classifications, constitutions, governance and the legal duties of officers vary markedly between and within countries.[26] It has been found that for different activities and at different times all these different forms of ownership can prove effective (Marshall 1946: 596).

This raises a fundamental question for those who discuss, advocate or oppose privatization policies: What does it mean, and why is it helpful, to classify a company as "private"? In other words, what are the characteristics that apply to all members of the class of "private" companies? If the response is that they are, by definition, ones which are responding to market forces in an efficient fashion, then privatization policy is tautologous: advocates are simply demanding that we create "good companies". If it is that they have a particular legal form, then it must be acknowledged that productive structures have many different legal forms in successful economies around the world.

Perhaps an example can help illustrate the point. We noted in Chapter 5 that following the extension of a loan to the Russian government, Oneximbank claimed to have found mismanagement at Norilsk Nickel. The bank sought to remove the board, and it was successful in doing so because it received the support of the government. Let us assume that these were the facts of the matter, and that the action taken was a positive one. However, it is not clear that these events took place because Norilsk Nickel was a private company. In fact, the government still owned the shares, and was critical in getting change to happen. The fact that better management had been applied to the enterprise was independent of who owned the shares.

Systems of exchange based on self-interest can prove enormously productive if that exchange is governed by competitive markets with no transaction costs. From that theoretical model, however, rules have been made for the real world: for example, one might be that private companies are more productive than public companies (although in some sectors, this cannot be demonstrated).

Thus, the definition of "private company" in reality embraces a variety of forms: not all firms are "owned" in the same way; what ownership means depends on context. Therefore, in pursuing privatization policies, the simpler bimodal classification may not produce the desired result. One may ask what are, and from where are derived, the characteristics of the standards to be created. To summarize, where, for policy purposes, there is a need to establish what is meant by "private ownership", it is important to be clear that the standards are not tautologous; for example, that private companies are not simply defined as those which give the economic outcomes which the policy maker seeks.

Applying this argument to Russia in the early 1990s suggests that different forms of ownership, as well as different methods for transfer of control and economic rights, could be appropriate in different situations. The transfer of small enterprises to their workers was deemed effective; the sale of oil and natural resource companies less so.

From a policy point of view, the question to be asked is not "Is this company private, or is it state-controlled?" That was the question posed by the Soviet communist government, which always erred on the side of state ownership. That same question can be answered equally simplistically in the other direction. But if the question asked is one of policy, rather than simply economics, surely the issue is whether, in a pragmatic sense, the distribution of (an often limited set of) ownership and control rights helps create the outcomes sought. For example, will those rights be effectively used; will they promote the fair and efficient distribution of resources, and the incentive to innovation? The policy question will have a different answer depending on the other economic institutions that shape incentives affecting enterprise behaviour.

What matters is what works well, what creates the best behaviours. And what will work well depends on the economy and society to which it is applied.

This observation about thinking on privatization applies equally to other economic paradigms, for example ownership, as Hansmann (2000), in his extensive exploration, shows. He emphasizes the importance of analysis of ownership results that are well grounded in observation. What, for example, do we mean when we say that someone "owns" an asset? Who, for example, "owns" British Petroleum (BP), one of the world's largest oil companies? Is it the fund managers whose names appear on the share register? Is it the pension funds whose assets they manage, or the trustees of those pension funds? Is it the beneficiaries, whose savings have been set aside, or the institution (usually their employer) which has established and contributes to the pension? Or is it the board of directors, which appoints the chief executive and oversees the strategy? Or the employees without whose collective labour the company would collapse? Or is it the governments of the various jurisdictions in which BP operates who can intervene in its operations? And if so, what part of the government?

The answer to all these problems is that they all do, albeit in different ways. If a fund manager owns 100 per cent of the shares s/he will enjoy different ownership rights than 100 fund managers with 1 per cent each. If the company is protected by a "poison pill", the board will have greater control. If the board is incompetent, ill-informed or under the influence[27] of another party, they will exert fewer ownership rights.[28] If workers are difficult to find, if they act as a body, they will have greater influence than if they do not. The point is that the economic concept of "ownership" cannot be divorced from the politics and power relations that affect the owned asset. The notion that there is some paradigm where there is a "unification of control rights and cash flow rights" is not one that is often found in the management of large companies. These rights are constrained by different checks and balances in the system.

We emphasize here that, if it is to be successful, economic reform, particularly something as fundamental as the Russian Privatization Programme, requires both pragmatic considerations regarding what is effective and what is not in privatization policies as well as planned coordination with other policies.

We do not here discuss, as would be appropriate in a longer or deeper book, the taxonomy used in Russian privatization. We merely comment that it is important to carefully define objectives and links between prescribed policy and expected outcome.

The work of economist Ronald Coase on property rights was cited in support of privatization (Boycko *et al.* 1995: 20–5). This is ironic. Coase specified that his concepts applied only where there were "zero transaction costs" (which is a general assumption of economic analysis). He writes that under these conditions, if ownership rights are clearly distributed, then efficient outcomes result. Known as the Coase Theorem (Coase 1988: 13), its expectations of property rights reform were cited as the key theoretical underpinning of the need to establish "ownership" in Russia (Boycko *et al.* 1995: 20–5).

Coase himself has been critical of the policy use of his writings, however. An extensive discussion in journals of the Coase Theorem, a proposition about the world of zero transaction costs, he writes, is a disappointing, if understandable, result of his theorizing. The theory poses many intellectual problems, but, as he insists, these are remote from the real world.[29] "That much of the discussion has been critical of my argument is also quite understandable since, if I am right, current economic analysis is incapable of handling many of the problems to which it purports to give answers" (Coase 1988: 15).

To emphasize again, in conclusion, our larger concern has been to recognize that despite its many imperfections, the Mass Privatization Programme in Russia contributed to the limiting of the "contested agenda" about the direction of economic transformation. Shops and factories were moving out of the hands of the state. An economic transition had begun. We also suggest that those who criticize the programme because of poor outcomes in the Russian economy need to suggest what alternative policy should have been adopted: What policy would not only have worked in theory (there are many of these), but would have worked in the circumstances in which the country found itself in the early 1990s? We have not found any such alternatives that appear convincing. There is therefore much to be said for the mass Privatization Programme in practice.

In regard to the LFS, in our view, economic theory used to justify practice sailed dangerously close to the rocks. As privatization moved from vouchers to cash, as the government used ever more creative devices to avoid parliamentary opposition, it may even have come to the view that ownership structure does not matter for the eventual outcome. If so, economic analysis will have become so remote from the real world that it will scarcely have a direct policy application.

Summary

It is now over 20 years since the passage of the Russian 1992 Privatization Programme. Few would argue that it succeeded in achieving the lofty goals set for it. We have attempted to provide some insight into why this was the case. However, if we can understand what failed in the past, are we better equipped to address the question of how this history might be useful to scholars and policy makers in the future?

We argue that privatization resolved a highly contested agenda, and in that sense was an effective political reform. It is also the case, however, that alone, without political, economic and cultural transformation, it could not have produced an efficient market economy, since the economic institutions Russia inherited were unfavourable for such an outcome. We further argue that expectations about the economic benefits of change in "ownership" were therefore unrealistic, perhaps because of a strictly disciplinary vision of key changes both by the reformers and by the parliamentarians who restricted rule by decree to economic policy. We see that the three disciplines, politics, economics and philosophy, are inter-related, and all are relevant for successful economic policy development.[30]

In this book we have aimed to write a history of decision making during the privatization of Russia in the early 1990s. We hope it is one upon which other scholars can build. We also hope it will be useful to policy makers more generally, in particular the architects of fundamental changes in economic structures.

And finally, we hope it may be of interest to students of Russian history, and to those who wish to understand how the country was shaped during those eventful years.

Appendices

Appendix 1

Text of the 1992 Privatization Programme

The following is the text of the 1992 Privatization Programme passed by parliament in June of that year. This is the key document agreed both by the government and the parliament.

State privatization programme of state and municipal enterprises in the Russian Federation in 1992

JUDGMENT of the Supreme Council of the RSFSR,
11 June 1992, N 2980-I (EJ 92–29)

1 Introduction

The state privatization programme of state and municipal enterprises of the Russian Federation in 1992 (hereafter: the Programme), developed in accordance with the requirements of the law of the Russian Federation On the Privatization of State and Municipal Enterprises in the Russian Federation, sets out the objectives, tasks and order of privatization in 1992, and defines the limits of this area.

The main objectives of privatization in 1992 are:

- the formation of a layer of private owners to promote the creation of a socially oriented market economy;
- the improvement of the performance of enterprises through privatization;
- the social protection of the population and the development of social infrastructure through funds received from privatization;
- the promotion of stabilization of the financial situation of the Russian Federation;
- the creation of a competitive environment and the promotion of demonopolization of the economy;
- the attraction of foreign investment;

- the creation of conditions and organizational structures to enhance the scale of privatization in 1993–1994.

The requirements established by the Programme are binding for execution by the organs of state power and the administrations of republics within the Russian Federation, by autonomous regions, autonomous districts, territories, regions, the cities of Moscow and St Petersburg, and local governments.

The facilities and state and municipal enterprise properties are distributed according to their possible privatization in 1992 into the following groups:

- those facilities and enterprises whose privatization is prohibited;
- those facilities and enterprises whose privatization may be carried out only by decision of the government of the Russian Federation or republics of the Russian Federation (depending on the type of state ownership);
- those facilities and enterprises whose privatization may be carried out only by the decision of the State Committee of the Russian Federation for the Management of State Property (hereafter the State Property Committee of Russia) in consideration of the opinion of the ministries;
- those facilities and enterprises whose privatization is allowed only in accordance with local programmes of privatization;
- those facilities, enterprises and structural subdivisions of enterprises privatized in cases stipulated by the law of the Russian Federation On the Privatization of State and Municipal Enterprises in the Russian Federation, with the consent of the labour collectives;
- those facilities and enterprises subject to mandatory privatization.

The privatization of property not included in the mandatory categories and where there are no restrictions on privatization may be carried out on the basis of local privatization programmes or applications for privatization.

The programme does not regulate the privatization of state farms, nor of land or housing funds.

2 Classification of facilities and businesses according to the possibility of privatization in 1992

2.1 FACILITIES AND ENTERPRISES WHOSE PRIVATIZATION IS PROHIBITED

2.1.1 subsoils, forest reserves, water resources, air space, and resources of the continental shelf, of territorial waters and the maritime economic zone of the Russian Federation, as well as the right to deployment and operation of communication satellites at defined points on the geostationary orbit

2.1.2 protected or specially used natural territories

2.1.3 facilities of historical and cultural heritage of the peoples of Russia

(unique cultural and natural monuments and facilities of nature, history, culture, science and technology, including the valuables stored in state museums, archives and libraries, including the premises and buildings where they are located)

2.1.4 funds of the federal budget of the Russian Federation, of the Republic foreign exchange (currency) reserves of the Russian Federation, of the Pension Fund of the Russian Federation and non-budgetary state funds, of the Central Bank of the Russian Federation, as well as the gold reserves and diamond fund

2.1.5 the Central Bank of the Russian Federation, the enterprises, organizations and agencies that ensure the production and storage of banknotes, government treasury bills, bonds and other government securities; facilities and enterprises for the sorting of gems, refineries

2.1.6 staff and reserve property under the operational management of the Armed Forces of the Russian Federation, the troops of the Ministry of Security of the Russian Federation and the Ministry of the Interior of the Russian Federation

2.1.7 institutions financed by budgets of all levels of the state

2.1.8 enterprises and institutions of cartography and geodesy, weather observation services, and inspection services for the state of the environment and conservation, and institutions of the geological services

2.1.9 enterprises and institutions of sanitary and epidemiological, veterinary, forest conservation and plant protection services

2.1.10 institutions for patents, standardization and metrology, and machine-testing stations

2.1.11 pipeline transport facilities, enterprises, organizations and institutions

2.1.12 water and drainage systems, as well as facilities and enterprises for their operation

2.1.13 television and radio transmitting centres

2.1.14 public roads and organizations carrying out their maintenance

2.1.15 enterprises for the production of state seals (signs)

2.1.16 enterprises for the production of narcotic and poisonous substances, as well as for the planting, cultivation and processing of cultures and their maintenance

2.1.17 port installations and facilities, atomic, educational, hydrographic, inshore fleet, fleet for rescue work and oil spills in the sea, and repair technology of the enterprise Atomflot, property of water production units, ways and channels, groups of Podvodrechstroya and ship inspections

2.1.18 facilities, enterprises and equipment for the disposal of industrial solid waste, solid and liquid radioactive waste, and animal burial

2.1.19 facilities and enterprises for medical production and corrective labour institutions

2.1.20 engineering infrastructure of cities and regions (including electricity, heat, gas and water supply, sanitation and urban outdoor lighting), and enterprises engaged in the exploitation, servicing and maintenance of these facilities

2.1.21 facilities and enterprises for gas fuel handling of nationwide and inter-regional scale

2.1.22 crematoriums and cemeteries

2.1.23 enterprises for the production of fissile and radioactive materials, nuclear weapons, space vehicles; enterprises and facilities that provide services, start-up and tracking of spacecraft, carrying out research and development activities in these areas

2.1.24 organizations and institutions of social protection, children's homes, orphanages, nursing homes, group homes, hospitals and sanitoriums for the disabled, children and the elderly, as well as organizations and agencies for the prevention and treatment of mental, neuropsychiatric and infectious diseases and cancer, substance abuse and for patients infected with HIV and AIDS

2.1.25 facilities and enterprises run by federal organs and representative authorities

Note: Restrictions on the privatization of enterprises referred to in paragraphs 2.1.11, 2.1.12, 2.1.14, 2.1.21 apply only to enterprise units within direct operation and the contents of the facilities and systems indicated herein.

2.2 FACILITIES AND ENTERPRISES WHICH MAY BE PRIVATIZED ONLY BY DECISION OF THE GOVERNMENT OF THE RUSSIAN FEDERATION OR GOVERNMENTS OF THE REPUBLICS OF THE RUSSIAN FEDERATION (DEPENDING ON THE TYPE OF STATE PROPERTY)

2.2.1 facilities and enterprises for the manufacture and repair of systems and elements of all types of weapons, ammunition, explosives and pyrotechnics, as well as research, design and development organizations carrying out work in these areas

2.2.2 facilities for civil defence and mobilization

2.2.3 facilities and enterprises of nuclear engineering

2.2.4 specialized elevators, refrigerators and warehousing facilities providing permanent placement of government reserves and storage of mobilization reserves

2.2.5 facilities and extractive industries enterprises (except for facilities and mining enterprises for the extraction of local raw materials), enterprises of the geological service

2.2.6 facilities and processing plants for ores of precious metals, precious and semi-precious stones, radioactive elements and rare earths

2.2.7 enterprises and associations of the fuel and energy complex (with the exception of construction organizations and enterprises), including enterprises of electric power generation, coal, oil and gas extraction and processing, export transhipment oil depots, and oil depots of nationwide or inter-regional scale

2.2.8 commercial banks (whose privatization is carried out by a special procedure)

2.2.9 communications enterprises (except for the retail network Rospechat)

2.2.10 information and news agencies of the Ministry of the Press and Information of the Russian Federation

2.2.11 facilities, enterprises and social and cultural institutions (health care, education, culture and sports) regardless of their formal bureaucratic affiliation, which are federal property or state property of the republics of the Russian Federation (except for the facilities among the balance sheets of the enterprises and organizations)

2.2.12 enterprises of wholesale trade, serving the Far North and similar locales, including rotational settlements

2.2.13 foreign trade union Ministry of External Economic Relations of the Russian Federation and other ministries and departments of the Russian Federation

2.2.14 printing enterprises and publishing houses

2.2.15 facilities and institutions of state sanatorium health resorts

Applications for the privatization of facilities and enterprises listed in Section 2.2 of the Programme go to the territorial agencies of the State Property Committee of Russia, which send them to the State Committee for Management of State Property of the Russian Federation with mandatory notification of the applicant. The decision on the application is taken by the Deputy Prime Minister of the Russian Federation by request of the State Property Committee of Russia and the relevant ministry. Decisions on such applications must be made within one month of their submission to the territorial agency of the State Property Committee of Russia.

The above procedure applies to those facilities and enterprises included in Section 2.2, which cannot be attributed to Section 2.1 of the Programme.

2.3 FACILITIES AND ENTERPRISES WHICH MAY BE PRIVATIZED ONLY BY DECISION OF THE STATE PROPERTY COMMITTEE OF RUSSIA IN CONSULTATION WITH THE RELEVANT MINISTRIES

2.3.1 enterprises of all sectors of the economy occupying a dominant position in the federal or local markets for goods, labour and services not included in Sections 2.1 and 2.2 of the Programme

2.3.2 large enterprises (whose average number of Employees is over 10,000 people or whose balance value of fixed capital as of 1 January 1992 was more than 150 million roubles), which were not included in Sections 2.1 and 2.2 of the Programme

2.3.3 movable and immovable property, released in connection with the reduction of the Armed Forces of the Russian Federation, except for weapons to be destroyed in accordance with the international obligations of the Russian Federation, and also property released by the

Ministry of Security of the Russian Federation and Ministry of Internal Affairs of the Russian Federation

2.3.4 enterprises of rail, air, sea and river transport

2.3.5 construction organizations and enterprises for the production of building materials and structures of national importance

2.3.6 state breeding and hours farms, breeding and hybrid centres, state seed inspectors and strain variety testing laboratories, strain variety testing stations and sites, enterprises and farms for the production of valuable and anadromous fish, fur farms

2.3.7 higher and secondary specialized educational institutions, research, design, exploration and other facilities, enterprises and institutions of the Russian Academy of Sciences, branches of the Academy, of the Ministry of Health of the Russian Federation, of the Ministry of Science, of Higher Schools and Technical Policy of the Russian Federation, of the Ministry of Education of the Russian Federation, of the Ministry of Ecology and Natural Resources of the Russian Federation, and facilities of state research centres

2.3.8 facilities and enterprises of the medical industry (including facilities and enterprises of the pharmaceutical industry and the industry of biomedical products), except those specified in paragraph 2.1.16 of the Programme

2.3.9 facilities and enterprises for the production of alcohol, alcoholic beverages, wine and tobacco products

2.3.10 facilities and enterprises for the production of children's food

2.3.11 mobilization reserves (under privatization of enterprises, mobilization reserves excluded from their property)

2.3.12 facilities for the provision of petroleum products

2.3.13 enterprises for folk arts and crafts

Decisions on the privatization of the facilities and enterprises included in Section 2.3 of the Programme shall be taken by the State Property Committee of Russia. Ministries and departments of the Russian Federation may give their opinion on these draft decisions if asked to do so by the committee.

The above procedure applies to those facilities and enterprises included in Section 2.3, which cannot be brought under Sections 2.1 and 2.2 of the Programme.

Under the privatization of these facilities and enterprises indicated in Sections 2.2 and 2.3 of the Programme, the State Property Committee of Russia may decide to maintain controlling interests in federal ownership for up to three years.

2.4 FACILITIES AND ENTERPRISES WHOSE PRIVATIZATION IS ALLOWED ONLY IN ACCORDANCE WITH LOCAL PROGRAMMES OF PRIVATIZATION

2.4.1 facilities and enterprises of urban passenger transport except for taxis, as well as enterprises for their repair
2.4.2 baths, laundries
2.4.3 enterprises, organizations and institutions that provide funeral (ritual) services, except for those indicated in paragraph 2.1.22
2.4.4 garbage processing plants
2.4.5 pharmacies (with mandatory state licensing for their activities)
2.4.6 facilities, enterprises, and social and cultural institutions (health care, education, culture and sports) regardless of their bureaucratic affiliation (except as noted in paragraph 2.2.11 and facilities in the balances of the enterprises and organizations)

Decisions on the privatization of facilities and enterprises included in Section 2.4 of the Programme shall be adopted by the committee on property management in accordance with the requirements of local programmes of privatization.

Restrictions on privatization as described in the Programme are binding on all organs of state power and administration and organs of local self-government. The introduction by these bodies of additional restrictions on privatization is not allowed.

Privatization of facilities and enterprises that are subject to the restrictions imposed by the Programme is not allowed without the permission of the corresponding organs.

Restrictions on privatization are established in Sections 2.2–2.4 of the Programme. Their application does not imply a ban on the transformation of state (municipal) enterprises into joint stock companies of the open type that are held among state (municipal) property.

The Programme prohibits the purchase and sale, transfer and exchange of shares (shares or parts of shares, stocks) between legal entities in their share of capital (fund) of which the share of state and municipal property is 25 per cent or more, unless otherwise established by legislative acts of the Russian Federation.

2.5 FACILITIES AND ENTERPRISES SUBJECT TO MANDATORY PRIVATIZATION

Facilities and enterprises subject to mandatory privatization are those that have the greatest influence on the formation and operation of the market infrastructure of the Russian economy, as well as facilities and enterprises whose ineffective operation constrains the pace of economic development in Russia and the formation of the market.

These facilities and enterprises are:

2.5.1 facilities and enterprises of the wholesale and retail trade (including those for the sale of products of technical-industrial significance), public food and domestic services (including departmental facilities of the open network of retail trade, public food and domestic services);
2.5.2 facilities and enterprises (organizations) of construction and the industry of construction materials;
2.5.3 state agricultural facilities and enterprises, including poultry (except farms [*sovkhoz*]);
2.5.4 enterprises engaged in processing agricultural products, serving agricultural production and making technological products of to support it;
2.5.5 enterprises of food processing and light industry;
2.5.6 loss-making enterprises in all economic sectors, except those specified in Section 2.1 of the Programme;
2.5.7 suspended facilities and unfinished buildings, for which the normative terms of construction have expired;
2.5.8 property of enterprises liquidated without establishing a right of succession;
2.5.9 enterprises of automotive transport, other than those indicated in paragraph 2.4.1.

3 Estimated figures (indicators) of privatization for organs of state power and management

3.1 Estimates figures for privatization in 1992 for the republics of the Russian Federation are contained in Table 1; those for territories [*kray*], regions [*oblast*], and the cities of Moscow and St Petersburg are in Table 2; and for autonomous regions and autonomous areas in Table 3.

3.2 Targets are defined in relative terms (the proportion of facilities being privatized as a percentage of the total number of facilities of the industry subject to privatization) and are minimal for the development of local privatization programmes.

Targets for the privatization of enterprises listed in paragraphs 2.5.6 and 2.5.7 are not to be established.

3.3 On the basis of the targets of the Programme, management committees for the property of the republics of the Russian Federation, autonomous regions [*oblast*], autonomous areas [*okrug*], territories [*kray*], regions [*oblast*] and the cities of Moscow and St Petersburg are to develop local programmes of privatization and forecast the consequent proceeds from privatization.

Approved relevant councils of people's deputies of the programme of privatization are to be submitted to the State Property Committee of Russia.

Personal responsibility for the fulfilment of the tasks of the Programme is assigned to the chairmen of the councils of people's deputies, heads of administrations, and chairmen of the asset management and property funds at all levels.

4 Norms of distribution of funds from privatization in 1992 and forecast of their revenues from 1992 to –1994

4.1 From 1992 to 1994 the privatization of state and municipal enterprises will be conducted on both a paid and an unpaid basis.

Forecast revenue from privatization on a paid basis in 1992 by sector is shown in Table 4, calculated on the basis of estimates of effective demand for the facilities of privatization in various sectors and regions of the Russian Federation. Income amounts to 72 billion roubles, including that:

- from personal means of citizens – 15 billion roubles;
- of funds for economic incentives (stimulation) of enterprises – 32 billion roubles;
- from the funds of enterprises, whose purchase is acknowledged in accordance with the law of the Russian Federation On the Privatization of State and Municipal Enterprises in the Russian Federation – 15 billion roubles;
- of funds from foreign investors – 10 billion roubles.

In the fourth quarter of 1992 the additional effective demand of the population will be provided with the introduction of personal privatization of accounts (privatization checks).

4.2 The forecast of revenue from privatization in 1993–94 is calculated on the basis of the effective demand for the facilities of privatization in various sectors and regions. Proceeds will consist of: 350 billion roubles in 1993; 470 billion roubles in 1994.

The main source of funds for the purchase of privatized facilities in this period will be personal privatization deposits (privatization checks) and the privatization funds of the enterprises.

4.3 The funds received from privatization are subject to distribution to the appropriate budgets and state organs according to the norms given in Table 5.

This distribution is to be made after the disbursement of funds to employees of privatized enterprises in accordance with the established Programme.

4.4 The Russian Federation has the right to adjust indicators for privatization (in consultation with the governments of the republics of the Russian Federation) and the norms of the distribution of funds accruing from privatization, in accordance with the state of the financial system of the Russian Federation and the market conditions for the facilities property.

4.5 All funds received from privatization are exempt from taxation.

4.6 The property management committee and property funds at all levels are exempt from taxation.

4.7 State duties are not charged on any acts and transactions of privatization.

5 Methods of privatization and the benefits provided by privatization in 1992

5.1 The particular method of privatization of an enterprise is determined by the committee on management of property based on the findings of the commission on privatization in accordance with requirements of the law of the Russian Federation On the Privatization of State and Municipal Enterprises in the Russian Federation, state and local privatization programmes, and normative acts of the State Property Committee of Russia, taking into account the views of the labour collective of the privatized enterprise.

Upon the transformation of state and municipal enterprises, joint stock companies of the closed type are not allowed.

It is not permitted to create joint stock companies (including holding enterprises), either by corporations, unions, associations or other groups of enterprises, including state (municipal) enterprises, except when bringing their organizational-legal form into compliance with the laws of the Russian Federation.

The property contributions made by state (municipal) enterprises to the authorized capital stock (fund) of enterprises created in any organizational-legal form, including the form of a union of enterprises, is considered to be state (municipal) property. These enterprises are permitted to make the indicated deposits only with the permission of the corresponding property management committee, and the sale and disposal of such in any form – only in accordance with the corresponding Russian legislation on privatization.

It is not permitted for unions of state (municipal) enterprises to create enterprises in any organizational-legal form, and it is likewise not permitted for organs of state power and management or organs of local self-government, except for committees for property management and property funds operating in their competencies as defined by the legislation of the Russian Federation.

The rightful successors of the indicated legal entities in the capacity of founders and participants (stockholders, shareholders) of previously established enterprises are exclusively the relevant property funds.

Decisions on the allocation of the structural sub-units of the enterprises in the process of privatization are to be adopted by the corresponding property management committees in accordance with the requirements of anti-monopoly legislation of the Russian Federation. In this case, an accord with the labour collective of the enterprise is not required. If the allocated structural sub-units are converted into joint stock companies of the open type, the officials of the administrative units receive the full range of benefits provided by Section 5.4 of the Programme.

5.2 All state (municipal) enterprises in relation to the methods used in privatization are divided into three groups:

Small enterprises whose average number of employees is less than 200 and whose balance value of fixed assets as of 1 January 1992 is no less than 1 million roubles are to be sold at auction (by competition), in accordance with the requirements of the Programme;

Enterprises whose average number of employees is over 1,000 and whose balance value of fixed assets as of 1 January 1992 is over 50 million roubles are to be privatized by conversion into joint stock companies of the open type.

All other enterprises can be privatized by any of the established methods in accordance with the requirements of the Programme.

5.3 In 1992, the following privatization methods may be used in accordance with the Programme:

- the sale of shares in joint stock companies of the open type;
- the sale of enterprises by auction;
- the sale of enterprises in a commercial competition (including competitions with a limited number of participants);
- the sale of enterprises by non-commercial investment competition (investment tenders);
- the sale of property (assets) of liquidating and liquidated enterprises;
- the purchase of leased property.

5.4 Upon the sale of shares of joint stock companies of the open type, created through the transformation of state and municipal enterprises (including those previously converted into joint stock companies of the closed type), at the request of the labour collective of the enterprise, one of the following options for granting benefits to the members of the labour collective of the privatized enterprise is to be used, and these benefits are granted to:

- workers for whom the enterprise is the primary place of employment;
- persons entitled under the legislation of the Russian Federation to return to their previous work at the enterprise;
- pensioners who have retired or former employees who worked at the privatized enterprise for at least 10 years for men and seven years and six months for women, and those dismissed at their own request or in order to reduce staff or number of workers;
- those removed from the enterprise to reduce the number of employees after 1 January 1992 and who are registered as unemployed.

OPTION ONE

All members of the labour collective of the privatized enterprise are provided, simultaneously and free of charge, with personal, privileged (non-voting) shares, amounting to 25 per cent of the charter capital, but in total amounting to no more than 20 times the established minimum wage in accordance with the legislation of the Russian Federation as calculated for one worker.

Ordinary shares of up to 10 per cent of the charter capital, but in total amounting to no more than six times the minimum monthly wage per employee established by the legislation of the Russian Federation, are to be sold by subscription to members of the labour collective at a reduction of 30 per cent of their nominal value and in instalments of up to three years, with an estimated cash down payment of no less than 15 per cent of the nominal value of the shares.

Responsible officials of the administration of the privatized enterprise (the head manager, his deputies, the chief engineer, the chief accountant), under the conditions of the contracts concluded with them, have the right (option) to purchase ordinary shares at the nominal value, amounting to a total sum of all of the indicated responsible officials of up to 5 per cent of the charter capital, but no more than 2,000 times the minimum amount of monthly wages per employee established by the legislation of the Russian Federation.

OPTION TWO

All members of the labour collective of the privatized enterprise are granted the right to purchase ordinary (voting) shares, comprising up to 51 per cent of the charter capital.

In this case:

- Free transfer of shares and the sale of shares on preferential terms is not carried out.
- The sale price of the shares is determined in accordance with the regulations approved by the State Property Committee of Russia.
- The transformation of state and municipal enterprises into joint stock companies of the open type the Property Committee, as proposed by the administration of the privatized enterprise and with the consent of the privatized enterprise's workforce, can personally provide employees of the enterprises belonging to a single technological complex with the privatized enterprise the right to participate in a private subscription to shares conducted among the employees of privatized enterprises.
- The total number of shares to be sold to employees of the privatized enterprises and employees belonging to a unified technological complex cannot exceed 51 per cent of the value of charter capital of the joint stock company.

OPTION THREE

If a group of employees of an enterprise takes responsibility for carrying out the plan of privatization of the enterprise to prevent its bankruptcy and with the consent of the general meeting of the labour collective to conclude the corresponding agreement, the period of which may not be more than one year (non-renewable), the members of the group have the right (option) at the conclusion of this period and in accordance with the conditions referred to in the agreement to purchase 20 per cent of the charter capital in the form of ordinary shares of the enterprise at nominal value. Should the group fail to meet the conditions of the agreement, the right (option) is lost and the stocks are sold in the established order.

During the period of effect of the agreement the indicated group shall be empowered to vote with 20 per cent of voting shares held by the relevant property fund.

The plan of privatization includes the terms of the agreement, the conclusion of which with the indicated group by the corresponding property fund is mandatory. The agreement specifies the obligations of the members of the group and limits their material liability of property belonging to them by the right of private property (to be contributed in the form of collateral), in an amount not less than 200 times the minimum monthly wage as established by the legislation of the Russian Federation for each member of the group.

Under this option, all employees of the enterprise (including members of the group) are sold ordinary shares constituting 20 per cent of the charter capital, but in an amount not more than 20 times the minimum monthly wage per employee as established by legislation of the Russian Federation, with a discount of 30 per cent of their nominal value and payment in instalments over three years.

In this arrangement the value of the initial contribution may not be less than 15 per cent of the nominal value of the shares.

Option Three can only be used in enterprises with employees numbering more than 200 and a balance value of fixed assets between 1 and 50 million roubles.

The decision to choose Option Two or Three for providing benefits is taken by the general meeting of the labour collective or is certified by the signatures of its members. The decision is considered adopted if it is voted for (signed) by not less than two-thirds of all the employees. In the absence of this decision, benefits are to be provided in accordance with the first of these options.

In all options, 10 per cent of the funds received from the sale of shares (excluding shares sold to members of the labour collective of the privatized enterprise) are credited to the private personal privatization accounts of its employees.

The order of distribution of shares transferred free of charge (by selecting the first version), and the distribution and transfer of funds to the personal privatization accounts, are determined by decision of the general meeting (conference) of the labour collective.

The sale of shares to employees within the limits of the benefits established by the Programme is carried out by private subscription in accordance with the regulations approved by the State Property Committee of Russia. If the subscription's sum exceeds the amount provided for by the selected option, the commission on privatization of the enterprise reduces the shares of all employees in the same proportion, in order to comply with the above restriction.

Shares acquired or granted free of charge in the indicated order, as well as those acquired on other terms in accordance with the regulations on the sale of shares, as approved by the State Property Committee of Russia, may be sold by the shareholders without restriction.

5.5 Sale by auction means the purchase by real individuals or legal entities as private property in a trading session of the objects of privatization in cases where the buyer is not required to comply with any conditions in relation to the object of privatization.

In this case, ownership is transferred to the buyer who made the highest bid during the trading session.

In this case, employees of privatized enterprises, and individuals dismissed from an enterprise to reduce the number of employees after 1 January 1992 and registered as unemployed who do not hold the right to own property as a result of the auction, receive up to 30 per cent of the selling price of the facility, but not more than 20 per cent of the minimum monthly wage per employee as established by the legislation of the Russian Federation.

5.6 Sale by competition (commercial or non-commercial investment) is the purchase by an individual or legal entity as private property of the objects of privatization when the buyer is required to perform any of the following conditions in relation to the object of privatization (saving the profile of the enterprise or purpose of the object, the number of work positions, the funding of social facilities, the required amount of investment).

In this case, employees of privatized enterprises, as well as individuals dismissed from an enterprise to reduce the number of employees after 1 January 1992 and registered as unemployed, receive up to 20 per cent of the selling price of the object, but not more than 15 times the minimum monthly wage per employee as established by the legislation of the Russian Federation.

Commercial competition is held in the form of an open auction or private tender. In the case of commercial competition the right to the acquisition of the belongings goes to the buyer who offered the highest price.

Sale by commercial competition with restrictions on the number of participants is allowed (in accordance with local programmes of privatization) only for privatizations that are located in rural areas, small towns or the Far North, and which privatize enterprises of trade, public food services and consumer services, and enterprises that process agricultural products and provide production and maintenance for agricultural production. Participants in this competition must be employees of the privatized enterprise, residents of the area or people deported from the given area (including those outside the Russian Federation) during periods of mass repression.

During the investment competition (for investment tenders) state and municipal enterprises are sold when the buyer is required to implement investment programmes. The right ownership is hereby transferred to the buyer whose offer best fits the criteria established by the privatization plan.

The provision on investment competitions (investment trading) is to be approved by the State Property Committee of Russia.

Through the sale of state and municipal enterprises (and property of enterprises being liquidated) by competition or by auction, a partnership (joint stock company), including at least one-third of the employees on the payroll of the privatized enterprise (sub-units), when purchased (unless it is leased property being purchased) is provided a trade discount of 30 per cent interest and paid in instalments over up to three years. In this case the amount of the down payment may not be less than 25 per cent of the sale price.

5.7 Individuals and legal entities who are the owners of privatized state-owned and municipal enterprises by auction (by competition) shall be entitled to enter into long-term (at least 15 years) leases for state (municipal) non-residential premises and buildings, but which are not incorporated into the property acquired by them, and also the right to acquire ownership of the indicated premises and buildings (not earlier than one year after the entry into force of the agreement for the sale of the enterprise) and the land occupied by the enterprise, in the order established by the government of the Russian Federation. Changing the conditions in comparison with the agreements previously signed by enterprises for the leases of buildings and structures is allowed only by agreement of the parties, unless otherwise provided by the terms of the agreement.

5.8 In cases where, during the auction (competition) for the sale of privatized enterprises, an individual or legal entity, recognized by the buyer in accordance with Article 9 of the law of the Russian Federation On the Privatization of State and Municipal Enterprises in the Russian Federation, is the only bidder in the auction (competition), the enterprise is sold to the indicated person at a price determined in the manner prescribed by the State Property Committee of Russia. This sale is made within two weeks of the date of the auction (competition) by the associated property fund. In this case, employees of the enterprise who are now its buyers receive no benefits.

5.9 The sale of the property (assets) of liquidating and liquidated enterprises is conducted exclusively at auction.

In this case, employees of such an enterprise, as well as those discharged from it in order to reduce the number of employees after 1 January 1992 and registered as unemployed, are paid up to 30 per cent of the selling price of the property (assets), but not more than 20 per cent of the minimum monthly wage per employee according to the legislation of the Russian Federation.

5.10 The privatization of state and municipal property that is leased is conducted in various ways, depending on the availability of foreclosure in the lease agreement and the permission of the labour collective of the lease-holding enterprise, by decision of not less than half its members.

Leaseholders with right of redemption in accordance with the contract lease may buy out according to the following order:

- in accordance with the lease agreement entered into prior to the entry into force of the RSFSR law On the Privatization of State and Municipal Enterprises in the Russian Federation, if the size, timing, terms and conditions to make the redemption are set according to the lease agreement;
- by transforming the enterprise, acting on a rental basis of leasing state (municipal) property into a joint stock company of the open type where the leaseholders hold a priority right to purchase shares owned by the state or the local soviets of people's deputies.

The staff of the structural sub-unit that is part of a trade, public food services, or a consumer service enterprise acting on the basis of the lease agreement with the option to purchase, shall be entitled to, if taking a decision to become an independent enterprise, buy out the enterprise's leased state (municipal) property, proportionally to its share in the total production (sale) of goods and services at a discount of 30 per cent of the value stated in the contract of the lease.

The provisions of this paragraph shall apply to leasing enterprises and cooperatives only if they bring the organizational-legal form into compliance with the requirements of the legislation of the Russian Federation.

5.11 The right to purchase leased property is provided to associations created by labour collectives of structural sub-units that have separated from the enterprises created by labour collectives of state (municipal) enterprises prior to the entry into force of the RSFSR law On the Privatization of State and Municipal Enterprises in the Russian Federation on the basis of leasing the property of enterprises that do not have this right in accordance with the leasing agreement.

In these cases, the specified associations are also granted the preferential right to conclude a long-term lease agreement (for a period of not less than 15 years) for state (municipal) non-residential premises, buildings, structures, as well as the right to acquisition of the property, but not earlier than one year after the purchase of the leased property in the manner prescribed by the State Property Committee of Russia.

5.12 In 1992, state and municipal enterprises (irrespective of the limitations of their privatization) with remaining economic incentive funds in their balance and profit remaining at their disposal may create privatization funds by opening personal private privatization accounts for employees. The funds are credited to the personal private privatization accounts of the employees and are not taxable.

In 1992, all remaining economic incentive funds on balance as of 1 January 1992 and up to 50 per cent of the actual profits remaining at the disposal of the enterprise after payment of taxes and other obligatory payments may be sent to the privatization fund.

Profits derived from the sale of fixed assets of the enterprise and amortization deductions are not sent to the privatization fund.

After the privatization of state (municipal) enterprises, the funds credited to the personal private privatization accounts of workers remain in their possession. When an employee is dismissed the money may be listed on his application for another personal privatization account by request.

Ownership of the funds in the personal private privatization account of the employee may be transferred to other persons as inheritance and gifts. Funds of personal privatization accounts of workers are to be used only for the purchase of any state- and municipal-owned facilities in the process of privatization.

5.13 In order to protect the interests of employees of the privatized enterprises, upon taking the decision to file a bid for the privatization of state (municipal) enterprises (sub-unit) or from the time of application by another person or legal entity until the time when the buyer gains the right to the property (the first meeting of shareholders), it is prohibited without the consent of the associated property management committee:

- to reorganize, liquidate or restructure the enterprise;
- to modify or terminate the agreements concluded earlier for leasing non-residential premises, buildings and structures occupied by privatized enterprises.

During this period it is also prohibited to change the staffing of the enterprise or reduce the number of its employees without the consent of the labour collective of the enterprise (sub-unit) or its authorized organ.

5.14 In 1992 the following additional benefits are established under the privatization of state (municipal) enterprises:

A partnership created by employees of an enterprise where the number of disabled exceeds 50 per cent of the total number of employees has a priority right to purchase the enterprise at the residual value; if the number of people with disabilities is less than 50 per cent but more than 10 per cent of the total number of employees, the conditions of sale of the business must include the buyer's obligation to preserve within the privatization plan the number of jobs for the disabled and provide them with special conditions.

A partnership created by at least two-thirds of the total number of workers in a state (municipal) enterprise of traditional arts and crafts of the peoples of the Far North (provided that at least half the members of the partnership belong to minority ethnic communities in relation to the indigenous population of the territory), and folk arts and crafts has a priority right to acquisition at the residual value.

Under the privatization of the mining industry located in the Far North and equivalent areas, the benefits of the Programme for the members of their labour collectives also apply to former employees of enterprises who had been with them for at least five years, and those members of prospectors' teams that lease the property of the enterprise who had been with them for at least five seasons.

Under the privatization of enterprises for the primary processing of agricultural products and the production-technical provision of agricultural production, shares may be sold by private subscription to agricultural producers, recognized by buyers in accordance with the law of the Russian Federation On the Privatization of State and Municipal Enterprises in the Russian Federation, on the territory of the indicated republic of the Russian Federation, autonomous region [*oblast*], autonomous area [*okrug*], territory [*kray*] or region [*oblast*].

6 Conditions offering credit for privatization in 1992

Commercial banks of the Russian Federation and foreign banks can to provide credit transactions for privatization without restrictions.

The Central Bank of Russia does not allocate loans for these purposes.

Local programmes of privatization may provide allocation of credit resources for these purposes from the funds held at the disposal of the relevant councils (soviets) of people's deputies.

7 The use of personal privatization deposits of citizens in 1992

7.1 The system of personal privatization accounts (privatization checks) is to be introduced no later than 1 November 1992. The government of the Russian Federation shall no later than one month prior to the payment of personal privatization accounts (privatization checks) submit for approval by the Supreme Council of the Russian Federation the total amount to be paid in the form of personal privatization deposits (privatization checks), and the possible extent of payments to a single citizen.

7.2 For the provision of the circulation and the distribution of funds from the registered privatization accounts, the State Property Committee of Russia and asset funds of all levels shall create and contribute to the creation of financial institutions (investment enterprises, funds and others) and provide for extensive involvement in their business structures.

7.3 The State Property Committee of Russia and local property management committees, in order to allow citizens to acquire privatized property at the expense of personal privatization accounts (privatization checks) by 1 September 1992, shall provide enterprises with the balance value of fixed assets as of 1 January 1992 of more than 50 million roubles in the joint stock companies of the open type, with the exception of enterprises that cannot be privatized in accordance with Section 2.1 of the Programme. To this end, the leaders of the indicated enterprises are in charge of drafting documents for the establishment of joint stock companies of the open type and plans for their privatization, prepared in accordance with the law of the Russian Federation On the Privatization of State and Municipal Enterprises in the Russian Federation, the Programme, and the typical documents to be approved by the government of the Russian Federation. As agreed with labour collectives, the privatization plans are to be submitted by the leaders of the enterprises to the relevant committees of property management by 1 September 1992.

8 The use of foreign investment

8.1 The use of foreign investment under privatization of state (municipal) enterprises is permissible in the following conditions:

Foreign investors may participate in auctions, competitions and investment trades. Upon completion of transactions with foreign investors, the exclusive sellers of the privatized property are the relevant property funds.

If the foreign investor is the sole participant in an auction, competition or investment trade, the sale of the enterprise is allowed. In this case, the relevant property fund does a special evaluation of the enterprise's property according to the method approved by the State Property Committee of Russia.

Participation of foreign investors in the privatization of facilities and trade enterprises, public food services and consumer services, as well as small enterprises (up to 200 workers on average with a balance value as of 1 January 1992 of up to 1 million roubles) and enterprises of industry and construction and automobile transport, is permitted only by decision of the local soviets of people's deputies or organs authorized by them.

The decision on allowing foreign investors to participate in the privatization of facilities and enterprises of the fuel and energy complex, and enterprises for the mining and processing of ores, precious and semi-precious stones, precious metals, radioactive elements and rare earths is taken by the government of the Russian Federation or the government of the republics of the Russian Federation (depending on the kind of state ownership) simultaneously with the taking of the decision on the admissibility of the privatization of the facilities and enterprises.

Other restrictions on the participation of foreign investors in privatization are not imposed.

8.2 Reciprocal payments with foreign investors upon completing transactions are conducted in the currency of the Russian Federation with special accounts opened in banks in accordance with the legislation of the Russian Federation.

The use under privatization of rouble shares of foreign investors and enterprises with foreign is to be in accordance with the legislation of the Russian Federation.

8.3 Foreign individuals who are not registered as entrepreneurs in their country of origin are recognized as foreign investors with respect to their participation in privatization.

9 The order of interrelations of state privatization organs among themselves, with other organs of state management and budgets of all levels

9.1 The sellers of state (municipal) enterprises and other facilities of state (municipal) property are the respective property funds.

When making decisions about privatization, within their competency within the Programme, the government of the Russian Federation and the Russian State Property Committee represent the interests of the autonomous regions [*oblast*], autonomous areas [*okrug*], territories [*kray*], regions [*oblast*], and the cities of Moscow and St Petersburg, and provide for their defence.

Control of the implementation and legality of the privatization transactions is assigned to the appropriate standing committees of the various soviets of people's deputies.

In regions where property funds (branches of the Russian Fund of federal property) are not set up, all of their functions given to the corresponding soviets of people's deputies (Russian Foundation federal property) are temporarily performed by the appropriate committees for property management.

9.2 From the moment the decision is taken to privatize an enterprise, the powers delegated by the relevant committee on property management to the ministries, agencies or organs of local administrations are repealed.

9.3 The ministries and departments of the Russian Federation are developing and reaching an accord with the State Committee of the Russian Federation for Anti-monopoly Policy and Support of New Economic Structures and submitting to the State Property Committee of Russia and the Russian Fund of Federal Property recommendations for accounting for special characteristics of the enterprises of the sector taken into account in the implementation of privatization and the exercise of the powers of the owner.

9.4 For the exercise of the powers of the owner at meetings of the shareholders of joint stock companies, the majority of whose controlling shares are assigned to the state, property funds of corresponding levels may draw upon on a contract basis representatives of the relevant ministries and departments of the Russian Federation and the officials of the administration of the enterprises.

10 Formation of special-purpose financial funds using the revenue received from privatization

10.1 The funds received from privatization means all the cash proceeds from the sale of the objects of privatization and other revenues obtained in the course of privatization (including the registration fee, deposit and so on).

Dividends and rental payments being received by property funds and property management committees are not included in the composition of the revenues of privatization and are subject to being transferred to the appropriate budget, accounting for the expenses of the banking operations.

10.2 The funds received from privatization, except for those of personal privatization accounts (privatization checks), at the disposal of the various soviets of people's deputies in accordance with the norms established by the Programme, shall be used for the formation of special purpose funds for:

- social security;
- implementation of environmental protection measures;
- de-monopolization and restructuring;
- development of the social and engineering infrastructure of cities and regions, as well as covering the budgetary deficit.

Using the funds received from the privatization of federal property held in the operational management of the Armed Forces of the Russian Federation, the Ministry of Security of the Russian Federation and Ministry of Internal Affairs of the Russian Federation, there shall be created a federal fund for the social security of military servicemen.

10.3 The order for the formation and consumption of the special purpose funds, as well as the amount of funds allocated for these purposes, are defined by the relevant councils of people's deputies.

11 Requirements for local programmes of privatization

11.1 Local programmes of privatization are developed by the committees of property management of the republics of the Russian Federation, autonomous regions [*oblast*], autonomous districts [*okrug*], territories [*kray*], regions [*oblast*], cities (except for those cities of regional subordination), districts [*raion*] (excluding those in cities), and are undertaken by the appropriate councils of people's deputies, who are free to establish for the lower organs of state power and management (organs of local self-governance) tasks of privatization in accordance with the Programme.

11.2 Local privatization programmes must be developed (revised) in accordance with the requirements of the Programme and approved (reinstated) no later than one month after its publication. After that the local programmes must be published in the organs of the press of the corresponding councils of people's deputies and presented to the State Property Committee of Russia.

11.3 The local privatization programmes are approved for one year and must meet the following mandatory requirements:

They must not contradict the Programme, not include proposals for the privatization of facilities and enterprises which are not eligible for privatization or have restrictions (other than Section 2.4) in accordance with the Programme, and not impose additional restrictions on the privatization of facilities and enterprises.

They must ensure full compliance with mandatory requirements and tasks established by the Programme.

They must list concrete facilities (groups of facilities), subject to mandatory privatization, in providing for the enforcement of calculation indicators and the obligatory tasks of the Programme.

They must include projections of the funds to be received from privatization and the order and direction for their use.

They must contain a list of the restrictions on privatization, established in accordance with Section 2.4 of the Programme.

They must contain specific measures for de-monopolization and the creation of a concrete environment, by the use of special purpose non-budget funds and foreign investment.

11.4 Property management committees of the republics of the Russian Federation, the autonomous regions [*oblast*], autonomous areas [*okrug*], territories [*kray*], regions [*oblast*], cities and districts [*raion*] with the consent of the corresponding supreme soviets, and the councils of people's deputies can make changes to republican and local privatization programmes.

11.5 The form and deadlines for reporting on the fulfilment of the tasks being established by the Programme are determined by the State Property Committee of Russia and the Russian Federal Property Fund by agreement with the State Committee of the Russian Federation Statistics.

11.6 Responsibility for the implementation of local programmes of privatization is given to representatives of the local councils of people's deputies and property funds, to the heads of the administrations and the representatives of local committees for the management of property.

11.7 Control over the implementation of local programmes of privatization is the responsibility of the State Property Committee of Russia.

Appendix 2

The role of associations

As discussed in Chapter 4 above, a key objective of voucher privatization was to avoid the threat from "associations". The following is the text of a memo from Bob Anderson and other consultants at GKI on the results of their investigations into these bodies.

From: Nicholas Barberis, Natasha Mamedova and Bob Anderson
Date: 30 June 1992
Re: Summary of what we know about "associations"

Over the past few weeks we have visited 15 industry "associations", meeting with their presidents or senior staff working on privatization. We wanted to know what an "association" is, what functions it performs, how it is paid for these services, and what its plans are for the future. Also of interest is the legal status of the firms within each association: are they state owned, leased, or joint-stock companies? This memo summarizes what we now know on the subject. For more details and information please turn to other memos (one was written for each association meeting)....

An association is simply a group of enterprises. The enterprises delegate functions to the association and pay a fee for the services performed.

Normally, but not always, an association contains the enterprises that were once controlled by one of the former ministries. For instance, 90 per cent of the enterprises in the former ministry of construction materials are now part of the construction materials association, Rosstrom. However, when the ministry for construction of heavy machinery for the energy industry broke up at the end of 1990, no fewer than nine associations were formed in its place.

Associations exist in two forms. They are either a "voluntary association" or a "joint-stock company". About half of our sample were joint-stock companies. They made transition to a JSC quite legally under the now famous "Statute 601" of December 1990. Some of the associations, while not JSC's themselves, do contain JSC's within them, such as banks or trading houses.

So what purpose do these structures serve? We give a list of the main functions and then go into each in more detail:

1 Representing the interests of the constituent firms
2 Supply coordination
3 Implementation of R&D
4 Marketing
5 Investment/financing
6 Production coordination

1 Representing the firms

This is perhaps the most important function. The associations act as a lobby in dealings with all kinds of organizations: the national government, governments of other republics, institutions abroad, and indeed the Ministry of State Property. For instance the transportation construction association Transstroi listed their most important role as representing the strength of the Russian construction industry on the world stage.

2 Supply coordination

What this involves is fairly clear: maintaining links between firms and their suppliers. There are two reasons why it is hard for the individual enterprises to do this themselves. First, some of the most important inter-firm links are those across republic boundaries. These have been breaking up recently leading to a large downturn in output in the Russian economy. It is difficult for an enterprise to conduct cross-republic negotiations and so it delegates this job to the association. For instance, the automobile construction association Avtoselkhozmash prides itself that it has managed to keep links across republics intact and thus kept the output level in the industry constant.

A second problem is that in this inflationary environment, suppliers do not want to receive money in return for their goods. Thus they engage in barter, and it falls to the association to arrange the complicated network of barter transactions.

3 Implementation of R&D

Associations often contain research institutes (which once belonged to the ministries) and so coordinate interaction between the firms and the institutes. However many of these institutes are independent and operate directly with the firms on a contract basis. Associations also have the technical expertise to advise firms whether they should receive R&D support from these institutes or others abroad. For example, the corporation of electrical technology and appliance building lists R&D support as one of their most important functions.

4 Marketing

This is taking on new importance as the government is no longer the sole customer. Some associations are actively seeking out foreign customers. They are also setting up so called "trading houses" within the association to act as an interface with the market. Marketing devices such as advertising are also dealt with by the association.

5 Investment/financing

Associations help their firms find investment partners for new projects, or, more often, projects which are unfinished through lack of funds. They often look abroad to do this.

Many associations are also attempting to set up "investment funds". These are a way of pooling resources from the constituent enterprises and using them for the good of the industry, or to help some ailing firm. The association may know which are the most profitable investment opportunities (they are better informed) and therefore firms' deposits could earn a good rate of return. In particular firms might do better this way than by turning to a bank. A more skeptical view is that the associations will squander deposits by supporting losing firms when it would be more efficient to liquidate them. In the new commercial environment, we doubt whether profitable enterprises will voluntarily agree to provide financial support to money-losing firms.

6 Production coordination

It is expected that over the next few years many firms will change their product mix to a more consumer-friendly one. Associations hope to organize such production within their industry so that the right amount of different kinds of output are produced to meet the prevailing level of demand.

At present these services are paid for in two ways, both based on a contract set-up: either a fixed fee is paid every year or the association takes a percentage of the deal. Some associations have a menu of services they offer; firms choose what they want and usually a combination of the two payment schemes is used.

The importance of associations is declining over time. Already the staff of these structures is often only a third of what it used to be when the former ministry existed. They correctly see their role as organizer of supplies diminishing over time, especially once the market system takes hold.

However they say that there will be a continuing role for them implementing R&D and as a lobby organization. They also claim their marketing and investment functions will grow in importance. In future they will advise firms on investment decisions and on their dealings with banks and the stock exchange. It is hard, however, to believe that these functions will remain with the associations beyond a few years.

One other function which we have not yet mentioned is helping the firms with the process of corporatization and privatization. This is closely tied up with the future structure of the associations, so we now turn to this topic.

Some of the "voluntary associations" are happy to remain as such. These are normally the associations that do not think they will be able to perform many useful functions in the future. Firms are free to leave them if they so wish, but at the moment, few of them are.

Other associations however have much more active plans, which almost always involve the formation of holding companies. It should be noted that GKI has no official policy on holding companies. We now describe how these companies might be formed.

First, each of the enterprises within the association will be corporatized and the usual initial distribution of shares made according to GKI plans: 35 per cent to the workers in total and 5 per cent to the managers. The remaining 60 per cent from each firm would be lumped together to form the founding capital of a holding company. But who will own shares in the holding company?

Many people misunderstand what the associations are really trying to do. They think that the associations want the government to own the holding company so that they can return to a ministerial style of governance i.e. of centralized planning. But it seems that this is mistaken. The real driving force behind the formation of these holding companies is the enterprises, in particular the managers. They want the holding company to be owned, not by the government, but by the enterprises. This may seem very strange, indeed meaningless, but to understand the motivation for their plans, we remind readers of the current ownership structure of firms.

Firms were once controlled by branch ministries, and owned by the government. As the branch ministries were phased out, although the government nominally remained the owner of the enterprises, the effective owners (in the sense of who had control rights) changed.

Managers, workers, and local governments began moving into the ownership vacuum created as the ministries declined. This distinction between nominal ownership and effective control is very important in what we discuss below. It means that the government is not now able to use its assets, the firms, as it sees fit. Others now have control rights as well. Thus the GKI programme of benefits to workers and managers can be interpreted as a "payment" or "bribe" to these parties so that they relinquish their control rights, enabling the government to sell the rest of the shares as it likes.

But let's get back to those holding companies. The associations are proposing a bizarre (to westerners) plan. First, as we said before, the holding company would own 60 per cent of each of the constituent enterprises. Second, this holding company would be owned, not by the property funds, but by the enterprises themselves! But wait a minute! That means the holding company owns part of the enterprises, and the enterprises own the holding company! So no one actually owns 60 per cent of the enterprises. To us, this seems bizarre: the privatization process which is meant to define ownership rights is leaving the ownership of 60 per cent of the shares unclear.

The enterprises, however, rather like this idea. Just as the managers and workers gained effective control when the branch ministries collapsed, so they hope that effective control over this unclaimed 60 per cent defaults to them over time. This could easily happen, because under their plan, no one has clear control over these shares.

This incredible scheme occurs again in a very popular (with the enterprises) plan for privatization which has been presented by the minister of industry, Mr. Titkin. He has a different proposal. Remember that 60 per cent of shares that does not go to the workers or managers? Only a small amount of this, say 20 per cent, would go to forming a holding company. Of course, this holding company will be owned by the enterprises, in accordance with the little trick we saw above.

The remaining 40 per cent of each firm, however, would be distributed to other firms in the association, especially suppliers. Note that what this effectively means is that all the enterprises own shares in each other. The associations say that the point of this plan is to strengthen ties between firm and supplier, to establish a stable relationship. However, the most striking feature of the proposal is the extent to which the managers stand to gain. One way of thinking about this is the following. The suppliers and other enterprises who own 40 per cent of the shares are probably long-time business partners of the manager and would probably agree not to exercise the control rights represented by the shares they own. One can imagine an agreement of the kind: "Don't meddle in my firm, and I won't meddle in yours". In this way the control rights of these shares would come straight back to the manager.

However, we have to think about this more carefully. For the ownership of these 40 per cent of shares is not defined. The supplier partly owns the firm, which partly owns the supplier etc. The ownership of the shares has been left open and again, managers hope that these unclaimed control rights default to them.

We repeat that we think it is the managers that support plans such as Titkin's. These plans were not conjured up by the association staff. They merely lobby on behalf of the enterprises, and try to explain the system as a means of strengthening ties between firms and suppliers. A discussion of whether the latter is a good idea is beyond the scope of this paper.

An important issue concerning the associations' activities and proposals for holding companies is their impact on competition. On the whole, associations no longer coordinate prices, though some do in external markets. The formation of holding companies, however, could easily lead to a monopoly in the industry and such structures are likely to come into conflict with future anti-trust legislation.... The majority of firms within each association are still government owned and would therefore go through the GKI programme. There are exceptions: in the Russian light industry association only 20 per cent of firms are still state owned. The rest are leased enterprises and joint-stock companies (closed type).

Another issue we discussed with the associations was their view of the GKI privatization programme. A number of comments emerged several times and we summarize them below:

- Associations varied in what they thought of the benefits given to workers in the programme. Some thought they were too generous, some not generous enough. We mentioned above that in the programme the government is effectively buying back control rights from the workers and it seems that the benefits given in the programme are a sufficient payment.
- The programme is not liked by very labor-intensive industries, nor by very capital-intensive industries. In the former, 25 per cent of the shares does not

represent a very generous payment, because of the low capital stock. In very capital-intensive industries, the limitation of 20 monthly salaries worth of shares is binding and so employees cannot receive the full 25 per cent.

- There is also a general sentiment that managers do not get enough benefits: 5 per cent of the shares at book value. It is believed that the government has to offer a lot more to buy back control rights from the managers. We are very sympathetic to this view.
- Another problem arises with enterprises that are leased without the right to buy. Under the GKI programme it appears that such enterprises will be treated like state enterprises and will have to go through the process specified in the programme. However they want to be given the right to buy on favorable terms, and it may be easier for the government to allow them to do this.

Conclusion

Associations are an important structure in the Russian economy. Firms delegate certain important functions to the associations and usually pay for the services by a contract system. Some of the functions will die away, but others will remain and indeed grow in importance.

We emphasize again that it is the enterprises (workers, but mostly managers) that are behind the formation of holding companies and that this is largely driven by their dissatisfaction with the benefits offered to them in the GKI programme. It seems to us that GKI is not "bribing" the managers enough to persuade them to relinquish their control rights over the firm, which they acquired after the demise of the ministries. To check these conclusions we plan to visit some enterprises and talk to the managers.

Appendix 3

Inter-enterprise debt

The buildup of inter-enterprise debt was one feature of the chaotic situation which faced Russian companies following price liberalization in January 1992. The following memorandum describes the nature of Russia's enterprise debt in summer 1992,[1] *and describes the plans developed by GKI and its consultants, working under a presidential decree, to resolve them in a way which would minimize inflationary impact, and how those plans were frustrated. It is included here to illustrate the lack of coordination and planning which surrounded reforms, and the disorder of policy making in 1992–93.*

Inter-enterprise debt background

At the end of June 1992, the indebtedness of state enterprises to each other had reached more than three trillion roubles. The main cause of this indebtedness was the failure of the banking settlement system.

There had been two methods of processing a payment between two enterprises through the banking system. The seller could send a payment demand to his bank, who forwards the demand through the banking system to the buyer's bank. If the buyer has insufficient funds to meet the payment, the unpaid demand had traditionally been recorded in the buyer's kartoteka 2 (K2) memo account. In general, no cash was credited to the seller's account; the K2 is off the bank's balance sheet. The K2 is therefore a partial listing of the buyer's accounts payable.

Alternatively, the buyer could place a payment order with his own bank. If there are no funds to cover the order, it is returned to the seller and should not be recorded in the K2. It is believed that the system of payment demands predominated for payments before 1.7.92, but that it was discontinued on this date.

The K2 should record all unpaid payment demands for goods and services which have been processed through the banking system and reached the buyer's account. It is not clear the extent to which the K2 also includes unpaid payment demands for other than goods and services.

The total value of items in K2 accounts had soared since January 1992, to represent a sum much greater than Russian GNP. The reasons for this growth are unclear, but are likely to include the following:

1. The number of unprofitable businesses, unable to meet their trading debts, has grown with price liberalization in January 1992, and with the removal of state subsidies to many firms.
2. The bank clearing system has fragmented with the break-up of the USSR and with the subsequent break-up of many banks.
3. Volumes passing through the clearing system have increased with the creation of more banks, the creation of small private enterprises, and with the decline of large single state orders for output.

Further reasons include the increased cost to enterprises of bank borrowing; inflation; and poor financial management at enterprises.

The direct consequences for the GKI of this growth of credit were twofold: the balance sheets of enterprises to be privatized are likely to include huge values of accounts payable and accounts receivable, sufficient to dissuade investors; and fundamentally unprofitable businesses, who should be bankrupt rather than privatized, survive. More broadly, the growth of credit undermines the strict macroeconomic monetary regime which is central to the reformists' agenda, of which privatisation is a part.

The Central Bank has initiated two procedures designed to reduce the value of items in K2 accounts. The Act on the Settlement of Payments (ASP) summarized the net indebtedness of enterprises as on 1.7.92. The scope and implementation of the ASP is unclear; it appeared to have had little effect.

The implementation of the ASP was interrupted by the creation of "725" accounts, the second Central Bank initiative. It is believed that a 725 account was set up for each state enterprise, and that 725 accounts, together with "160" accounts at commercial banks, formed a closed system, administered entirely by the banks.

Each 725 account was then credited with an amount equal to the lesser of: the value of unpaid payment demands for goods and services from other state enterprises, recorded in K2 on 1.7.92; and the value of all debtors on the balance sheet of the firm on 1.7.92. Qualifying K2 items were then processed through the 725 accounts using the central bank opening credit. To the extent that the 725 accounts remained closed, the central bank credits were not money, but quasi-money. Each enterprise should end up with a positive, zero or negative balance on its 725 account. The sum of 725 balances across enterprises should be zero. The size and distribution of net balances on 725 accounts was for a long time unknown.

However, prior to these Central Bank initiatives, on 1 July 1992, by Decree No. 720, President Yeltsin made the GKI responsible for creating an Agency to "Normalise Payment and Accounting Relations in the Economy of Russia", shifting responsibility for inter-enterprise debt onto the GKI.

In September, the Strategic Design group of the Consortium were asked to present a plan for handling the inter-enterprise debt in such a way as to minimize any inflationary impact there might be. Under the proposed plan, all 725 balances would be vested in the GKI Agency for Inter-enterprise Debt. The Agency would thereby have become the debtor or creditor of the enterprises. Creditors would only receive cash to the extent that debtors had paid cash to the Agency. If the Agency had no cash, it would have been empowered to issue long-term paper to the creditor enterprises which would represent assets of the enterprise. The total effect would therefore have been noninflationary.

WORK DONE

On October 15th, the Consortium were asked to set up such an agency. A team was rapidly assembled and detailed action plans drawn to establish the Agency.

The Central Bank, however, having not been consulted by the GKI, was proceeding to the next part of its plan to resolve the situation: it allowed credit balances to be used to pay indebtedness to the Government or to commercial banks. It also allowed commercial banks to lend money to enterprises for the settlement of debit balances, even making short term loans to the banks to facilitate this.

The ultimate effect of these actions was to reduce the Inter-enterprise Debt to an irreducible debit balance of 215 billion roubles by the end of October. (This balance represented only the debts which were on the books of banks and enterprises at the end of June 1992.) The Central Bank's action injected nearly one trillion roubles into the economy.

Without the assistance of the Central Bank, it would be impossible to define the true extent of the remaining Inter-enterprise Debt, since all information about the debtor enterprises is held at the level of the commercial bank (accessible only through the Central Bank). Hence the role of the Agency was undermined; furthermore, hyperinflation was now threatening to reduce the remaining balances even further. Less than a month after giving the go ahead to the Agency, the GKI were forced to suspend its work. [Consulting] staff were reassigned to more pressing areas.

NEXT STEPS

The Central Bank and the GKI still need to resolve the question of how to deal with the remaining balances. The GKI have not set up the Agency required by Yeltsin's Decree, and take the position that Inter-Enterprise Debt is the Central Bank's problem; the Central Bank have stated that the IED is the GKI's problem…

Appendix 4

The conduct of voucher auctions in the Russian regions

This appendix consists of two notes written for this book by senior western consultants employed to monitor and assist with voucher auctions in Smolensk and Novosibirsk. Between them, they give a sense of the degree of control which the central Moscow authorities had over the privatization process, and how in practice they were carried out. For further discussion, see Chapter 4 above.

Smolensk voucher auctions

NICOLA RAMSDEN

My diaries record 16 visits to the city of Smolensk between 28 February 1993 and 24 January 1994. Each visit was for two to four days. We cancelled visits in October 1993 during the siege of the White House but returned to Smolensk immediately following the elections in December 1993.

The first visit in February 1993 included a briefing from the western consultancy that had made first contacts for the EBRD there. They had already set up an office in the local administration's building, staffed by two bright young languages graduates from Smolensk. A junior consultant from Deloitte & Touche moved to Smolensk shortly after. This team ensured continuity in between visits from me and other senior consultants based in Moscow. It's easy to forget that we were still communicating mainly by phone and fax.

Subsequent visits over the following year went through the cycle of voucher auctions and follow-up work, such as advising on share registration systems. At an early stage we were asked to provide good computers for the auction process. It was difficult to buy modern PCs locally at that time, and bureaucracy and primitive payment systems meant that we had to use a colleague's credit card to buy imported equipment in Moscow. The Smolensk administration sent a van with guards to drive the computers to Smolensk at the end of April. I drove my own car behind the convoy and remember thinking that the van's flashing light was a good way of alerting highway robbers. When we added a laser printer to the equipment the following month, I drove it there myself without mentioning it to the local officials.

The Smolensk auctions were on a smaller scale than other regional cities. We had expected to be needed to help to run the auctions (we had been through earlier training on the Zil auction in Moscow) and were bemused to find ourselves kept generally at arm's length from the auctions themselves.

In the nine-week gap between our first visit and delivering the computers we saw that the Property Fund staff had already set up the auction systems on their existing computers. After we delivered ours, expecting that they would replace the old ones, we never saw them again. When I mentioned this to the GKI in Moscow the response was that they would be just as useful as sweeteners for officials in the local GKI and Property Fund.

We received detailed reports of the auction outcomes after the event. The official in charge of these was keen to demonstrate that correct procedures were being followed, but was otherwise a master of stonewalling impassiveness. He gave the impression that it was insulting to suggest that he might need help – he'd had his instructions from Moscow and knew how to get on with them.

We asked a Russian member of the consultancy team to investigate whether there was any significant pattern to the auction results and he soon confirmed that the outcome in Smolensk was similar to that being reported elsewhere. The general directors of many of the firms being auctioned had bought or bartered vouchers from their employees so that by the time the auctions took place, they (and/or their family and friends) could bid for a controlling stake.

The GKI in Moscow and the EBRD seemed relaxed about this – by then they seemed to take the view that the existing managers were probably the best people to own as well as run local firms, and if an effective management buy-out was the result, it was not necessarily a bad thing. We found it hard to tell whether this had been the expected – even intended – outcome all along and whether models of share-owning democracy were never thought to be realistic at that stage. My recollection is that pragmatism prevailed and we moved quite quickly to projects connected with developing secondary markets. Perhaps it was hoped that the need for further capital would eventually result in more widespread share ownership.

Privatization in Novosibirsk

JOSHUA BOWER SAUL

> "Do Moskvy daleko, do tsarja esche vyshe."
> *Moscow is far away and the Tsar still further.*

The privatization process

The case of western Siberia is particularly instructive due to the close ties of the economic establishment with Moscow and its strategic importance as an R&D hub for the 50 years since the Akademgorodok was founded there to bring together the brightest minds of the USSR. Their original focus was to provide the military and the economic establishment with innovations and engineering capability.

The USAID in conjunction with the EBRD made the western Siberia effort a keystone in its experiments to support privatization. The hope was that by privatizing the Novosibirsk industrial R&D centres a plethora of innovative companies would arrive on the Russian market. In this framework, the programme envisaged not only a series of "Entrepreneurial Centres" in these provincial cities, but, in the case of Novosibirsk, likewise a new stock market linked electronically to Moscow, a separate privatization centre and an auction centre with several new banks providing the management of stocks, bonds, vouchers and financial support to the companies involved.

At the time the process began in western Siberia some 700 major enterprises were meant to come to auction and 1,000 lesser companies could be considered as well. Given that the rhythm that the GKI had set for what the privatization process was to achieve, including the entire corporatization within nine months, the 20 administrators and 50 consultants that cycled in and out of the region had to achieve a throughput of more than 20 businesses per week give or take. The task was clearly impossible and the region was left more or less on its own in terms of how it was to achieve the goal.

Given the 40 or more years that many of the officials and business officers of the corporatized entities had been working under a plan mentality, the plan to privatize was treated just the same as the old plan: "exaggerate the need for inputs and overstate the output, and keep the difference". In this regard, the GKI at local levels blatantly told consultants what values they would expect or accept for this or that enterprise and charged the teams representing the case in Moscow to play the role of the Soviet era "Tolkach" (or "Fixer"). The fixer was meant to get ministries and Plan Officials to agree to "reality" and bring targets down or carry volumes over into the next plan period when production or supply issues menaced bonuses for plan completion.

Often, privatizations took place in a totally uncontrolled process even before a company was "listed" for auction. In the local jargon this was called "spontaneous privatization" and amounted to blatant administrative transfer of state assets to a small group of like-minded managers or cronies. This process again involved transfer of share packages and money to decision makers. Some of the organizers of spontaneous privatization openly became very rich.

Setting up a privatization centre

The pressure on local teams was high enough that when in 1993 a plan was developed to open a series of privatization centres and auction houses as a means of "industrializing" the process, regional officials jumped on the bandwagon. Such centres existed in Moscow and had been successful in channeling operations in such classic privatizations as the Red October Confectionary Factory and others. In Siberia, operating such a centre was not so clear cut. The local and regional administrators of the Novosibirsk region basically gave carte blanche to consultants to choose, design, build and operate the Auction Centre.

The best and only available building in the short term turned out to be the first floor grocery store that supplied dairy and meat products to the workers of the state engineering and design facility in the middle of downtown. This business was a supplier of ventilation systems to military factories and to some military vehicles and was classified top secret, meaning no foreigner could enter even the front door theoretically. The problem was resolved by the creation of a Russian identity card with top secret clearance for one of the consultants, allowing him to run the site and operate the auction centre. When it was determined that the second floor would also be required as a back office for managing vouchers and "blind auction" processes, the institute demurred at allowing foreigners up the stairs. When the western team recommended building a spiral staircase up from the auction floor toilets into the back office area, the welders were called within 24 hours. To the news that the auction house must open on 9 March in order for the plan to be fulfilled, the furniture first chosen by the team was cancelled and a local wood shop and designer engaged to conceive, source and deliver the auction centre's furnishings within two weeks. The consultants worked alone with the carpenters many a long night and weekend gluing and painting the furniture. Delivery and installation was done on the March 8th women's day holiday under driving snow – covered by the local television as a "milestone in privatization's progress in the regions". The holiday being traditionally quite a well-lubricated affair, the installation party went rather well.

This type of efficiency of decision making and execution was unheard of in Russia at that time, and translated the clear motivation of the officials to be seen fulfilling their privatization "plan".

Voucher trading

With 150 million vouchers distributed, they soon became an instrument for speculation. At the outset prices for the voucher began to vary around the $9 mark in the key centres where considerable numbers of enterprises were up for sale. The most striking aspect was that very early discrepancies arose in the spot market for vouchers as a function of exactly what was being privatized where and by whom. Mixed cash and voucher schemes arose in Siberia in the auction houses to deal with the shortage of vouchers created by the concentration of the "most attractive" enterprises in the western part of the country. It was on this basis that a number of operators in the eastern reaches of Russia, and indeed some western investment banks managed the process of arbitration on voucher values.

In essence, the provincial rate of exchange of a voucher varied at about a 20 to 30 per cent discount to the Moscow or St Petersburg rates in dollars and these rates were carefully monitored by a few tech savvy boys in the East who built brokerages to buy and trade vouchers and later privatized company share blocks obtained with the vouchers. Their principal clients were the celebrated trusts. By buying up vouchers in the hinterland of Siberia these teams gathered considerable quantities of the vouchers and then flew them to Moscow or St Petersburg in time for key auctions taking place in those markets. The vouchers would then be sold on the grey market for dollars. Of course the dollar rate for roubles was better as well in the hinterland, so the double arbitration yielded profits of 20 to 30 per cent per week.

Notes

Introduction

1 Among numerous surveys of the Soviet economy on the eve of privatization, see Åslund (1994); Gaddy and Ickes (2002); Hanson (1993; 2003); and the collection of articles in Hewett (1991).
2 Or "orgy of plunder", see Hedlund (2008: 191).
3 For a recent review of the economic theory associated with transition policies in Central Europe and the CIS, see Mickiewicz (2005: 26) and Chapters 2–4. See also Åslund (2008); Åslund *et al.* (1993); Shleifer and Treisman (2000); Granville (1995); Gustafson (1999).
4 An extended discussion of the groups forming around "models" is in Mau (2010: III, 364–8).
5 "On Implementation of the USSR Law: On Individual Labour Activity." *Ved SSSR* (Supreme Soviet USSR), 19 November 1986, No. 47, Item 965, sec. 1.
6 On the Establishment in the Territory of the USSR and Operation of Joint Ventures with the Participation of Soviet Organizations and Firms from Capitalist and Developing Countries, No. 49, *Sobrfanie Postanovlenii [SP] SSSR,* No. 9, Item 40.
7 On State Enterprise, *Ved. SSSR*, 30 June 1987, No. 26, Item 385.
8 On Cooperatives, *Ved. SSSR*, 26 May 1988, No. 22, Item 355.
9 See Feldbrugge (1922).
10 Principles of Legislation of the USSR and of the Union Republics on Lease. *Ved. S''ezdov Narodnykh Deputatov i Verkhovnogo Soveta 1989*, 23 November 1989, No. 25, Item 481.
11 On Approving Regulations on Joint Stock Companies and Companies with Limited Liability and Regulations on Securities, Decree No. 590 of the USSR Council of Ministers, 19 June 1990.
12 Such as Gazprom, Rosugol', Rosneft and Mosfil'm (see Ustiuzhanina 2001: 83).
13 Russian Law On Property, 24 December 1990, *Ved. S''ezdov Narodnykh Deputatov RSFSR i Verkhovnogo Soveta*, No. 30, Item 416; law On Enterprises and Entrepreneurial Activity, 25 December 1990, ibid., Item 418.
14 On the Privatization of State and Municipal Enterprises in the RSFSR, *Ved. RSFSR*, 3 July 1991, No. 29, Item 927; On Fundamental Basis of De-statization and Privatization of Firms, Regulation of Supreme Soviet USSR, 1 July 1991, No. 2279-1.
15 Before then, numerous forms of privatization, called "spontaneous" privatization by the popular press, were evident: "imprecise legislation, policy paralysis at all levels of government, the breakdown of the state supply system, and continued excess demand, have allowed managers of state firms to initiate 'spontaneous privatization' – through which managers and other individuals are effectively obtaining property rights which previously belonged to ministries, planners and the Communist Party" (Johnson 1992: 1).

1 Privatization and the Russian transition: perspectives

1 Also known as "voucher privatization".
2 Mikhail Gorbachev (1931–), President and General Secretary of the Communist Party of the Soviet Union (1985–91).
3 See also Åslund (1994) for an analysis of economic reforms in the late Soviet era, and Appel (2004: 71–6) for a survey of works on early reform efforts.
4 For instance, the 1987 Soviet Law on State Enterprises broadened the parameters for private ownership without delineating the relationship between the central government and firms. Similarly, the Law on Privatization of State and Municipal Enterprises, ratified by the Russian parliament in 1991, was so general in its formulation that most of its contents were later superseded by presidential decrees.
5 "CPSU Panel Views Destatization, Privatization", *Pravda*, 20 May 1991, p. 2 (FBIS-SOV-91–099, 22 May 1991).
6 Interview with Mikhail Gorbachev, 17 June 1991 (FBIS-SOV-91–116, 17 June 1991).
7 Boris Yeltsin (1931–2007), first president of Russia (1991–99).
8 The Supreme Soviet of the RSFSR (Verkhovniy Sovet RSFSR), later Supreme Soviet of the Russian Federation, was the supreme government institution of the Russian SFSR in 1938–90. Between 1990 and 1993, it was a permanent parliament, elected by the Congress of People's Deputies of the Russian Federation.
9 The supreme legislative body in the Soviet Union (1989–91), created by Gorbachev.
10 For a study of the politics of this period, see Mau (1996); Gustafson (1999); McFaul (2004: 58), among others.
11 Ruslan Khasbulatov (1942–) left the Communist Party in August 1991; he became speaker of the Supreme Soviet in 1991, and in 1993 led the Supreme Soviet in its power struggle against Boris Yeltsin.
12 Anatoly Chubais reported:

> As soon as the decision on commencing privatization was approved by the Russian government (this happened at its last session in 1991) Boris Yeltsin interrupted the session and got in touch with Ruslan Khasbulatov, the speaker of the Russian parliament. Originally, the program was expected to be put through parliament, implying its adoption no earlier than February, and hence a halt in the course of the entire reform. Khasbulatov seemed to appreciate Yeltsin's arguments, convened the Supreme Soviet's Presidium and the same night the program received unanimous support at a joint meeting of the government and parliament's leadership.

See interview with Anatoly Chubais, Chairman of the Russian Federation State Committee for Control and Management of Property, *Moscow News*, 19–26 January 1992, p. 10 (FIBIS-SOV-92–026, 7 February 1992).
13 The point regarding incentives is made in Stavrakis (1993), cited in Huskey (1996: 365). See also Vasiliev *et al.* (1999).
14 The leadership of the Supreme Soviet passed to its chief executive in 1990 (Boris Yeltsin to 10 July, Ruslan Khasbulatov as acting chairman after 10 July and then chairman from 29 October 1991 to 4 October 1992).
15 On 12 June 1991, he became the first popularly elected chief executive in Russia, as president of the Russian Soviet Federative Socialist Republic, with 57 per cent of the vote.
16 "Khazbulatov Warns against 'Dictatorship'", *TASS International Service*, 16 January 1992 (FBIS-SOV-92–013, 21 January 1992); "Critical of Privatization Strategy", *INTERFAX*, 20 January 1992 (FBIS-SOV-92–014, 22 January 1991).
17 Cited in Colton (2008, ebook location 3504, 3513).
18 Yegor Gaidar (1956–2009) was a Soviet and Russian economist, politician and author, and acting prime minister of Russia from 15 June 1992 to 14 December 1992 and, as such, the key author of the radical reforms.

19 Interview on PBS programme "The Commanding Heights", transcript at: www.pbs.org/wgbh/commandingheights/shared/minitext/int_yegorgaidar.html#5, accessed on 13 October 2012. Also see McFaul (2004: 140).

20 "Economic Official Discusses Privatisation", *Moscow Russian Television Network*, 18 February 1992 (FBIS-SOV-92–035, 21 February 1992).

21 "Psychological Barriers to Market Economy Persist", *Izvestiia*, 26 March 1991 (FBIS-SOV-91–063, 2 April 1992).

22 Ibid.: 44.

23 See Bruno (1992) for a consideration of the few alternatives available to Central and Eastern European states at that time, with each scenario likely to result in output collapse.

24 In Soviet times, inter-company trades were not conducted in roubles, which could be monetized for purchases other than those from other enterprises that had been agreed in the plan. They might be thought of as "accounting entries" rather than "money".

25 Viktor Gerashchenko (1937–), president of Gosbank of the USSR 1989–91, and, from 17 June 1992 to 14 October 1994, head of the Central Bank of the Russian Federation.

26 Private interview with Viktor Gerashchenko, 18 October 2010.

27 Inflation not only made trading difficult, it also made it very difficult, for example, to decide upon any rouble valuation of an enterprise that was to be sold, or to interpret its "book value" from historical records.

28 By comparison, for example, with Poland, where the initial rise in the price level was only 80 per cent; see Gros and Steinherr (1995: 410).

29 Gaidar's prognosis was that in January and February of 1992, prices would rise by about 100 per cent a month, thus tripling in three months, with stabilization beginning in February on the consumer market. By March and April, "inflation will have fallen to about 10–12% a month", at which time more prices would be liberalized. By the end of the year, he wrote, "the price rise will be limited to a few percentage points, the exchange rate will be stabilized, and objective conditions for an inflow of foreign investment will appear" (E. Gaidar, "Budushchee prineset nam novye tseny i zabytye tovary", *Izvestiia*, 2 January 1992, cited in Krotov 2010: 422). The actual monthly rate was over 1,000 per cent by the end of March 1992.

30 Yeltsin, television address 30 December 1991, quoted in McFaul (2001: 144).

31 Gosudarstvennaia Programma Privatizatsii gosudarstvennykh i municipal'nykh predpriatii v Rossiiskoi Federatsii na 1992 god, 11 June 1992.

32 Two options were originally proposed. A third option, which was not widely used, was introduced during the bill's passage through parliament.

33 Government Decree No. 490, 15 July 1992, and Edict of the President, No. 914, On the Introduction of a System of Privatization Checks in the Russian Federation, *Vedomosti RSFSR*, 1992, No. 35, 14 August 1992, Item 2001; see "Legislative Survey of the Russian Federation, May–August 1992", *Review of Central and East European Law,* 1993, 19: 585.

34 For surveys of this literature, see Megginson and Netter (2001), Estrin (2002a); Estin *et al.* (2009).

35 "Chubays Gives Briefing on Privatization Program", *Nezavisimaya Gazeta*, 24 September 1992, p. 1 (FBIS-SOV-92–186, 24 September 1992).

36 The Washington Consensus formed a general guide for international assistance (IMF, World Bank, USAID, US Treasury and the EU).

37 Although missions were sent to Russia, and advisers from Harvard and elsewhere advised policy makers, large-scale assistance to privatization from the international financial institutions did not begin until the passage of the June 1992 programme.

38 World Bank and the EBRD, "Mass Privatisation in Russia", 25 March 1992.

39 GAO/NSIAD-95–156, USAID Projects in Russia (Washington, DC: GAO, 1995), p. 27.

40 GAO/NSIAD-95–156, p. 29.
41 As well as the critique given in the text, others noted the partial nature of the price and trade liberalization as a policy flaw.
42 See Chapter 5 of this book. Accepting, after modification, a proposal by Vladimir Potanin, the government adopted a loans-for-shares scheme to lease some of the largest state industrial assets (including state-owned shares in Norilsk Nickel, Yukos, Lukoil, Sibneft, Surgutneftegas, Novolipetsk Steel and Mechel) through auctions in return for loans to the government. The loans were not returned as contracted, and thus these assets were sold at the very low market price available at the time.
43 A critical study of the results of the IMF and World Bank missions to Russia can be found in Woods (2006). However, there is no evidence that advice from these institutions was the cause of state capture and corruption or resulted in damaging effects.
44 See also Boone (1996).
45 Wedel's book cannot be taken as a comprehensive history of US aid to those countries – it is focused on a few top-level projects, and it does not follow aid through its monitoring procedures or local administration. There was considerable donor credibility in central and regional government agencies and non-governmental organizations in Russia. It can be noted, too, that the USA was not the most important source of bilateral assistance to Russia. Germany, the most significant donor, gave almost twice the amount given by the USA, and its contribution has not been negatively reviewed. Bilateral aid from Development Assistance Committee (DAC) donors was provided by advisers representing departments of agriculture, ministries of finance, European banks, law firms and other groups, which assisted a variety of Russian agencies by providing information about international standards in areas as important as contracting, property rights, budgeting, statistical services, poverty targeting, income determination, programme development and monitoring, and regulating conflicts of interest. Any scholarly review of aid to Russia must begin elsewhere than the USA and must embrace a larger mission.
46 Joseph Stiglitz (1943–), who received the Nobel Prize in economics in 2001, was prominent in the Clinton administration as the chair of the President's Council of Economic Advisors from 1995 to 1997, and at the World Bank, where he served as senior vice-president and chief economist from 1997 to 2000.
47 See a recent review of this literature in Hamm *et al.* (2012).
48 A. Åslund, paper presented at CEELBAS Conference "Privatization in Russia: Decisions and Outcomes, 1991–1997", St Antony's College, Oxford, 12–13 November 2010.

2 The Mass Privatization Programme: the ideas, their evolution and their embodiment in law

1 Conflicts over sovereignty between the Union government and those of the subnational governments in the last years of the Soviet Union.
2 http://en.wikipedia.org/wiki/War_of_Laws.
3 Private interview with Maxim Boycko, 18 October 2010.
4 Despite the relatively peaceful dissolution of the Soviet Union, the Caucasus proved the exception, with the 1988–94 dispute between Armenia and Azerbaijan over Nagorny-Karabakh, internal conflicts in Georgia between 1989 and 1993, and the Chechen wars. See Zurcher (2007).
5 O predpriatiiakh i predprinimatel'skoi deiatel'nosti, Zakon RSFSR, 25 December 1990, No. 445–1.
6 To last until 1 December 1992, presidential decrees and other acts guaranteeing economic reform have priority in legislation, and they are to go into effect if the Supreme Soviet – or its Presidium, during its recess – does not overturn them within seven days (Postanovlenie SND RSFSR, 1 November 1991, No. 1831–1, O pravovom obespechenii

ekonomicheskoi reformy); other measures were passed allowing the president to make all appointments in and restructure the executive (Postanovlenie SND RSFSR, 1 November 1991, No. 1830-I, Ob organizatsii ispolnitel'noi vlasti v period radikal'noi ekonomicheskoi reform (in effect until 1 December 1992)), to approve all of the economic reform plans announced in the President's address (SND RSFSR, 1 November 1991, No. 1829-I).

7 Letter from Ira Lieberman to Anatoly Chubais, from Private papers, World Bank, 25 March 1992.

8 This is illustrated in a number of papers of the Consortium, in particular Braxton Associates/Deloitte, "Strategic Issues Raised by the MPP", 15 August 1992.

9 Private interview with Petr Mostovoi, 19 October 2010.

10 Private interview with Patrick Naegeli, 13 November 2010.

11 Private interview with Maxim Boycko, 18 October 2010.

12 Postanovlenie Verkhovnogo Soveta RSFSR, December 1990, No. 446–1; Zakon RSFSR, 25 December 1990, No. 445–1.

13 Zakon RSFSR, No. 445-1, Article 6.

14 Ibid.

15 World Bank private paper addressed to Anatoly Chubais, "An Approach to Rapid Privatisation", 25 March 1992.

16 Yegor Gaidar, first vice-premier of the Russian government and economic minister, appointed acting premier in 1992 from 15 June until 14 December, and again first vice-premier in September 1993; resigned in January 1994.

17 Gaidar was the leader in the late 1980s of a group of economic reformers who met regularly in Moscow and St Petersburg, and, in June 1990 with Anatoly Chubais, Petr Aven and others in Hungary, with economists Nordhaus, Dornbush and others to discuss reform. See Iasin (2002). *Rossiiskaia ekonomika: istoki i panorama rynochnykh reform, kurs lektsii*, Chapter 6, Moscow: Higher School of Economics, 2002, cited in http://ru.wikipedia.org/.

18 Both had some experience in government, but they were better known in party and intellectual circles. Yegor Gaidar, the editor of a major journal and member of a Politburo Commission on Economic Reform in the 1980s – "one of these rare Soviet economists able to discuss economics in modern micro and macro economic terms with his Western professional counterparts" (LePage 1990) – was chosen by Mikhail Gorbachev as part of a team of economists to present new economic thinking to western economists and government leaders. Anatoly Chubais, also an economist, served first as deputy mayor and then economic adviser to the mayor of St Petersburg, and, in 1991, was appointed by the mayor and by the Nobel Prize Winner Vasilii Leontieff as the president of the new Leontieff Research Center in St Petersburg.

19 OA uses a network of academic contributors to comment on world events. Its publications are peer-reviewed with the aim of being politically neutral.

20 David Pitt-Watson, co-author of this book, currently serves as a non-executive director of OA.

21 Oxford Analytica, "Political Obstacles to Privatisation in Russia", 1992.

22 Ibid.

23 Ruslan Khasbulatov supported Yeltsin in his successful resistance to the coup attempt in August 1991. He became chairman of the Supreme Soviet of the RSFSR in 1991.

24 Private interview with Ruslan Khasbulatov, 16 October 2010. Among the laws that were inspired by parliament, he cited the privatization of housing from July 1991. This law, however, predated Gaidar's appointment to the government.

25

> Privatizatsiia v Rossii do 97 goda voobshche ne byla ekonomicheskom protsessom. Ona reshala sovershenno drugogo masshtaba zadachi, chto malo kto ponimal togda, a yzh tem bole na Zapade. Ona reshala glavnyiu zadachu – ostanovit' kommunizm. Etu zadachu my reshili. My reshili ee polnost'iu. My reshili ee s togo

momenta, kogda na vyporakh v 96-om godu Ziuganov otkazalsia ot lozunga "nat-sionalizatsiia chastnoi sobstvennosti".

[Up to 1997, privatization in Russia was not an economic process. It decided a completely different and enormous task, which few at the time understood, not to mention in the West. It was decisive in resolving the main problem of ending communism. This we did, we did entirely. We decisively achieved it at the moment when Ziuganov, in the election year of 1996, rejected the platform, "Nationalization of Private Property".]

(A. Chubais, "Privatizatsiia voobshche ne byla ekonomicheskim protsessom. Ona reshala glavnuiu zadachu – ostanovit' communism", Interview, Aleksandr Gentelev, 2001, http://forum-msk.org/material/video/2493684.html)

26 Little provision was made for the systemic effect of price liberalization. In particular, no reform was undertaken to the inter-enterprise payments system, which hitherto had assumed that the buyer was willing and able to pay at regulated prices.
27 Similar anecdotes can be found in Gaidar (2003).
28 Private interview with Ruslan Khasbulatov, 16 October 2010.
29 Ob uskorenii realizatsii programmy privatizatsii na 1992 god, Postanovlenie Pravitel'stva RF, 29 1992, No. 52; O vvedenii v deistvie Gosudarstvennoi programmy privatizatsii gosudarstvennykh i munitsipal'nykh predpriatii v Rossiiskoi Federatsii na 1992 god, Postanovlenie Verkhovnogo Soveta RF, 11 June 1992, No. 2980–1. For the text of the programme, see Appendix 1.
30 Postanovlenie Verkhovnogo Soveta RSFSR, 3 July 1991, No. 1532–1, Zakon RSFSR, 3 July 1991, No. 1531–1. See Boycko *et al.* (1995).
31 Medium-sized enterprises of between 200 and 1,000 employees were to be sold by a combination of the methods available to large and small companies.
32 World Bank private paper addressed to Anatoly Chubais, "An Approach to Rapid Privatisation", 25 March 1992.
33 O vvedenii v deistvie sistemy privatizatsionnykh chekov v Rossiiskoi Federatsii, ukaz Prezidenta RF, 14 August 1992, No. 914.
34 Private interview with Ruslan Khasbulatov, 16 October 2010.
35 See, for example, World Bank, "Strategic Issues Raised by the Mass Privatisation Process", August 1992. This document outlines the key challenges facing the programme.

3 Reforming the communist inheritance: the goals and limits of privatization

1 The EBRD cites the IMF *et al.* (1991) and the CSFB publication *Historical Precedents for Economic Change in Central Europe and the USSR*. Quoting from the former, the EBRD goes on to note the limits of private enterprise:

> Households were allowed to hold some "personal" property with income generating potential – such as private plots, livestock, automobiles and housing – but resale was prohibited.... Other capital was banned, as was employment of hired labour, and supplies were often difficult to obtain through legal channels. The main legally sanctioned private activity was crop production on the household plots of collective farm members.
>
> (EBRD, "Privatisation in Russia", 8 June 1993, p. 8)

2 For those interested in the topic, there are contemporary textbooks, such as Gregory and Stuart (1994), which trace the development of the Soviet economy in its later years.
3 Separate savings banks existed until 1963, when they were incorporated into Gosbank, which constituted an extension of the government's monetary and economic policy,

carrying out central bank and commercial functions. In 1988, in a major banking reform, Gorbachev separated out functions, bringing back Sberbank, among others, to serve as a savings and loan bank for workers and other citizens.

4 One might note the difference in the relative price of oil which had arisen between the Soviet estimate in 1988 and the IEA three years later, an illustration of the inflexibility of prices or the reliability of statistics, or perhaps both.
5 See World Bank (1992: 182).
6 The Central Bank of the Soviet Union, and the only bank on the territory of the Soviet Union from the 1930s until 1987.
7 See also Pistor (2006); Andreev (1992); Sachs and Pistor (1997).
8 See background in EBRD, "Privatisation in Russia", 8 June 1993.
9 Ibid., p. 27. See also Black and Kraakman (1996).
10 See Humphrey (1999); Shleifer (1997); Volkov (1999); Varese (2001, 2005).
11 EBRD, "Privatisation in Russia", 8 June 1993, p. 28.
12 Ibid.
13 EBRD, "Privatisation in Russia", 8 June 1993, p. 31.
14 On unemployment in the Soviet economy, see Gregory and Collier (1988); Bergson (1964); Granick (1987); Ofer and Vinokur (1980); Roxburgh and Shapiro (1996).
15 A residence registration system that was replaced in 1993 by the statute On the Right of Russian Citizens to Liberty of Movement and Choice of Temporary or Permanent Residence within the Russian Federation (Council of Europe, 13 November 2001, 25). The change allowed simple notification of local authorities to replace official permission to register one's residence (see www.unhcr.org/refworld/country,,IRBC,,RUS,,3f7d4e0f38,0.html, accessed 23 October 2012).
16 See also Rubins (1998).
17 D. Pitt-Watson *et al.*; EBRD, "Privatisation in Russia", 8 June 1993.
18 World Bank March 1992.
19 World Bank, "An Approach to Rapid Privatisation", *c.* March 1992.
20 Quoted Goldman (2004: 81–2).
21 Braxton Associates/Deloitte.
22 World Bank, Staff Appraisal, 23 November 1992.
23 Ibid.: 96.
24 Cited in ibid.: 96.
25 Staff Appraisal, World Bank, *c.* March 1992.
26 Braxton, 12 August 1992, p. 5.
27 As illustrated in Appel (2004: 82).
28 Braxton Associates/Deloitte 8/92 (Most of this is in presentation form and unpaginated).
29 Ibid.
30 Ibid.
31 Ibid.
32 World Bank, "An Approach to Rapid Privatisation", *c.* March 1992.
33 Braxton Associates/Deloitte, "Final Presentation and Report", 22 December 1992.
34 Ibid.
35 Ibid.
36 Ibid.

4 Implementation of privatization, 1992–1994

1 Presidential Edict No. 914 (14 August 1992), On the Introduction of a System of Privatization Checks in the Russian Federation, with the statute of checks annexed; Presidential Edict No. 1228 (14 August 1992), On the Sale of the Housing Fund, Land Plots and Municipal Property by Privatization Checks (Vouchers); Presidential Edict No. 1229 (14 August 1992), On Developing the System of Privatization Checks;

Presidential Edict No. 1391 (16 November 1992), On Selling Objects of Privatization for Vouchers; Presidential Edict No. 1705 (31 December 1992), On Expanding the Opportunity for the Population to Participate in Specialized Check Auctions.

2 EBRD, "Privatisation in Russia", 8 June 1993, p. 8.

3 Ibid.: 14.

4 Ibid.: 15.

5 Braguinsky and Yavlinsky (2000: 5) write that "anyone who starts a small business in Russia will encounter extortion demands from the mafia, so there is no incentive for entrepreneurship".

6 Private interview with Khasbulatov, 16 October 2010. Note that different versions of non-tradable privatization vouchers were introduced in Ukraine and in Kazakhstan.

7 Private note from Andrei Shleifer, undated, summer 1992.

8 Later notes suggest decree 160 was not approved.

9 "Meeting with Machine Tool Manufacturing Association", Memo from Bob Anderson to Maxim Boycko and Jonathan Hay, 3 June 1992.

10 Machine tools (500,000 employees); transport construction (400,000 employees); general purpose machinery construction (500,000 employees); electrical technology (400,000 employees).

11 Braxton Associates/Deloitte, "Strategic Issues Raised by the MPP", 15 August 1992.

12 Ibid.

13 The notion that managers were "bribed" occurs openly in the writings of many of the advisers and reformers, including Shleifer, Boycko and Hay. Readers can also note its use in the memo on associations (Appendix 2).

14 Scott Griffith, "Summary of Interview Results", 24 August 1992.

15 Ibid.

16 Braxton Associates/Deloitte, "Strategic Issues Raised by the MPP", 15 August 1992.

17 Private conversation with Ruslan Khasbulatov, 2010, Moscow.

18 "Implementation of the Voucher Scheme", Memo from David Pitt-Watson to Chubais, Vasiliev, Boycko and Hay.

19 This figure is obtained by subtracting the number of vouchers received at voucher auctions from the total issues.

20 FMSU Statistics on Voucher Investment Funds in Russia, presented to OECD conference, Paris, 2–4 March 1994. The largest voucher funds were Pervii Vouchernii Fond (2,100,000 shareholders); Alpha Capital (1,012,000 shareholders); MN-Fond (900,000 shareholders).

21 See press conference by Anatoly Chubais, official Kremlin International News Broadcast, 21 August 1992, and discussion in Appel (2004: 91).

22 Around 149 million vouchers were issued. Of these, 116,395,000 were returned at voucher auctions, leaving 33,000,000, or 22 per cent, that were used in other ways, presumably by the workforce (Blasi *et al.*, 1997: 192).

23 See Blasi *et al.*, (1997: 192–3), using Russian National Survey and other sources. Note the inequity in value between insider subscription and outsider ownerships may not be as great as the figures initially suggest, since companies which had a higher value would tend to have a greater proportion of outside shareowners.

24 At CEELBAS Conference, Oxford, 10–11 November 2010.

25 See Appendix 4.

26 It might be noted that in the UK insider trading was not made illegal until the 1980s.

27 In order to make values comparable, in accounting for rouble inflation, these values are expressed in dollars.

28 In Appendix 3, we outline the Consortium's observations on this topic in the spring of 1993.

29 The rise of the oligarchs is discussed in more detail in Chapter 5.

5 Implementation of privatization after 1994

1 "Fewer Deputies Support Privatization Bill", Reuters, 21 July 1994, accessed on 6 October 2012 from Factiva Database, access by University of Oxford.

2 Ob osnovnykh polozheniiakh Gosudarstvennoi programmy privatizatsii gosudarstvennykh i munitsipal'nykh predpriiatii v Rossiiskoi Federatsii posle 1 iulia 1994 goda. Ukaz Prezidenta RF, 22 July 1994, No. 1535.

3 See Timothy Frye (2000: 190–1).

4 "Reducing the numbers of prohibited companies – those enterprises still treated as 'untouchable' with regard to privatization": see Kokh (1998: 84).

5 Barnes (2006: 127) describes the distribution to members of his family of valuable assets by Alexander Rutskoi, former vice-president and a leader of the parliamentary revolt against Yeltsin, who was elected governor of Kursk region in 1996.

6 "The deals themselves neither created the oligarchs nor bought their support for the reelection run" (Barnes 2006: 114). The conventional loans-for-shares story fits the cases of Abramovich (in 1995–97 a junior partner of Berezovsky), Khodorkovsky and, especially, Potanin. The other two winners were the oil sector insiders Vagit Alekperov and Vladimir Bogdanov, who obtained stakes in firms they already controlled. However, most of those listed in Table 5.1 did not become oligarchs through the loans-for-shares programme. Some of the 22 largest owners tried to participate in the loans-for-shares and even offered more competitive bids, but were excluded by those in charge of auctions; some even raised their concerns in public (Guriev and Rachinsky 2005: 139; Treisman 2010).

7 See Treisman (2010: 218–20) on asset stripping.

8 Note that targets for government revenue are difficult to compare with actual revenues because of hyperinflation. Budgets usually underestimated inflation and, of course, sales at year end would be expected to raise more than those earlier in the year. Nevertheless, the points made in the text remain valid (OA Daily Brief, 9 October 1995).

9 Vladimir Potanin (1961–), an engineer and senior official in Soyuzpromexport (1983–90), was president of the Interros Foreign Trade Association, which he co-founded with Mikhail Prokhorov, vice-president and then president of the International Company for Finance and Investments (MFK) (1992–93). President of the United Export–Import Bank (Oneximbank) from 1993, he was the principal author of the loans-for-shares programme. He supported Yeltsin's re-election and, in 1996–97, served as first deputy prime minister in charge of the economy; in 2005 he became a member of the Public Chamber. See www.themoscowtimes.com/mt_profile/vladimir_potanin/433790.html.

10 "'Of course these banks are not offering any favors,' he said, 'they want to make money. But if this will be profitable for Russia's banks, it should be profitable for Russia's government as well'" (Elif Kaban, "Banks' Loan-for-Shares Offer", *Moscow Times,* 31 March 1995). The financial crisis in 1998 showed the vulnerabilities of the banking sector, which was weakened by non-performing loans and limited investment in the real economy.

11 On 24 August interbank trading in Moscow actually collapsed.

12 Sergei Aleksashenko was; he told reporters that he supported the measure as a means to reduce the role of the state in the economy (Natasha Mileusnic, "Alexashenko Supports Banks' Plan", *Moscow Times*, 26 April 1995).

13 Fuel and Energy, Communications and the State Precious Metals Committee (Kaban 1996).

14 "Is Russia Less Attractive?", *Moscow Times*, 9 February 1995, www.themoscowtimes.com/news/article/is-russia-less-attractive/342954.html#ixzz1wuZgaoce, accessed 5 June 2012.

15 www.pjsymes.com.au/articles/MMM.htm, accessed 30 October 2012.

16 www.themoscowtimes.com/news/article/officials-take-steps-to-control-securities/349980.html#ixzz1wjz2YDTt, accessed 3 June 2012.

17 According to the BBC: see http://investorswatchdog.com/blog/investorswatchblog/?p=7459; www.themoscowtimes.com/news/article/mmms-mavrodi-voted-into-duma/346594.html#ixzz1wk2GZmRm, accessed 3 June 2012.

18 "Yeltsin Appoints Privatization Minister", *Moscow Times*, 16 November 1994, www.themoscowtimes.com/news/article/yeltsin-appoints-privatization-minister/346068.html#ixzz1wtsKOXtC, accessed 12 June 2012.

19 Dmitry Vasiliev, head of Federal Securities and former deputy head of the GKI, told a press conference: "Because of Polevanov, we lost several hundred million dollars in funds not invested in Russia", *Moscow Times*, 26 January 1995, www.themoscowtimes.com/news/article/polevanov-out-sell-offs-up-in-the-air/343607.html#ixzz1wuWMi6rs, accessed 30 October 2012.

20 Russian newspapers quoted Vladimir Polevanov, deputy premier and head of the State Property Committee, as saying he would insist on the nationalization of "wrongly privatized" industry, especially in the aluminium, energy and military-industrial sectors. See *Moscow Times*, 31 December 1994, www.themoscowtimes.com/news/article/privatization-chief-says-sell-off-drive-is-threat/344452.html#ixzz1wuUefDtK, accessed 5 June 2012.

21 News Brief, 11 April 1995, www.imf.org/external/np/sec/nb/1995/nb9511.htm, accessed 3 June 2012.

22 Arrears in company tax payments rose from 2.3 per cent to 8.2 per cent of GDP from 1994 to 1998 (*Russian Economic Trends*, 1 December 1999: 124; see Table 58, "Sources of Company Financing"). A tax collection "emergency" was declared in 1996, when the government realized only 56 per cent of taxes had been levied. The tax system in 1995–96 taxed the profits of enterprises heavily, especially in comparison with the tax burden of personal income, and many non-wage sources of income were not captured: Russians kept $30 billion to $60 billion in foreign banks to avoid taxation. VAT, experiencing uneven compliance, was set at 21.5 per cent. Export taxes became more important in the 1990s. Tax on the extraction and sale of natural resources yielded an important source of revenues, but the ad hoc granting of tax exemptions, which distorts the overall revenue system, undermined the authority of administrators especially in the natural gas industry. See information provided for the 1990s by the US Congress's research service: www.country-data.com/cgi-bin/query/r-11459.html.

23 "Russia Threatens Stet", *New York Times, International Briefs*, 30 December 1995, www.nytimes.com/svyazinvest, accessed 12 June 2012.

24 Federal budget revenues due to privatization in 1995 emerged from: (1) pledge auctions of the stocks of 12 enterprises for 5.1 trillion roubles (by contrast with expected 2–3 trillion roubles from auctions of 29 enterprises); (2) blocks of stock sold for 1.5 trillion roubles instead of 4–5 trillion expected from the sales of 136 enterprises; (3) the floating of a one trillion rouble convertible bond issue of the Lukoil Company (the sale of 25 per cent of the stocks of Svyazinvest for 1.9 trillion roubles did not materialize: see Radygin (1996: 5–19).

25 "After Ruble? Some Legal Stabilization", *Moscow Times*, 7 August 1995, www.themoscowtimes.com/news/article/after-ruble-some-legal-stabilization/336249.html#ixzz20J6xvr1x, accessed 11 July 2012.

26 OA Daily Brief, 5 February 1996.

27 Note that Kokh believed that such purchasers were fully legal (see Kokh 1998: 214).

28 Boycko was removed from office days before the privatization of VNK (the Eastern Oil Company), which he had overseen. That auction far exceeded expectations for the amount of money to be raised, and was perhaps one of the few examples of good practice during the period.

29 As Kokh (1998: 152) notes, "the budget projection of receipts from privatization in

1996 was set purely arbitrarily, i.e. as the difference between the actual receipts and the budget deficit set by the IMF".

30 The results were formulated by a critical regulation, Postanovlenie Gosudarstvennoi Dumy Federal'nogo Sobraniia Rossiiskoi Federatsii ot 11 iunia 1997 goda, No. 1517-II GD: "O khode privatizatsii v Rossiiskoi Federatsii i dopushennykh narusheniiakh zakonodatel'stva Rossiiskoi Federatsii pri ee osushestvlenii".

31 O privatizatsii gosudarstvennogo imushchestva i ob osnovakh privatizatsii munitsipal'nogo imushchestva v Rossiiakoi Federatsii, 21 iulia 1997, No. 123-FZ.

32 "Interview with Mikhail Khodorkovsky: Money, Power and Politics", *Frontline/World*, 31 October 2003, http://419.bittenus.com/serguizakhagcv/pbs.htm, accessed 16 October 2012.

33 Tax revenues in 1994 were 60 per cent of the amount expected: "Soaring Tax Evasion 'Threatens' State", *Moscow Times*, 24 March 1994, www.themoscowtimes.com/news/article/soaring-tax-evasion-threatens-state/341285.html, accessed 5 June 2012.

Conclusion

1 Centre for East European Language Based Studies Conference, "Privatization in Russia: Decisions and Outcomes, 1991–1997", St Antony's College, Oxford, 12–13 November 2010.

2 Petr Petrovich Mostovoi (1949–), lawyer and statesman, one of the early authors of Russian privatization, was in the Leningrad *kruzhok* of economists with Anatoly Chubais in the late 1980s. He became the deputy head of the State Property Committee of the Russian Federation in early 1992. See his detailed history of his own participation, "V poiskakh pravovogo polia", on the website of the Soiuz Pravykh Sil: Nashe delo pravoe www.sps.ru/?id=206210, and this and other articles in A. Chubais, *Privatizatsiia po Rossiiskii* (1999), www.ru-90.ru/content/приватизация-по-российски-под-ред-анатолия-чубайса, accessed 29 October 2012.

3 Maksim Vladimirovich Boycko (1959–), economist, associate of the National Bureau for Economic Research, sector head at the Institute of the World Economy and International Relations RAN (IMEMO) (1985–92), lead economic adviser for consultancy to the State Property Committee of the Russian Federation, 1992–95, deputy head of the Russian Federation Government Committee for Economic Reform (1995), general director of the Russian Privatization Center (1993–96), privatization minister August–November 1997.

4 See a recent review in Hamm *et al.* (2012).

5 See Mostovoi, "V poiskakh pravovago polia".

6 S. Medema in "Ronald Coase on Economics and Economic Method", *History of Economics Review*, 24 (Summer 1996): 1, thus quotes Coase and, more precisely, states that economics is the study of "the social institutions which bind the economic system together, markets for goods and services, labour markets, capital markets, the banking system, international trade, and so on".

7 To review, the Law on the Privatization of State and Municipal Enterprises in the RSFSR, *Vedomosti RSFSR* 1991, No. 27, Item 927, assigns to the RF State Property Committee (Goskomimushchestvo) responsibility for drafting the programme and to the Russian Fund for Federal Property and subsidiary funds the administrative responsibilities. It establishes four means: buy-out of leased enterprises, distribution of shares, auction (encumbered), unencumbered sale. See "Legislative Survey of the Russian Federation: July–December 1991", *Review of Central and East European Law* (1993), 19: 336–7.

8 This criticism also applies to the post-reform economic arrangements: see Filatotchev *et al.* (1999: 481): "The authorities were less concerned about the structure of share ownership that would initially result from privatization, believing that the tradability of shares would ensure a rapid evolution of ownership structure, whatever the initial allocation."

9 Marek Paweł Dąbrowski (1951–), the chairman of the Supervisory Council of the Center for Social and Economic Research (CASE) in Warsaw and chairman of the Supervisory Board of CASE-Ukraine in Kyiv, was first deputy minister of finance of Poland (1989–90), member of Poland's parliament (1991–93), and member of the Monetary Policy Council of the National Bank of Poland (1998–2004).

10 See Blasi *et al.* (1997); Shleifer and Treisman (2001: 2–3); "Analiz" (2004), and others.

11 In the sense that the compromises made by reformers to include a large role for insiders in privatization were blamed as a Russian policy failure, rather than seen as part of a successful political strategy (Dewatripont and Roland 1995; Filatotchev *et al.* 1999; Black *et al.* 2000). But see Popov (1998: 123): "Massive and quick privatization became socially acceptable and politically feasible at the cost of establishing the control of insiders over most privatized enterprises."

12 Private interview with Maxim Boycko, 16 October 2010.

13 See, for example, an interview from 2001 on board a plane by documentary film maker, Aleksandr Gentelev in which A. Chubais said "Privatizatsiia voobshche ne byla ekonomicheskim protsessom. Ona reshala glavnuiu zadachu – ostanovit' kommunizm" [Privatization was generally not an economic process. It addressed the main task – to end communism], http://forum-msk.org/material/video/2493684.html, made available on YouTube 18 February 2010, accessed 21 October 2012.

14 Vice-President Alexander Rutskoi, who complained to a Portuguese newspaper in December 1991 that he was practically excluded from the mechanisms of decision making, with reportedly only three personal staff members compared with the ten allotted to other high-ranking leaders, was referring to Yeltsin's key advisers when he spoke at a stop in the Siberian city of Barnaul, of "little boys in pink pants": Irina Gushchenko and Renfrey Clarie, "A Good Season for demagogues", *GreenLeft*, 22 January 1992.

15 Gaidar, who advised Gorbachev and served as his emissary to the World Bank, and Chubais, who had served briefly as deputy mayor of St Petersburg and was at the time of his appointment the president of the Leontieff Centre, were the leading economists in Russia, widely recognized in the United States, the European Commission and Central European economists in the late 1980s.

16 Vladimir Alexandrovich Mau (1959–), economist, a politician close to Yegor Gaidar and Anatoly Chubais, rector of the Presidential Academy of the National Economy and Public Administration (2002–).

17 A. Ilarianov quotes V. Mau from the Round Table, "Twenty Years of Market Reforms", Plenary Session, 3 April 2012, "The Strategy for the Development of Russia" in his blog "No One Wanted Power?", *Ekho Moskvy*, 4 May 2012.

18 Yeltsin's appeal to the voters and, indeed, his mandate, were personal, emotional. Tim Colton (2008: 213) cites Burbulis on pro-Yeltsin voters, who bore "a purely religious form of protest and hope". They "threw in with 'a savior' and not a reform plan".

19 A plan that raised expectations that Russia could overcome in a few years the economic crisis at the end of the 1980s by means of forging a market economy. Proposed by Grigory Yavlinsky, it was further developed by a work group under the direction of Stanislav Shatalin (an economic adviser to Mikhail Gorbachev). See Desai (2006).

20 Private interview with Ruslan Khasbulatov, 16 October 2010, Moscow.

21 Ibid.

22 Braxton Associates/Deloitte, 1992.

23 For a review of the literature about its results and an updated summary, see Estrin *et al.* (2009).

24 In one Consortium document (MPP, Technical Assistance Programme, Board Meeting, 7 August 1992), there is a discussion of the value of advice: that given on "policy" was deemed to have a perspective of two months, on operations two weeks, on immediate response, two hours. It was the latter two that were demanded by the GKI.

25 For reviews of the literature, see Hansmann (2000); Learmount and Roberts (2006).

26 The issue of how contracting and principal-agent issues can be resolved is one that has engaged economists for some time. Adam Smith (1937), for example, would have advised against "a separation of management from ownership". Smith believed that managers, rather than owners, lacked the "anxious vigilance" necessary to look after someone else's investment and, therefore, "negligence and profusion" would prevail in such enterprises (Smith [1776] 1909–14) Book V, Ch. 1, 311). Alfred Marshall (1946: 596ff.) noted the increasing delegation of management, and that it depended on "a spirit of honesty and uprightness in commercial affairs" to make it a success. Berle and Means (1932) argue the need for broader social obligations by those who control large corporations.

27 Ross Johnson, the CEO of RJR Nabisco, famously provided private jets for his entire board on the grounds that "I know that if I'm there for them, they'll be there for me": see Davis *et al.* (2006: 103).

28 For further discussion, see ibid., 100.

29 Boycko *et al.* (1995: 25), to be sure, understand that "the Coase theorem shows how efficiency can be restored but only if property is protected and contracts enforced".

30 For example, the Philosophy, Politics and Economics degree at Oxford was developed with the training of civil servants in mind (http://en.wikipedia.org/wiki/Philosophy,_Politics_and_Economics). It has been criticized for being an overly generalist degree for modern times. "Why does PPE rule Britain?", www.bbc.co.uk/news/magazine-11136511). However, we would argue that an interdisciplinary approach, including history as well, is important for effective economic policy making.

Appendices

1 Russian Mass Privatization Programme, Final Extension Phase Report, Components 1, 2, 3, Braxton Associates, Deloitte and Touche, Touche Ross, March 1993.

References

Selected private papers referred to in this book

Anderson, Bob, Natasha Mamedova and Nicholas Barberis, "What We Know About Associations", 30 June 1992.

Anderson, Robert (for GKI), "The 1992 Privatisation Program", 3 July 1992.

Anderson, Robert and Goohoon Kwon, "Corporation of Russian Enterprises", 25 June 1992.

BBDO Ditto Component 4, 27 May 1992.

Blasi, Joseph and Scott Griffith, "General Advice on Improving MPP".

Blasi, Joseph, "Note on Management Buy Outs to Maxim Boycko and Jonathan Hay", 23 August 1992.

Boycko, Maxim, Interview for this book, 18 October 2010.

Boycko, Maxim and Andrei Shleifer, "The Debt Agency: Memo from to Chubais", 2 July 1992.

Braxton Associates/Deloitte, Interim discussions with A. Chubais.

Braxton Associates/Deloitte, "Strategic Issues Raised by the MPP", 15 August 1992.

Braxton Associates/Deloitte, "Technical Assistance Programme: Consortium Final Phase 1 Report", October 1992.

Braxton Associates/Deloitte, "Final Presentation and Report", 22 December 1992.

Braxton Associates/Deloitte, Ditto Introduction, Background, Issues and Overall Approach.

CFF, Ditto Component 6, 27 May 1992.

CCF, "Recommendation Paper on Investment Funds", 27 July 1992.

Deloitte, Questionnaire of MKIs in *oblasts*.

Deloitte, "Proposal for TAP Component 2", 27 May 1992.

Deloitte, Inter-Enterprise Debt Agency, 19 October 1992.

Deloitte, "TAP Final Extension Phase Report Component 1, 2, 3", March 1993.

Deloitte, "Program for Intensive Enterprise Support (PIES)", 8 July 1996.

Deloitte Consortium, "Technical Assistance Programme: Consortium Interim Report Component 2–6", 30 August 1992.

Deloitte *et al.* Various internal notes showing discussions and debate among Consortium members about the issues, timing, practicality and results of the privatization programme.

DNA, Inter-enterprise debt briefing document, 28 October 1992

EBRD, "Technical Assistance Programme: Proposal Request", 11 May 1992.

EBRD, "Privatisation in Russia. A Discussion Paper for the Consultative Group in Paris", 8 June 1993.

Gerashchenko, Viktor, Interview for this book, 15 October 2010.
Griffith, Scott, Summary of interview, results with managers, 24 August 1992.
Khasbulatov, Ruslan, Interview for this book, 16 October 2010.
Kwon, Goohoon, "The Regional Distribution of Russian Industrial Enterprises and its Implications for Export", 16 March 1993.
MacDonald, Paul, Notes on likely participation in programme.
Mostovoi, Piotr, Interview for this book, 19 October 2010.
Oxford Analytica, "Political Obstacles to Privatisation in Russia", and subsequent briefings, 1992.
Oxford Analytica, Daily brief on Russia 1992–94.
Pitt-Watson, David, Notes on visit to Russia, April 1992.
Pitt-Watson, David, Three notes on inter-enterprise debt, ? Summer 1992.
Pitt-Watson, David, Notes/Write-up, *c.* 1993/94.
Russian Federation President, Decree on organizational measures regarding the transformation of state enterprises and voluntary associations of state enterprises into joint stock societies, 1 July 1992.
Russian Federation President, Decree on commercialization and transformation of government and municipal enterprises into open stock companies (voucher legislation), 22 June 1992.
Russian Soviet Federative Republic, Law of Russian SFSR on Enterprise and Entrepreneurship, 25 December 1990.
Russian Soviet Federative Republic, Law on privatization of State and Municipal Enterprises in the RSFSR 3 July 1991.
Shleifer, Andrei, Discussion of Titkin's privatization programme, 1992.
Shleifer, Andrei and Maxim Boycko, "A Voucher Programme for Russia", June 1992.
White and Case, Ditto Component 5, 27 April 1992.
White and Case, "Decree on Inter Enterprise Debt: Note to Deputy Prime Minister Chubais", 24 June 1992.
White and Case, Draft investment fund legislation.
World Bank, "An Approach to Rapid Privatisation in the Russian Federation", *c.* March 1992.
World Bank, "Report on Vouchers and Mass Privatisation", 25 March 1992.
World Bank, "Privatization Implementation Assistance Project Staff Appraisal Report", 23 November 1992.

Published sources

Abal'kin, L. and A. Miliukov, eds. 1990. *Ekonomicheskaia Reforma: Poisk Reshenii* (Moscow: Politizdat).
Afanasev, M., P. Kuznetsov and A. Fominykh. 1997. "Korporativnoe Upravlenie Glazami Direktorata: po Materialam Obsledovanii 1994–1996 gg". *Voprosy Ekonomiki* 5: 84–101.
Aghion, P. and Olivier Blanchard. 1994. "On the Speed of Transition in Central Europe". *NBER Macroeconomic Annual* 9: 283–330.
Alchian, Armen A. and Harold Demsetz. 1972. "Production, Information Costs, and Economic Organization". *The American Economic Review* 62 (5): 777–95.
Amurzhuyev, O. and V. Tsapelik. 1989. "How to Conquer the Diktat of the Monopolies". *Ekonomicheskaya Gazeta* 49 (7).
"Analiz Protsessov Privatizatsii Gosudarstvennoi Sobstvennosti v Rossiiskoi Federatsii za Period 1993–2003". 2004. Moscow: Audit Chamber RF, 23 November.

Andreev, Vladimir. 1992. "Privatization of State Enterprises in Russia". *Review of Central and East European Law* 18 (3): 265–76.
Angelo, Georgi. 1993. "Legal Framework of Privatization in Russia". *Minnesota Journal of Global Trade*, Winter: 207–28.
Appel, Hilary. 1997. "Voucher Privatisation in Russia: Structural Consequences and Mass Response in the Second Period of Reform". *Europe-Asia Studies* 49 (8): 1433–49.
Appel, Hilary. 2004. *A New Capitalist Order: Privatization and Ideology in Russia and Eastern Europe*. Pittsburgh, Pa.: University of Pittsburgh Press.
Aron, Leon. 2000. *Yeltsin: A Revolutionary Life*. New York, NY: St Martin's Press.
Åslund, A. 1989. *Gorbachev's Struggle for Economic Reform: the Soviet Reform Process, 1985–1988*. Ithaca, NY: Cornell University Press.
Åslund, A. 1994. *Economic Transformation in Russia*. New York: St Martin's Press.
Åslund, A. 1995. *How Russia Became a Market Economy*. Washington, DC: Brookings Institution.
Åslund, A. 1997. *Russia's Economic Transformation in the 1990s*. London and Washington, DC: Pinter.
Åslund, A. 2002. *Building Capitalism: the Transformation of the Former Soviet Bloc*. Cambridge, UK, and New York: Cambridge University Press.
Åslund, A. 2004. "Russia's Economic Transformation under Putin". *Eurasian Geography and Economics* 45 (6): 397–420.
Åslund, A. 2007. *How Capitalism Was Built: the Transformation of Central and Eastern Europe, Russia, and Central Asia*. Cambridge and New York: Cambridge University Press.
Åslund, Anders and P. Layard. 1993. *Changing the Economic System in Russia*. New York: St Martin's Press.
Åslund, Anders, Peter Boone and Simon Johnson. 1996. "How to Stabilize: Lessons from Post-Communist Countries". *Brookings Papers on Economic Activity* 1: 217–313.
Barnes, Andrew. 1998. "What's the Difference? Industrial Privatisation and Agricultural Land Reform in Russia, 1990–1996". *Europe–Asia Studies* 50 (5): 843–57.
Barnes, Andrew. 2001. "Property, Power, and the Presidency: Ownership Policy Reform and Russian Executive–Legislative Relations, 1990–1999". *Communist and Post-Communist Studies* 34 (1): 39–61.
Barnes, Andrew Scott. 2006. *Owning Russia: the Struggle over Factories, Farms, and Power*. Ithaca, NY, and London: Cornell University Press.
Bergson, A. 1964. *Economics of Soviet Planning*. New Haven, Conn., and London: Yale University Press.
Berle, A. 1931–32. "For Whom Corporate Managers are Trustees". *Harvard Law Review* 45: 1365–73.
Berle, A. and G. Means. 1932. *The Modern Corporation and Private Property*. New York: Macmillan.
Berliner, Joseph S. 1976. *The Innovation Decision in Soviet Industry*. Cambridge, Mass., and London: MIT Press.
Berliner, Joseph S. 1988. *Soviet industry from Stalin to Gorbachev*. Aldershot: Elgar.
Black, B. and R. Kraakman. 1996. "A Self-enforcing Model of Corporate Law". *Harvard Law Review* 109 (8): 1911–82.
Black, B., R. Kraakman and A. Tarassova. 2000. "Russian Privatization and Corporate Governance: What Went Wrong?", *Stanford Law Review* 52 (6): 1731–808.
Blanchard, O. and P. Aghion. 1996. "On Insider Privatization". *European Economic Review* 40 (3–5): 759–66.

Blanchard, Olivier, Rudiger Dornbusch, Paul Krugman, Richard Layard and Lawrence Summers, eds. 1991. *Reform in Eastern Europe*. Cambridge, Mass.: MIT Press.

Blasi, Joseph R., Maya Kroumova and Douglas Kruse. 1997. *Kremlin Capitalism: the Privatization of the Russian Economy*. Ithaca, NY: ILR Press.

Boone, Peter. 1996. "Politics and the Effectiveness of Foreign Aid". *European Economic Review* 40 (2): 289–329.

Borensztein, Eduardo and Manmohan S. Kumar. 1991. "Proposals for Privatization in Eastern Europe". *IMF Staff Papers* 38 (2): 300–26.

Bornstein, Morris. 1999. "Framework Issues in the Privatisation Strategies of the Czech Republic, Hungary and Poland". *Post-Communist Economies* 11 (1): 47–77.

Boycko, Maxim, Andrei Shleifer, and Robert Vishny. 1993. "Privatizing Russia". *Brookings Papers on Economic Activity* 2.

Boycko, Maxim, A. Shleifer and Robert Vishny. 1995. *Privatizing Russia*. Cambridge, Mass.: MIT Press.

Braguinsky, S. and G. Yavlinsky. 2000. *Incentives and Institutions: the Transition to Market Economy in Russia*. Princeton, NJ: Princeton University Press.

Brenton, Paul, Daniel Gros and Guy Vanadille. 1997. "Output Decline and Recovery in the Transition Economies: Causes and Social Consequences". *Economics of Transition* 5 (1): 113–30.

Breslauer, George. 2002. *Gorbachev and Yeltsin as Leaders*. Cambridge: Cambridge University Press.

Brovkin, V. "Democrats in Disarray", *Moscow Times*, 4 January 1994, www.themoscowtimes.com/news/article/democrats-in-disarray/216222.html#ixzz1xOlZu5Q7, accessed 11 June 2012.

Brown, A., Barry Ickes and R. Ryterman. 1994. *The Myth of Monopoly: A New View of Industrial Structure in Russia*. Washington, DC: Transition Economics Division, World Bank.

Brown, David, Sergei Guriev and Natalya Volchkova. 1999. "Financial-Industrial Groups in Russia: Virtue or Vice". *Russian Economic Trends* (1 September): 6–12.

Bruno, Michael. 1992. "Stabilization and Reform in Eastern Europe: a Preliminary Evaluation". *IMF Staff Papers*. Washington, DC: IMF.

Buck, Trevor, Igor Filatotchev and Mike Wright. 1998. "Agents, Stakeholders and Corporate Governance in Russian Firms". *Journal of Management Studies* 35 (1): 81–104.

Butler, W. E. (2003). *Russian Law*. Oxford: Oxford University Press, 2nd edition.

Carlin, Wendy, John Van Reenen and Toby Wolfe. 1995. "Enterprise Restructuring in Early Transition: the Case Study Evidence from Central and Eastern Europe". *Economics of Transition* 3 (4): 427–58.

Chebankova, Elena. 2008. "Adaptive Federalism and Federation in Putin's Russia". *Europe-Asia Studies* 60 (6): 989–1009.

Choksi, Armeane and Demetris Papageorgiou. 1986. Economic Liberalization in Developing Countries, at Washington, DC.

Chubais, A. 1999a. "Kak My 'Probivali' Nashu Programmu". In A. Chubais, ed., *Privatizatsiia Po-Rossiiski*. Moscow: Vagrius.

Chubais, A. 1999b. "Kak My Zashchishchali Privatizatsiu". In A. Chubais, ed., *Privatizatsiia Po-Rossiiski*. Moscow: Vagrius.

Chubais, A. 1999. "Rozhdenie Idei". In A. Chubais, ed., *Privatizatsiia Po-Rossiiski*. Moscow: Vagrius.

Coase, R. 1988. "Nature of the Firm: Origin, The Lectures". *Journal of Law, Economics and Organization* 4 (3): 3–18.

Colton, Timothy J. 2008. *Yeltsin: a Life*. New York: Basic Books.
Cornia, Giovanni Andrea and Vladimir Popov. 2001. *Transition and Institutions: the Experience of Gradual and Late Reformers*. Oxford: Oxford University Press.
Dąbrowski, Marek. 1997. "The First Half Year of Russian transformation". In A. Åslund, ed., *Russia's Economic Transformation in the 1990s*. London and Washington, DC: Pinter.
Dallin, Alexander and Gail Warshofsky Lapidus. 1991. *The Soviet System in Crisis: a Reader of Western and Soviet Views*. Boulder, Colo.: Westview Press.
Davis, S., J. Lukomnik and D. Pitt-Watson. 2006. *The New Capitalists: How Citizen Investors Are Reshaping the Corporate Agenda*. Boston, Mass.: Harvard Business School.
De Melo, Martha, Cevdet Denizer and Alan Gelb. 1996. "Patterns of Transition from Plan to Market". *The World Bank Economic Review* 10 (3): 397–424.
De Melo, Martha, Cevdet Denizer, Alan Gelb and Stoyan Tenev. 1997. "Circumstance and Choice: the Role of Initial Conditions and Policies in Transition Economies". In *Policy Research Working Paper 1866*. Washington, DC: World Bank.
Desai, Padma. 2006. *Conversations on Russia: Reform from Yeltsin to Putin*. Oxford and New York: Oxford University Press.
Desai, Raj and Itzhak Goldberg. 2001. "The Politics of Russian Enterprise Reform: Insiders, Local Governments, and the Obstacles to Restructuring". *The World Bank Research Observer* 16 (2): 219–40.
Dewatripont, Mathias and Gérard Roland. 1995. "The Design of Reform Packages under Uncertainty". *The American Economic Review* 85 (5): 1207–23.
Durden Smith, Jo. 1995. "Slaying the National Myth", *Moscow Times*, 17 January 1995, www.themoscowtimes.com/news/article/slaying-the-national-myth/343991.html, accessed 30 October 2012.
Ellerman, David P. 1998. *Voucher Privatization with Investment Funds: an Institutional Analysis*. Washington, DC: Office of the Senior Vice President, World Bank.
Ellerman, David P. 2003. "On the Russian Privatization Debate". *Challenge* 46 (3): 6–28.
Estrin, S. 1997. "Transforming the Core: Restructuring Industrial Enterprises in Russia and Central Europe". *Economics of Transition* 5 (2): 517–18.
Estrin, S. 2002a. "Competition and Corporate Governance in Transition". *Journal of Economic Perspectives* 16 (1): 101–24.
Estrin, S. 2002b. "Corporate Governance and Privatisation: Lessons from Transition Economies". *Journal of African Economies* 11: 68–104.
Estrin, Saul and Robert Stone. 1997. "A Taxonomy of Mass Privatization". In I. Lieberman, N. Stilpon and R. Desai, eds, *Studies of Economies in Transformation No. 23*. Washington, DC: World Bank.
Estrin, S., J. Hanousek, E. Kocenda and J. Svejnar. 2009. "The Effects of Privatization and Ownership in Transition Economies". *Journal of Economic Literature* 47 (3): 699–728.
Favarel-Garrigues, Gilles. 2011. *Policing Economic Crime in Russia: from Soviet Planned Economy to Privatisation*. London: C. Hurst.
Feige, Edgar. 1991. "Perestroika and Ruble Convertibility". *The Cato Journal* 10 (3): 631–53.
Feldbrugge, F. 1992. *The Emancipation of Soviet Law*. Leiden: Martinus Nijhoff Publishers, vol. 1.
Feldbrugge, F. 2009. "The Codification Process of Russian Civil Law". In J. Arnscheidt, B. Van Rooji and J. Otto, eds, *Lawmaking for Development: Explorations into the*

Theory and Practice of International Legislative Projects. Chicago: University of Chicago Press, ch. 10.

Fidrmuc, Jan. 2003. "Economic Reform, Democracy and Growth during Post-communist Transition". *European Journal of Political Economy* 19 (3): 583–604.

Filatotchev, Igor, Mike Wright and Michael Bleaney. 1999. "Privatization, Insider Control and Managerial Entrenchment in Russia". *Economics of Transition* 7 (2): 481–504.

Fish, M. Steven. 1997. "The Determinants of Economic Reform in the Post-communist World". *East European Politics & Societies* 12 (1): 31–78.

Freeland, Chrystia. 2000. *Sale of the Century: Russia's Wild Ride from Communism to Capitalism*. New York: Crown Business.

Frydman, Roman, Andrzej Rapaczynski and John S. Earle. 1993. *The Privatization Process in Russia, Ukraine and the Baltic States: Economic Environment, Legal and Ownership Structure, Institutions for State Regulation, Overview of Privatization Programs, Initial Transformation of Enterprises*. Budapest and London: Central European University Press.

Frye, Timothy. 2000. *Brokers and Bureaucrats: Building Market Institutions in Russia.* Ann Arbor: Michigan University Press.

Gaddy, Clifford and Barry Ickes. 2002. *Russia's Virtual Economy.* Washington, DC: Brookings Institution Press.

Gaidar, E. T. 1999. *Days of Defeat and Victory.* Seattle, Wash., and London: University of Washington Press.

Gaidar, E. T. 2003. *State and Evolution: Russia's Search for a Free Market.* Seattle, Wash.: University of Washington Press.

Gaidar, E. T. 2005. *Dolgoe vremia: Rossiia v mire: ocherki ekonomicheskoi istorii.* Moscow: Delo.

Gaidar, E. T. 2006. *Gibel' imperii: uroki dlia Sovremennoi Rossii.* Moscow: ROSSPEN.

Gogek, D. (1995). "Russian Company Law Reform: Have Flawed Laws Impeded the Transition to a Market Economy?", *McGill Law Journal* 41: 271–83.

Goldman, Marshall I. 2004. *The Piratization of Russia: Russian Reform Goes Awry.* London: Routledge.

Goldman, Philip, Gail Warshofsky Lapidus and Victor Zaslavsky. 1992. "Introduction: Soviet Federalism – its Origins, Evolution and Demise". In From Union to Commonwealth: Nationalism and Separatism in the Soviet Republics. G. W. Lapidus and V. Zaslavsky, eds, Cambridge: Cambridge University Press.

Graney, K. 2001. "Ten Years of Sovereignty in Tatarstan: End of the Beginning or Beginning of the End?", *Problems of Post-Communism* 48 (5): 32–41.

Granick, David. 1987. *Job Rights in the Soviet Union: their Consequences.* Cambridge: Cambridge University Press.

Granville, Brigitte. 1993. "Russian Economic Reform in 1992: the Threat to Stabilization". *Business Strategy Review* 4 (1): 29–44.

Granville, Brigitte. 1995. *The Success of Russian Economic Reforms.* London and Washington, DC: Institute for International Affairs and Brookings Institution Press.

Granville, Brigitte and P. Oppenheimer, eds. 2001. *Russia's Post-Communist Economy.* Oxford: Oxford University Press.

Gray, C. and Kathryn Hendley. 1997. "Developing Commercial Law in Transition Economies: Examples from Hungary and Russia". In J. Sachs and K. Pistor, eds, *The Rule of Law and economic reform in Russia.* Boulder, Colo.: Westview Press.

Gregory, Paul R. and Irwin Jr Collier. 1988. "Unemployment in the Soviet Union: Evidence from the Soviet Interview Project". *The American Economic Review* 78 (4): 613–32.

Gregory, Paul and Robert Stuart. 1994. *Soviet and Post-Soviet Economic Structure and Performance*. New York: Harper Collins.

Grigoriev, Leonid. 1992. "Ulterior Property Rights and Privatization: Even God Cannot Change the Past". In A. Åslund, ed., *The Post-Soviet Economy: Soviet and Western perspectives*, New York: St Martin's Press.

Gros, Daniel and Alfred Steinherr. 1995. *Winds of Change: Economic Transition in Central and Eastern Europe*. London and New York: Longman.

Gros, Daniel and Alfred Steinherr. 2004. *Economic Transition in Central and Eastern Europe: Planting the Seeds*. Cambridge: Cambridge University Press.

Guriev, S. and A. Rachinsky. 2005. "The Role of Oligarchs in Russian Capitalism". *Journal of Economic Perspectives* 19 (1): 131–50.

Gustafson, Thane. 1999. *Capitalism Russian-style*. Cambridge, England, and New York: Cambridge University Press.

Hahn, G. 2003. "The Past, Present and Future of the Russian Federal State". *Demokratizatsiya* 11 (3): 343–62.

Hamm, P., L. P. King and D. Stuckler. 2012. "Mass Privatization, State Capacity, and Economic Growth in Post-Communist Countries". *American Sociological Review* 77 (2): 295–324.

Hanauer, Laurence S. 1996. "Tatarstan's Bid for Autonomy: Tatarstan as a Model for the Devolution of Power in the Russian Federation". *Journal of Communist Studies and Transition Politics* 12 (1): 63–82.

Hanson, P. 1993. "Local Power and Market Reform in Russia", *Communist Economies and Economic Transformation* 5 (1): 45–61.

Hansmann, H. 2000. *The Ownership of Enterprise*. Cambridge, Mass.: Harvard University Press.

Hay, Michael and Alan Peacock. 1992. "Giving Advice to Government: the Case of Russia". *Business Strategy Review* 3 (2): 59–77.

Hedlund, Stefan. 2008. "Such a Beautiful Dream: How Russia Did Not Become a Market Economy". *The Russian Review* 67 (2): 187–208.

Hewett, A., ed. 1991. *Milestones in Glasnost' and Perestroyka. The Economy*. Washington, DC: Brookings Institution Press.

Heybey, Berta and Peter Murrell. 1999. "The Relationship between Economic Growth and the Speed of Liberalization during Transition". *The Journal of Policy Reform* 3 (2): 121–37.

Hoffman, David E. 2002. *The Oligarchs: Wealth and Power in the New Russia*. New York: Public Affairs.

Humphrey, Caroline. 1999. "Russian Protection Rackets and the Appropriation of Law and Order". In J. Heyman, ed., *States and Illegal Practices*. Oxford: Berg.

Huskey, E. 1996. "Making an Economic Policy in Russia: Changing Relations between Presidency and Government". *Review of Central and East European Law* 22: 365–86.

Iasin, E. 2002. *Rossiiskaia Ekonomika: Istoki i Panorama Rynochnykh Reform, Kurs Lektsii*. Moscow: Higher School of Economics.

Ickes, B. 2002. *Russia's Virtual Economy*. Washington, DC: Brookings Institution.

International Energy Agency (IEA). 1994. *Russian Energy Prices, Taxes and Costs 1993*. Paris: OECD.

International Monetary Fund (IMF), World Bank, OECD and EBRD. 1991. *A Study of the Soviet Economy*. Paris: OECD.

Jensen, Michael C. and William H. Meckling. 1976. "Theory of the Firm: Managerial Behavior, Agency Costs and Ownership Structure". *Journal of Financial Economics* 3 (4): 305–60.

Johnson, Simon. 1991. "Spontaneous Privatization in the Soviet Union: How, Why and for Whom?" WIDER Working Paper No. 91 (September).

Johnson, Simon and Heidi Kroll. 1991. "Managerial Strategies for Spontaneous Privatization". *Soviet Economy* 7 (4): 281–316.

Kaban, Elif 1995. "Top Securities Official Blasts Consortium", *Moscow Times*, 22 April 1995, www.themoscowtimes.com/print/article/top-securities-official-blasts-consortium/340062.html, accessed 3 May 2012.

Kennet, Jim 1995. "Cash Strapped State Targets Tax Shelters", *Moscow Times* (23 September 1995), www.themoscowtimes.com/news/article/cash-strapped-state-targets-tax-shelters/334239.html#ixzz20JAFhUyu, accessed 11 July 2012.

Kikeri, Sunita, John R. Nellis and Mary M. Shirley. 1992. *Privatization: the Lessons of Experience*. Washington, DC: Country Economics Department, The World Bank.

Klebnikov, Paul. 2000. *Godfather of the Kremlin: Boris Berezovsky and the Looting of Russia*. New York: Harcourt.

Kokh, Alfred. 1998. *The Selling of the Soviet Empire: Politics and Economics of Russia's Privatization: Revelations of the Principal Insider*. New York: S.P.I. Books: Liberty Publishing House.

Kolodko, G. 2000. *From Shock to Therapy: the Political Economy of Postsocialist Transformation*. Oxford: Oxford University Press.

Kornai, Janos. 1986. "The Soft Budget Constraint". *Kyklos* 39 (1): 3–30.

Kornai, Janos. 1992. *The Socialist System: the Political Economy of Communism*. Princeton, NJ: Princeton University Press.

Kroll, Heidi. 1991. "Monopoly and Transition to the Market". *Soviet Economy* 7: 143–74.

Krotov, Nikolai. 2010. *Zhizn' i Udivitelnye Prikluchenia Bankira Viktora Geraschenko*. Moscow: ANO Ekonomicheskaia Letopis.

Krueger, Gary and Marek Ciolko. 1998. "A Note on Initial Conditions and Liberalization during Transition". *Journal of Comparative Economics* 26 (4): 718–34.

Kubicek, Paul. 1996. "Variations on a Corporatist Theme: Interest Associations in Post-Soviet Ukraine and Russia". *Europe–Asia Studies* 48 (1): 27–46.

Lane, David and Cameron Ross. 1999. *The Transition from Communism to Capitalism: Ruling Elites from Gorbachev to Yeltsin*. New York: St Martin's Press.

Lapidus, G. W. 1994. *The New Russia: Troubled Transformation*. Boulder, Colo.: Westview Press.

Lapidus, G. W. 1998. "Contested Sovereignty – the Tragedy of Chechnya". *International Security* 23 (1): 5–49.

Lapidus, G. W. 1999. "Asymmetrical Federalism and State Breakdown in Russia". *Post-Soviet Affairs* 15 (1): 74–82.

Learmount, S. and J. Roberts. 2006. "Meanings of Ownership of the Firm". *Journal of Interdisciplinary Economics* 17 (1): 139–62.

Leeds, Roger and Michael Harman. 1995. "Securities Market Development and Privatization". In I. Lieberman and J. Nellis, eds, *Russia: Creating Private Enterprises and Efficient Markets*. Washington, DC: The World Bank.

Leonard, Carol. 2011. *Agrarian Reform in Russia: The Road from Serfdom*. Cambridge: Cambridge University Press.

LePage, Henri. 1990. "A Little Known Part of Russian History". In Yegor Gaidar and Ljubo Sirc, *A Russian-Slovene Conversation*. London: Centre for Research into Post Communist Economies, quoted in http://yourfreedomandours.blogspot.co.uk/2009/12/yegor-gaidar-1956-2009.html, accessed 12 March 2013.

Lieberman, I. and S. Rahuja. 1995. "An Overview of Privatization in Russia". In I. Lieberman and J. Nellis, eds, *Russia: Creating Private Enterprises and Efficient Markets*. Washington, DC: The World Bank Working Paper 15.

Lieberman, Ira W. and Daniel J. Kopf. 2007. *Privatization in Transition Economies: the Ongoing Story*. Bingley, UK: Emerald.

Liesman, Steve. 1994. "Cabinet Approves Privatization", *Moscow Times*, 1 July 1994, www.themoscowtimes.com/news/article/cabinet-approves-cabinet-approves-privatization-plan/350922.html#ixzz1xUUej9cV, accessed 11 June 2012.

Lipton, D. and Jeffrey Sachs. 1990. "Privatization in Eastern Europe: the Case of Poland". *Brookings Papers on Economic Activity* 2 (293–341).

McFaul, Michael. 2001. *Russia's Unfinished Revolution: Political Change from Gorbachev to Putin*. Ithaca, NY: Cornell University Press.

McFaul, M. 2004. "Gorbachev and Yeltsin as Leaders". *Slavic Review* 63 (1): 200–1.

Marshall, Alfred. 1946. *Principles of Economics*. London: Macmillan.

Matthews, Mervyn. 1993. *The Passport Society: Controlling Movement in Russia and the USSR*. Boulder, Colo.: Westview Press.

Mau, V. A. 1996. *The Political History of Economic Reform in Russia, 1985–1994*. London: Centre for Research into Communist Economies.

Mau, V. A. 2010. *Sochineniia v shesti tomakh*. Moscow: "Delo".

Mau, V. A. and Irina Starodubrovskaia, eds. 2001. *The Challenge of Revolution: Contemporary Russia in Historical Perspective*. Oxford: Oxford University Press.

Megginson, W. L. and J. R. Netter. 2001. "From State to Market: A Survey of Empirical Studies on Privatization". *Journal of Economic Literature* 39 (2): 321–89.

Mickiewicz, T. 2005. *Economic Transition in Central Europe and in the Commonwealth of Independent States*. London: Palgrave.

Milgrom, Paul and J. Roberts. 1992. *Economics, Organization and Management*. London: Prentice Hall.

Moser, Robert and Frank Thames. 2003. "Compromise amidst Political Conflict: the Origins of Russia's Mixed-Member System". In M. Shugart and M. Vattenberg, eds, *Mixed-Member Electoral Systems: The Best of Both Worlds?* Oxford: Oxford University Press.

Mostovoi, P. 1999a. "Kak Sozdavalas' Programma". In A. Chubais, ed., *Privatizatsiia po-Rossiisk*. Moscow: Vagrius.

Mostovoi, P. 1999b. "V poiskakh pravovogo polya". In A. Chubais, ed., *Privatizatsiia po-Rossiiski*. Moscow: Vagrius.

Naishul, Vitaly. 1992. *The Supreme and Last Stage of Socialism*. London: Centre for Research into Communist Studies.

Nellis, John. 1995. "Introduction". In I. Lieberman and J. Nellis, eds, *Russia: Creating Private Enterprises and Efficient Markets*. Washington, DC: The World Bank.

Nellis, John R. 1999. *Time to Rethink Privatization in Transition Economies?* Washington, DC: World Bank.

Nelson, L. D. and Irina, Y. Kuzes. 1994. "Evaluating the Russian Voucher Privatization Program". *Comparative Economic Studies* 36 (1): 55–67.

Nelson, L., L. Babaeva and R. Babaev. 1992. "Perspectives on Entrepreneurship and Privatization in Russia: Policy and Public Opinion", *Slavic Review* 2 (Summer 1992): 271–86.

OECD. 2005. "Performance and Appraisal. Russia: Building Rules for the Market". *OECD Reviews of Regulatory Reform*. Paris: OECD.

Ofer, Gur and Aaron Vinokur. 1980. *Private Sources of Income of the Soviet Urban Household*. Santa Monica, Calif.: Rand.

Pickles, John and Adrian Smith. 1998. *Theorising Transition: the Political Economy of Post-Communist Transformation*. London: Routledge.

Pistor, Katharina. 2006. "Patterns of Legal Change". In M. Fox and M. Heller, eds, *Corporate Governance Lessons from Transition Economy Reforms.* Princeton, NJ: Princeton University Press.

Pistor, Katharina and Andrew Spicer. 1997. "Investment Funds in Mass Privatization and Beyond". In I. Lieberman, S. Nelson and R. Desai, eds, *Between State and Market.* Washington, DC: The World Bank.

Popov, Vladimir. 1998. "Preparing the Russian Economy for World Market Integration". In A. Jilberto, ed., *Regionalization and Globalization in the Modern World Economy: Perspectives on the Third World and transitional economies*. London: Routledge.

Popov, Vladimir. 2000. "Shock Therapy Versus Gradualism: the end of the Debate (Explaining the Magnitude of Transformational Recession)". *Comparative Economic Studies* 42 (1): 1–57.

Popov, Vladimir. 2007. "Shock Therapy versus Gradualism Reconsidered: Lessons from Transition Economies after 15 Years of Reforms". *Comparative Economic Studies*, 49 (1): 1–31.

Puffer, Sheila M. and Daniel J. McCarthy. 2003. "The Emergence of Corporate Governance in Russia". *Journal of World Business* 38 (4): 284–98.

Radygin, A. 1996. "The Privatization Process in Russia in 1995". *Problems of Economic Transition* 39 (7): 5–19.

Radygin, A. 2000. "The Redistribution of Property Rights in Post-privatization Russia". *Problems of Economic Transition* 42 (11): 6–34.

Remington, Thomas. 2001. *The Russian Parliament: Institutional Evolution in a Transitional Regime, 1989–1999*. New Haven, Conn.: Yale University Press.

Rodrik, D. 2006. "Goodbye Washington consensus? Hello Washington Confusion? A Review of the World Bank's Economic Growth in the 1990s: Learning from a Decade of Reform". *Journal of Economic Literature* 44 (4): 973–87.

Rogoff, K. "Has Russia Been on the Right Path? Commentary", *IMF Vedomosti*, 26 August 2002, http: //www.inf.org/external/np/vc/2002/082602.htm.

Roland, G. 2000. *Transition and economics: Politics, Markets, and Firms*. Cambridge, Mass., and London: MIT Press.

Roxburgh, Ian, and Judith Shapiro. 1996. "Russian Unemployment and the Excess Wages Tax". *Communist Economics & Economic Transformation* 8 (1): 5–27.

Rubins, N. 1998. "The Demise and Resurrection of the Propiska: Freedom of Movement in the Russian Federation". *Harvard International Law Journal* 39 (2): 545–66.

Rutland, Peter. 1992. *The Politics of Economic Stagnation in the Soviet Union: the Role of Local Party Organs in Economic Management*. New York: Cambridge University Press.

Rutland, P. 2009. "Putin and the Oligarchs". In S. Wegren, ed., *Putin's Russia*. Lanham, Md: Rowman and Littlefield.

Sachs, Jeffrey and Katharina Pistor. 1997. *The Rule of Law and Economic Reform in Russia*. Boulder, Colo. and Oxford: Westview Press.

Sakwa, Richard. 2002. *Russian Politics and Society*. London: Routledge.

Sakwa, Richard. 2008. "Putin and the Oligarchs". *New Political Economy* 13 (2): 185–91.

Sakwa, Richard. 2009. *The Quality of Freedom: Khodorkovsky, Putin and the Yukos Affair*. Oxford: Oxford University Press.

Shlapentokh, Vladimir. 1993. "Privatization Debates in Russia: 1989–1992". *Comparative Economic Studies* 35 (2): 19–32.

Shleifer, Andrei. 1997. "Government in Transition". *European Economic Review* 41 (3–5): 385–410.

Shleifer, A. and D. Treisman. 2000. *Without a Map: Political Tactics and Economic Reform in Russia*. Cambridge, Mass.: MIT Press.

Smith, Adam. [1776] 1909–14. In C. J. Bullock, ed., *Wealth of Nations*. The Harvard Classics. New York: P. F. Collier & Son, vol. X.

Solnick, Steven. 1998. "Will Russia Survive: Center and Periphery in the Russian Federation". In B. Rubin, ed., *Post-Soviet Political Order: Conflict and State Building*. London: Psychology Press.

Spulber, Nicolas. 1969. *The Soviet Economy: Structure, Principles, Problems*. New York: W. W. Norton.

Standing, Guy. 1991. *In Search of Flexibility: the New Soviet Labour Market*. Geneva: International Labour Office.

Standing, Guy. 1994. "Employment Restructuring in Russian Industry". *World Development* 22 (2): 253–60.

Stavrakis, Peter J. 1993. *State Building in Post-Soviet Russia: the Chicago Boys and the Decline of Administrative Capacity*. Washington, DC: Kennan Institute for Advanced Russian Studies.

Steele, J. 1994. *Eternal Russia: Yeltsin, Gorbachev and the Mirage of Democracy*. London: Faber and Faber.

Stiglitz, Joseph E. 2002. *Globalization and its Discontents*. London: Allen Lane.

Suraska, Wisla. 1999. *How the Soviet Union Disappeared: An Essay on the Causes of Dissolution*. Durham, NC: Duke University Press.

Sutela, P. 1991. *Economic Thought and Economic Reform in the Soviet Union* (Cambridge University Press).

Svejnar, Jan. 1990. "A Framework for the Economic Transformation of Czechoslovakia". *Eastern European Economics* 29 (2): 5–28.

Svejnar, Jan. 2002. "Transition Economies: Performance and Challenges". *The Journal of Economic Perspectives* 16 (1): 3–28.

Thomas, Scott. 1993. "The Politics and Economics of Privatization in Central and Eastern Europe". *The Columbia Journal of World Business* 28 (1): 168–78.

Tolkacheva, Julie. 1994. "Top Companies to Go Under the Hammer", *Moscow Times*, 24 March 1994, www.themoscowtimes.com/news/article/top-companies-to-go-under-the-hammer/213985.html#ixzz1xUfQRg2G, accessed 12 June 2012.

Treisman, D. S. 1998. "Fighting Inflation in a transitional regime: Russia's Anomalous stabilization". *World Politics* 50 (2): 235–65.

Treisman, Daniel. 2009. "Elections in Russia, 1991–2008". In *Working Paper WP7*. Moscow: Higher School of Economics.

Treisman, D. 2010. "'Loans for Shares' Revisited". *Post-Soviet Affairs* 26 (3): 207–27.

Treisman, D. 2011. "Presidential Popularity in a Hybrid Regime: Russia under Yeltsin and Putin". *American Journal of Political Science* 55 (3): 590–609.

Troxel, Tiffany. 2003. *Parliamentary Power in Russia, 1994–2001: a New Era*. Basingstoke: Palgrave Macmillan.

Tsikata, Tsidi M. 1998. "Aid Effectiveness: a Survey of the Recent Empirical Literature". *IMF Papers on Policy Analysis and Assessments* 98/1. Washington, DC: International Monetary Fund.

Ustiuzhanina, E. V. 2001. "'Drugaia' chastnaia sobstvennost': privatizatsiia no-russki". *Ekonomicheskaia Nauka Sovremennoi Rossii* 2: 74–95.

Varese, F. 2001. "Is Sicily the Future of Russia? Private Protection and the Rise of the Russian Mafia". *Archives Européennes de Sociologie* 42 (1): 186–220.

Varese, Federico. 2005. *The Russian Mafia: Private Protection in a New Market Economy*. Oxford: Oxford University Press.

Vasiliev, Sergei, A. B. Chubais and Andrei Illarianov. 1999. *Ten Years of Russian Economic Reform: a Collection of Papers*. London: Centre for Research into Post-Communist Economies.

Volgin, Andrei and Yuri Milner. 1995. "Voucher Investment Funds". In I. Lieberman and J. Nellis, eds, *Russia: Creating Private Enterprises and Efficient Markets*. Washington, DC: The World Bank.

Volkov, Vadim. 1999. "Violent Entrepreneurship in Post-Communist Russia". *Europe-Asia Studies* 51 (5): 741–54.

Vysokov, V. V. 1995. *Privatization in Russia: the Way: to Wealth?... to Bankruptcy?* Rostov-on-Don: Centre of Economic Assistance to Market Transition.

Walker, Edward. 2003. *Dissolution: Sovereignty and the Breakup of the Soviet Union*. Lanham, Md.: Rowman and Littlefield.

Wedel, Janine. 1998. *Collision and Collusion: the Strange Case of Western Aid to Eastern Europe*. Basingstoke: Palgrave Macmillan.

Weisskopf, Thomas. 1998. "Economic Perspectives on Privatization in Russia: 1990–1994". In D. Iatridis and J. Hopps, eds, *Privatization in Central and Eastern Europe: Perspectives and Approaches*. Westport, Conn.: Greenwood Publishing Group.

Williamson, O. 1979. "Transaction–Cost Economics: the Governance of Contractual Relations". *Journal of Law, Economics and Organization* 22 (October 1979): 233–61.

Williamson, O. 1985. *The Economic Institutions of Capitalism*. New York: Free Press.

Woods, N. 2006. *The Globalizers: the IMF, the World Bank, and their Borrowers*. New York: Cornell University Press.

World Bank. 1992. *Russian Economic Reform: Crossing the Threshold of Structural Change*. Washington, DC: World Bank.

Yeltsin, Boris. 1994. *The Struggle for Russia*. New York: Belka.

Zürcher, Christoph. 2007. *The Post-Soviet Wars: Rebellion, Ethnic Conflict and Nationhood in the Caucasus*. New York, NY: New York University Press.

Index